The Scottish Idealists

Selected Philosophical Writings

Edited and Introduced
by David Boucher

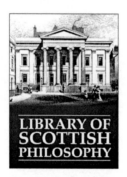

LIBRARY OF
SCOTTISH
PHILOSOPHY

ia

IMPRINT ACADEMIC

Published in the UK by Imprint Academic
PO Box 200, Exeter EX5 5YX, UK

Published in the USA by Imprint Academic
Philosophy Documentation Center
PO Box 7147, Charlottesville, VA 22906-7147, USA

ISBN 0 907845 72X

A CIP catalogue record for this book is available from the
British Library and US Library of Congress

Contents

Series Editor's Note

The principal purpose of volumes in this series is not to provide researchers with scholarly editions, but to make the writings of Scottish philosophers accessible to a new generation of modern readers. In accordance with this purpose, certain changes have been made to the original texts:

- Spelling and punctuation have been modernized.
- In some cases, the selected passages have been given new titles.
- Some original footnotes and references have not been included.
- Some extracts have been shortened from their original length.
- Quotations from Greek have been transliterated, and passages in foreign languages translated, or omitted altogether.

Care has been taken to ensure that in no instance do these amendments truncate the argument or alter the meaning intended by the original author. For readers who want to consult the original texts, full bibliographical details are provided for each extract.

The Library of Scottish Philosophy was launched at the Third International Reid Symposium on Scottish Philosophy in July 2004 with an initial six volumes. Attractively produced and competitively priced, these appeared just fifteen months after the original suggestion of such a series. This remarkable achievement owes a great deal to the work and commitment of the editors of the individual volumes, but it was only possible because of the energy and enthusiasm of the publisher, Keith Sutherland and the outstanding work of Jon M.H. Cameron, Editorial and

Administrative Assistant to the Centre for the Study of Scottish Philosophy.

Acknowledgements

Grateful acknowledgement is made to the Carnegie Trust for the Universities of Scotland for generous financial support for the Library of Scottish Philosophy in general, and to Mr George Stevenson for a subvention for this volume in particular.

Acknowledgement is also made to the University of Aberdeen Special Libraries and Collections for permission to reproduce the engraving of the Edinburgh Faculty of Advocates from *Modern Athens* (1829).

Gordon Graham
Aberdeen, June 2004

Introduction

There was a time, not so long ago, when modern analytic philosophy dominated the Anglophone world, when Idealism as a philosophy was looked on with derision because of the alien character of its mode of analysis, heavily metaphysical, often impenetrable in its supposed mysticism, and all encompassing in its refusal to acknowledge dualisms and divisions of any kind. Everything had to be explained and understood in relation to broader and broader contexts, and ultimately in relation to experience, or the universe, as a whole. At a time when the unit of philosophical analysis had become smaller and smaller, and the clarification of concepts and the use of language almost anal-retentive, the grand theory of Idealism, thoroughly permeated as it was with religion and poetry, did not figure on the philosophical landscape. The possible exception is F.H. Bradley because, despite the fact that his logic and metaphysics were Idealist in character, his philosophical manner and rigour was more compatible with the analytic method.

The revival of interest in philosophical Idealism was at first historical. Melvin Richter's *The Politics of Conscience* was an important milestone in this process, with the modest aim, not of reviving T.H. Green's reputation, nor of endorsing the low esteem into which he had fallen, but instead of understanding him in his historical context.[1] Since then there has been a proliferation of interest, not only historically oriented, but also acknowledging and exploiting the Idealists' contribution to developing a communitarian theory of the relation of the individual to society, and of formulating a widely accepted theory of rights in opposi-

---

[1]   Melvin Richter, *The Politics of Conscience: T.H. Green and His Age* (Bristol: Thoemmes Press, 1996: first published in 1964).

tion to natural rights-grounded theories, namely one that rests upon social recognition as part of what it means to have a right, with their justification resting on the criterion of the common good.[2]

In the process of rehabilitating Idealism, both in historical and philosophical scholarship, the tendency has been to see it as a British, or more narrowly, as an English, phenomenon. It is not at all surprising since the histories of both Scotland and Wales have mostly been tangential or a mere adjunct to English and European history. What has been little noticed about British Idealism is the extent to which it was heavily dominated by Scotsmen, and the degree to which Scotsmen were the main exporters of it. There are a number of reasons why England has been seen as being at the centre of the importation of Hegelian Idealism into Britain. First, the figures who have since come to be represented as canonic in this loosely cohering group of Kantians and Hegelians are T.H. Green, Bernard Bosanquet, and F.H. Bradley, all Englishmen. Bosanquet is the only one of these three to have had a chair in Scotland (St. Andrews 1903–8). There were, nevertheless very strong links between T.H. Green and the philosophy students of Glasgow University. Edward Caird, the doyen of the Scottish Idealists, went to Balliol College, Oxford, in 1860 on a Snell Exhibition from Glasgow. There he struck-up an enduring friendship with T.H. Green. On returning to Glasgow Caird encouraged many of his students to study at Balliol as Snell exhibitioners, or Clark Fellows. Among those who took this route were W.P. Ker, taught by T.H. Green; John Henry Muirhead, taught by both Green and R.L. Nettleship; and David George Ritchie, taught by Green and Arnold Toynbee (of Toynbee Hall fame).

The second reason why the contribution of Scotland to Idealism has not been adequately acknowledged is that it was quite alien from the Scottish philosophy that preceded it, and what gave it a distinctive quality, a heavy emphasis upon poetry and literature, was not itself philosophical. Carlyle contributed significantly to making the British climate hospitable to Idealism. The empiricism of Dugald Stewart and his colleague Thomas Browne at Edin-

---

[2]   See Rex Martin, *A System of Rights* (Oxford: Oxford University Press, 1993), and more recently 'Rights and Human Rights' in Peter Sutch and Bruce Haddock, eds., *Multicultural Identity and Rights* (London: Routledge, 2003), pp. 176–95.

burgh University was in Carlyle's view, as expressed in his *Miscellaneous Essays*, a mere preparation for philosophy, and in particular, a preparation for what was to be found in Kant. In his essay, 'Signs of the Times' he encapsulated in the phrase 'the Mechanical Age' his pejorative characterization of the main features of the age.[3] The problem in his view was that from Locke onwards metaphysics in Britain was both physical and mechanical, obsessed with the origins of consciousness and the genetic history of the content of the mind at the expense of exploring the mysteries of freedom and our relations to God, the universe, space and time. Carlyle gave the impression, not wholly justified, that he was ignorant of philosophical systems and dismissive of philosophical method. Even someone sympathetic to Carlyle could argue that 'something more thoroughgoing than the literary methods of poetry and prophecy was called for to meet the intellectual demands of the new time'.[4] While many of his contemporaries viewed him as a philosopher, he has rarely been described so in the last century and a half.

A number of the Scottish Idealists were first and foremost men of literature, for example Mungo MacCallum who became professor of English literature at Sydney University and who was responsible for organizing Henry Jones's visit to lecture on Idealism in Australia.[5] In addition, W.P. Ker became professor of Poetry at Oxford. One of those who were philosophers with literary frames of reference was, of course, Edward Caird, who famously wrote on matters literary, including Wordsworth and Carlyle. His protégé, Henry Jones's first book was *Browning as a Philosophical and Religious Teacher*, and he also wrote on Walter Scott, Tennyson, Robert Browning and Shakespeare.[6]

A third reason why Scotland did not figure prominently in the mind of the person who invoked British Idealism was that one of

---

[3]   Thomas Carlyle, *The Works of Thomas Carlyle*, ed. H.D. Traill. 30 volumes (1896-9), vol. 27, p. 59.

[4]   John H. Muirhead, *The Platonic Tradition in Anglo-Saxon Philosophy: Studies in the History of Idealism in England and America* (London: George Allen and Unwin, 1931), p. 146.

[5]   For an account of this tour and of the Scottish Idealists in Australia see my 'Practical Hegelianism: Henry Jones's lecture tour of Australia', *Journal of the History of Ideas*, 51 (1990), pp. 423–52.

[6]   Henry Jones, *Browning as a Religions and Philosophical Teacher* (Glasgow: Maclehose, 1891); and *Essays on Literature and Education*, ed. H.J.W. Hetherington (London: Hodder and Stoughton, 2nd edition, 1892).

its Scottish proponents, in tracing the history of Hegelianism in Britain, fails to differentiate between England and Scotland.[7] Hegel's transformation of the philosophical vocabulary, far more radical than anything Kant or Fichte effected, made his passage into Anglo Saxon discourse doubly difficult. Understanding Hegel required at once the acquisition of the German language with a philosophical idiom whose weight it could barely sustain. Scotsmen proved themselves to be particularly brave in this respect, if not always wholly successful. James Frederick Ferrier (1808–64), for example, travelled to Germany in 1834 to acquaint himself with the growing tide of German philosophy. He expounded his ideas in opposition to Reid and Hamilton, but nevertheless thought his philosophy Scottish to the core. He maintains a position that, like Idealism, denies false dichotomies, such as the distinctions between subject and object, the real and the ideal, sensation and intellect. He recognized the necessity of a rational philosophy that could overcome the division that reason created. He ultimately claims as the culmination of his argument that: 'All absolute existences are contingent *except one*; in other words, there is One, but only one, Absolute Existence which is strictly *necessary*; and that existence is a supreme, and infinite, and everlasting Mind in synthesis with all things.'[8] He nevertheless confessed that he understood little of Hegel, unlike James Hutchison Stirling, a gentleman scholar from Glasgow, resident just outside Edinburgh, who somewhat recklessly claimed to have found the secret of Hegel.[9] The rather terse translations of the *Logic* and commentary are presented in a Carlyleian style, with the observation that the secret was to be found in Kant and his idea of *a priori* categories and in Hegel's idea that every concrete concept included within itself two antagonistic elements that are found to be at once through and in the other. The book drew much favourable attention from, for example, Benjamin Jowett, Caird's predecessor as Master of Balliol College, Oxford, T. H. Green, the doyen of British Idealism, and Ralph Waldo Emerson, America's counterpart of Carlyle, but it is the infamous

---

[7]   Muirhead, *The Platonic Tradition*.

[8]   James Frederick Ferrier, *Institutes of Metaphysic: the Theory of Knowing and Being* (Edinburgh: Blackwood, 1856: first edition, 1854), p. 522.

[9]   James Hutchison Stirling, *The Secret of Hegel: Being the Hegelian System in Origin, Principle, Form, and Matter* (Edinburgh: Oliver and Boyd, 1898: first edition 1865).

unkind review that persists, in which Stirling is accused of keeping Hegel's secret uncommonly well.[10] Even those sympathetic to Stirling described the book as lacking in method and 'almost as difficult as the original'.[11] Whereas Stirling did an undoubted, if dubious, service to Britain in attempting to reveal the secret of Hegel, no further ground would have been made if it had not been for the important translations by philosophers of Hegel's principal works. Again it was Scotsmen who were the pioneers. The principal translations were: *The Logic of Hegel* (1874), and *The Philosophy of Mind* (1894) by William Wallace of Cupar, Fife; *The Philosophy of Art* (1886) by William Hastie of Wandlockhead, Dumfries; *Lectures on the History of Philosophy* (1892–6) by E.S. Haldane of Edinburgh, younger sister of the Idealist Richard Burden Haldane; and *The Phaenomenology* (1910) by J.B. Baillie of Edinburgh and Aberdeen Universities.

At the turn of the twentieth century there were only a small number of Universities in Britain: six in England — Oxford, Cambridge, London, Birmingham, Durham and Victoria (Manchester), all essentially federated: one in Wales with colleges in Cardiff, Aberystwyth and Bangor: and four in Scotland — Glasgow, St. Andrews, Aberdeen and Edinburgh. Departments tended to be small and therefore opportunities for the aspirant Scottish Idealist philosopher were few. Most began their careers outside Scotland, and in some cases spent all their working lives away from their native country. Many went to Australia, for example William Mitchell to Adelaide, Henry Laurie to Melbourne and Francis Anderson and Mungo McCallum to Sydney, both later plagued by Henry Jones's student John Anderson, the architect of Australian Realism, and who lectured on T. H. Green up until the end of the 1940s. John Watson, one of Caird's star students, spent almost all his career at Queen's University, Kingston, Canada. In Britain, outside Scotland, Cardiff extended a friendly welcome, providing a home at one time or another for Andrew Seth, W.P. Ker, W.R. Sorley, J.S. Mackenzie and H.W.J. Hetherington. At Oxford, William Wallace, D.G. Ritchie, Edward Caird, W.P. Ker and J.A. Smith were stalwarts of Idealism. At Cambridge, the only notable Scottish Idealist was W.R. Sorley. J.M.E.

[10]   W.H. Greenleaf, *Oakeshott's Philosophical Politics* (London: Longmans, 1966), p. 1.
[11]   Muirhead referring to Andrew Seth in *The Platonic Tradition*, p. 170.

McTaggart, although having a Scottish name, was born in London as an Ellis, adding McTaggart under the terms of a bequest. In Scotland the centres of Idealism were St Andrews, where Ferrier, Henry Jones, David Ritchie and Bernard Bosanquet worked; Edinburgh, home to Campbell Fraser, and James and Andrew Seth; and Glasgow, where John Nicol and the formidable Edward Caird reigned. From 1866 Caird held the prestigious Chair of Moral Philosophy — previously held by Francis Hutcheson, Adam Smith and Thomas Reid — until he took up the Mastership of Balliol College, Oxford in 1893. He was succeeded by his former student the Welshman Henry Jones who held the chair until his death in 1922. Jones had been a student at Glasgow and had held the chair of Logic, Rhetoric and Metaphysics at St. Andrews. Jones is included in this volume because of his contribution to Scottish philosophy and his immense personal influence on Scottish philosophers, including a negative influence on John Anderson the leading light in Australian empricism. While never losing his love for Wales, he spoke in a Scottish accent, used Scottish words and phrases in conversation and is buried at Kilbride. When a young man, forced to leave Glasgow to take up a position in Aberystwyth, he wrote to Andrew Seth expressing the sentiments that were never to leave him: 'It is a trial to leave my Glasgow friends and Caird has been a father to me. Nor do I know that I have sufficient strength to live the higher life in my new surroundings: but I must try it, and hope that now and then I shall get a glimpse of the stronger race of philosophers and thinkers of the Scottish Universities.'[12]

This collection of readings, the first of its kind, has been chosen with a view to displaying the variety, richness and strength of the Scottish Idealist tradition. The collection begins with a general statement of the purpose and task of philosophy from an Idealist vantage point, followed by an exploration of the place of aesthetic experience in experience as a whole. The first two essays represent the dominant Absolute Idealist tendency among Scottish Idealists. The third mounts a full frontal attack on the Hegelian system and its assumptions, and constitutes the beginnings of Personalism, or Personal Idealism in Britain. The fourth is a two

---

[12] Letter from Henry Jones to Andrew Seth dated 30 October, 1882. Thomas Jones Collection, Class U, vol ii, fol. 25/2. National Library of Wales.

part essay, one of the most powerful statements of Absolute Idealism in English, that addresses the critics, and especially the Personalists. The remainder of the essays demonstrate the importance of moral, social and political questions to Idealist philosophy. Unlike Hegel, for example, who believed that philosophy was non injunctive and prescribed no solutions because it comes on the scene after the event, the British Idealists, including the Scots, tended to see a very close relation between philosophical enquiry and practical reform. This entailed a positive role for the state, and a conception of rights that was firmly grounded in the social community and not in abstract conceptions of natural rights.

Scottish Idealism was immensely spiritual in character and recognized no hard and fast distinctions between philosophy, religion, poetry and science. I begin this collection with the most influential of the Scottish Idealists, that is Edward Caird's exploration of philosophical enquiry in general. In the true spirit of Idealism Caird takes the purpose of philosophy to be the reconciliation of what the modern age has fragmented and divided. He wanted to give all aspects of human experience a fair hearing in the face of the dissolving and disintegrating tendencies of the times to sever them from each other and to consider them in abstraction. The tendencies were on the one hand Subjective Idealism that had 'infected' British philosophy since the time of Berkeley and on the other hand the Realism and Naturalism that was equally as one-sided in dismissing the subjective, and in conceiving everything as a mechanical system.[13]

From the Hegelian starting point of the unity of experience, in which all dualisms have to be overcome, the issue of how the unity becomes differentiated into its various modes has to be addressed. When thinking is taken to be the process by which Spirit or God realizes itself, the subjective and objective are not separated by ideas, but instead are the differentiations of the one comprehensive unity.[14] Caird sums up Hegel's position thus: the highest aim of philosophy 'is to reinterpret experience, in the light of a unity which is presupposed in it, but which cannot be made conscious or explicit until the relation of experience to the think-

[13]   See Henry Jones and J.H. Muirhead, *The Life and Philosophy of Edward Caird* (Glasgow: Maclehose, Jackson and Co., 1921), chapter viii.
[14]   Edward Caird, *Hegel* (Edinburgh: Blackwood, 1903), p. 55.

ing self is seen — the unity of all things with each other and with the mind that knows them'.[15]

For Caird philosophy effects a reconciliation of ourselves to ourselves and to the world. This entails nothing less than placing human life in the context of the universe. Implicit in his argument is a philosophy of history in which there is pattern and meaning to human history exhibited in an observable tendency towards greater unity and organization. The contribution of Caird to this volume demonstrates the very close relation in which the Scottish Idealists held natural science, religion and poetry. All three could perceptively reveal something profound about life, but it is philosophy that unifies them in the higher synthesis of the whole. Poetry, for example, can characterize philosophical positions, but without the endless argumentation. Hence the quotation from Geothe's *Faust* to illustrate the call to philosophy to restore the unity between faith and reason, or from Omar Khayyam to illustrate how the wealth of modern life and science distracts us from seeking the ultimate synthesis and directs us to scepticism and agnosticism.

The most famous of Scottish Idealist books was *Essays in Philosophical Criticism* (1883), a book that set out the future direction of enquiry for this group of thinkers who shared a 'common purpose or tendency'. From this testament of Scottish Idealism, edited by Andrew Seth and R.B. Haldane, I have chosen W.P. Ker. The significance of W.P. Ker's essay was that more or less for the first time since Coleridge we have a philosophical treatment, as opposed to the polemics of Ruskin and Morris, of how the content and meaning of art constitutes one of the principal ways in which reality reveals itself to us. For him the rationale of the philosophy of art is to determine whether the creations of art are contingent and fortuitous, inexplicable appearances from the point of view of the methods of science, which of course they are, or if they merit a different context, not in the history of events, but of the achievements of the mind and of reason in this world.

Andrew Seth is of immense importance in the history of British Idealism because four years after he edited what was the manifesto of Scottish Hegelianism he more fully developed doubts he had hinted at earlier. He now questioned the metaphysical con-

[15]   Edward Caird, 'Metaphysic', *Essays on Literature and Philosophy*, vol. 2 (Glasgow: Maclehose, 1892), p. 442.

clusions that Absolute Idealism projected and was at the forefront in Britain of leading the revolt against them and championing the cause of Personal Idealism. Personalism, as it came to be known, was to be taken-up by McTaggart and Sorley at Cambridge, and a group of eight philosophers, including Hastings Rashdall and W.R. Boyce Gibson in Oxford, who called themselves Personal Idealists, and who in 1902 produced a manifesto equivalent to that of Seth and Haldane, edited almost twenty years before.[16] Personal Idealism, or Personalism, took as its starting point a dissatisfaction with the place of individual personality in the post-Kantian Hegelian programme. However important a place self-consciousness may have, the self of which we are conscious seemed to be completely absorbed into the Absolute. Both Bradley and Bosanquet were widely criticized for maintaining that the individual's mode of being is 'adjectival' as opposed to 'substantive'.[17]

The Idealists acknowledged Kant's important Copernican revolution in philosophy, but recognized in addition Hegel's rejection of the epistemological problems to which both Descartes and Kant gave rise. Instead of the mind conforming to reality, on Descartes' model, or making reality dependent upon mind, along the lines of Berkeley, reality had to conform to mind whose *a priori* categories reveal an intelligible order in the world.[18] The Idealists could not accept, however, the Kantian dualism between the phenomenal or empirical world of appetites and instincts and the noumenal world of intelligence and spirit. The idea of things in themselves, the reality of which is inaccessible to the mind, and as they are known to the mind, constituted an advance on Descartes and Berkeley, but still posited an unresolved dualism. Andrew Seth, for example, complained that thinking involves a relation between the thinker and an objective world, and that it was a fallacy to begin by assuming that one side of the dualism exists inde-

[16] Henry Sturt, ed., *Personal Idealism: Philosophical Essays by Eight Members of the University of Oxford* (London: Macmillan, 1902).

[17] For a clear and informed discussion see William Sweet, ' "Absolute Idealism" and Finite Individuality', *Indian Philosophical Quarterly*, xxiv (1997), pp. 431–62.

[18] Henry Jones, *The Philosophy of Martineau* (London: Macmillan, 1905), pp. 6–7. Also see Henry Jones, *Philosophy of Lotze* (Glasgow: Maclehose, 1895), p. 371.

pendently of the other.[19] John Watson argued that Kant's view was perverse in positing that thought actually prevents us from knowing reality. Kant, then, denied that the world known by us is identical with reality, while Hegel contended 'that the known world is for us necessarily a world that exists only because we are thinking beings'.[20] Watson is not suggesting that every being knows reality, but instead that reality embodies thought that is intelligible and capable of being known only by a being that thinks.[21] Hastings Rashdall sums up the position when he says that Idealism assumes 'that there is no such thing as matter apart from mind, that what we commonly call *things* are not self-subsistent realities, but are only real when taken in their connection with mind — that they exist for mind, not for themselves'.[22]

The Scottish Idealists in general maintained that there could be no thought without a thinker, and no thinker without thought, but there were still significant disputes over the question of the extent to which denying the distinction between subject and object put the self at risk of being subsumed entirely by the Absolute. Seth constantly reminded Idealists of the importance of the self in any account of the nature of experience. In his contribution to *Essays in Philosophical Criticism* Seth already intimates his dissatisfaction with the way Idealists characterize individuality and the self. Seth argues that the self exists only through the world, and the world only through the self. Self and the world are the same reality looked at from different points of view, but we must never lose sight of the fact that the basic unity, or identity, can only be grasped from the point of view of the subject, or person.[23] As Hastings Rashdall argued some years later: 'Our idea of a per-

---

[19] Andrew Seth, *Scottish Philosophy* (Edinburgh: Blackwood, 1890: 2nd edn.), p. 11. Seth became one of the leading exponents of Personal Idealism which took its lead from Lotze and Rudolf Eucken. This development will be highlighted below.

[20] John Watson, *The Interpretation of Religious Experience*, the Gifford Lectures 1910–12, part I (Glasgow: Maclehose, 1912), p. 289.

[21] John Watson, *Interpretation of Religious Experience*, part I (New York: AMS, Press, 1979: reprinted from the edition of 1912), p. 292.

[22] Hastings Rashdall, 'Personality: Human and Divine', in Henry Sturt, ed., *Personal Idealism: Philosophical Essays* (London: Macmillan, 1902), p. 370. Rashdall, as a Personal Idealist, distinguished himself from Absolute Idealists. See below.

[23] Andrew Seth, 'Philosophy as Criticism of the Categories', *Essays in Philosophical Criticism*, ed. Andrew Seth and R.B. Haldane (London:

son is then the idea of a consciousness which thinks, which has a certain permanence, which distinguishes itself from its own successive experiences and from all other consciousness — lastly, and most important of all, which acts. A person is a conscious, permanent, self-distinguishing, individual, active being'.[24]

Seth's *Hegelianism and Personality* constitutes the first systematic fully informed critique of Hegel in Britain, and given its importance the final chapter and conclusion are reproduced in this collection. Seth attempts to sustain the integrity of personality by use of a criterion that is not merely given, but is instead the extent to which each, by the exercise of reason, attains unity in his or her life by genuine membership of a kingdom of ends.

Bradley and Bosanquet, in the view of Personal Idealists, constituted the greatest danger to the integrity of the self. Indeed they criticized Bradley for casting doubt on the usefulness of the idea of a person for comprehending or understanding experience as a unity in diversity, and for characterizing the absolute as unknowable, something beyond human experience, which he refers to as 'mere' appearance. Seth had the highest regard for Bradley in freeing British Idealism from a slavish imitation of Hegel, but was extremely critical of Bradley's vagueness and inability to go beyond the suggestion that all contradictions are resolved in the absolute, and all differences are fused and overcome. The question of how the multiplicity of selves and diversity of experience become a unity is avoided in the admission that we know not how, only that somehow, they do.[25]

Subjective, or Personal Idealists, who objected to the propensity of Absolute Idealism to undervalue the individual and to run the risk of allowing the individual to become absorbed into the Absolute, acknowledged that some exponents of Monism were closer to them than others. One of Henry Jones's students at Glasgow, W.G. Boyce Gibson, was among those philosophers, led by Andrew Seth Pringle-Pattison in Britain and Rudolph Eucken on the continent, who wanted to rescue personality from being con-

---

Longmans Green, 1883), p. 38. Muirhead fails to see how these remarks foreshadow Seth's defence of a Kantian position against Hegel in his *Hegelianism and Personality*.

[24] Hastings Rashdall, *Personal Idealism*, ed. Henry Sturt (London: Macmillan, 1902), p. 372.

[25] Andrew Seth, 'A New Theory of the Absolute' in Seth, *Man's Place in the Cosmos* (Edinburgh: Blackwood, 1897), pp. 188–9.

signed to oblivion. Personal Idealism defended the metaphysical autonomy of personality against, on the one hand, naturalism which made personality the outcome of nature, and, on the other, the form of Idealism that made personality an 'adjective' of the Absolute. W.R. Boyce Gibson recognized that Absolute Idealists, such as Caird and Jones, while agreeing with the monistic unity of the whole, gave much more emphasis than Bradley or Bosanquet to the reality of the appearances. Gibson's exposure to Eucken clarified for him the main problems that needed to be addressed in philosophy. Following Rudolph Eucken, Boyce Gibson contended that the central idea of Absolute Idealism, that the real is rational, is upheld by Personal Idealism, but 'from the point of view of the personal experient'.[26]

Although Jones was viewed less suspiciously than Bosanquet or Bradley by Personal Idealists he nevertheless, like R.B. Haldane, felt that Personalists constituted a serious danger to Hegelian philosophy. Haldane, Seth's former co-editor, hit out against Personalists in *Mind* as someone who felt betrayed. Seth complained that: 'I am treated as a culprit who ought to know better.'[27] It was Subjective Idealism that for Jones constituted a threat to Absolute Idealism in that the former accused the latter of dissolving individual consciousness into experience as a whole, and postulating that the universe is itself a system of cohering worlds of ideas. Critics accused Absolute Idealism of positing a view of experience that was at once unstable and insubstantial, offering worlds of ideas unattached to the subjective consciousness at the one end, and to reality at the other. These floating worlds, the critics contend, need to be anchored at both ends to reality; at one end to the individuals whose thoughts they are, and at the other end to the external facts that the thoughts represent. Philosophy, therefore, must be divided into three spheres: psychology that deals with the thinking person; ontology that is concerned with the nature of things, which includes thinkers; and epistemology that focuses upon the relation between thoughts and reality. Drawing upon the strange combination of idealism and realism in Lotze, subjective Idealists accused Absolute Ideal-

---

[26]   W. R. Boyce Gibson, 'A Peace Policy for Idealists', *The Hibbert Journal*, 5 (1906-7).

[27]   Andrew Seth, 'Hegel and his Recent Critics', *Mind*, 14 (1889), p. 116.

ists of having no epistemology, and of continuing to confuse it with metaphysics and ontology.

Jones addressed these criticisms in the two-part article reprinted in this volume. He defiantly argued that not only did idealism have no epistemology, it denied the very possibility of having one. The charge that Absolute Idealism had been unable to account for the link between thought and reality because it made the latter the product of the former was, in Jones's view, fundamentally misconceived. No Idealist, Jones argued, would want to deny the distinction between thought and reality, nor maintain that knowledge of a fact or event is that fact or event itself.[28] 'It is', he said, 'inconsistent with the possibility of knowledge that it should *be* the reality which it represents'.[29] Jones is denying, then, that Absolute Idealism entails the assertion that experience is a world, or worlds, of cohering ideas. It is the critics themselves who want to maintain the existence of a world of ideas that mediates between psychic states, or indubitable data, and the reality we seek to know. The problem of epistemology is to explain how we make the transition from our conscious states to the reality of which we are conscious. In viewing the problem from this subjectivist starting point the critics themselves have been unable to transcend the dichotomy between thought and reality.[30]

Idealism arose from the consciousness of this insurmountable gulf which frustrates the 'movement from within outwards, or from ideality to reality'.[31] All reasoning, Jones contends, rests upon hypotheses, and those that postulated the knowing subject as the starting-point of philosophy have proved untenable. A hypothesis is more than a guess: it is suggested to the intellect by the world whose intelligibility we seek, and is held 'only so long as the realm of reality seems to support it'.[32] Hypotheses are never ultimately proven, but always in the process of being proved. All

---

[28] Jones, 'Idealism and Epistemology', pp. 460–1.

[29] Jones, *Philosophy of Lotze*, p. 273.

[30] *Ibid.*, pp. 113 and 368.

[31] *Ibid.*, p. 369.

[32] Henry Jones, 'The Immortality of the Soul in the Poems of Tennyson and Browning', a lecture (London: Macmillan, 1905), p. 32. Jones maintained that: 'Except for hypotheses, facts and events would seem to us to stand in no relation of any kind to one another'. Henry Jones, *A Faith That Enquires* (London: Macmillan, 1922), p. 93.

forms of enquiry require 'working hypotheses'[33] before any advance can be made in understanding experience. A hypothesis, while lacking certainty, 'commends itself to our notice by the range and clearness of the light it seems to throw on the manifold data of our experience'.[34]

It was Kant who made the first step in formulating a new hypothesis from which to work. He wondered whether we could dispense with the demand that thought must correspond to things, and assume instead that things must correspond to thought.[35] Kant, however, in trying to reconcile opposites was unable to reconcile thought and things. Things were ultimately unable to reveal their central character in thought.[36] It was Hegel who self-consciously completed the Copernican revolution in philosophy by identifying what Richard Norman calls the 'Dilemma of Epistemology'.[37] The epistemologist has to presuppose what he, or she, sets out to prove. The examination of forms of knowledge and their relation to reality with a view to declaring which are genuine and which are not requires a criterion of true knowledge in advance of the enquiry which is supposed to establish it.[38] Instead of reconciling differences as Kant had persistently attempted to do, Hegel first assumed unity and then proceeded to differentiate it. The starting point of his philosophy is the conception of reality as Absolute Self-Consciousness, or spirit, which finds expression and knows itself in all things. Ideas do not stand between the thinking intelligence and the world of reality; the

---

[33] Henry Jones, 'The Present Attitude of Reflective Thought Towards Religion', *Hibbert Journal*, 1 (1902-3), p. 233.

[34] Henry Jones, 'The Nature and Aims of Philosophy', *Mind* ,N.S. 6 (1893), p. 164.

[35] Henry Jones, *The Philosophy of Martineau* (London: Macmillan, 1905), pp. 6-7. Also see Jones, *Philosophy of Lotze*, p. 371.

[36] Henry Jones, 'Mr. Balfour as a Sophist', *Hibbert Journal*, III (1904-5), p. 458; Henry Jones, *Browning as a Philosophical and Religious Teacher* (Glasgow: Maclehose, 1891), p. 174; Jones, 'Idealism and Epistemology', p. 304; Jones, *Philosophy of Lotze*, p. 371; Henry Jones, 'Morality as Freedom', *Time* (London) NS 7 (1888), pp. 314-15. Jones makes similar points in his lectures on Kant delivered in University College, Bangor ,in 1888. Notes taken by Edward Edwards, National Library of Wales, Aberystwyth, NLW 9394C.

[37] Richard Norman, *Hegel's Phenomenology: a Philosophical Introduction* (New York: Oxford University Press, 1976), chapter one.

[38] G.W.F. Hegel, *The Phenomenology of Mind*, trans. J.B. Baillie (London, 1931: second edition), pp. 139-40.

ideas are reality expressing itself in the thinker who in that expression makes it his, or her, own. It is therefore not with thoughts disengaged from the thinker, nor with abstract worlds of ideas, that Hegel is concerned, but with the process of thinking as the realization of spirit, or God, in all reality. The subjective and objective are not separated by a world of ideas, but are differentiations of the one all encompassing unity. In answer to the critics who accused Idealism of lacking an epistemology Jones emphasized that Hegel did not need one because, 'to him there is no activity which, ultimately, is not the activity of Spirit. And, in consequence, the laws of its operations are laws of thinking — not the laws of thoughts. On this account his Metaphysic is also a Logic, a science, not of the connexions of ideas, but of the *operation of mind*'.[39] Hegelianism, then, was to be recommended for its radical new starting point of differentiating unity rather than reconciling, or unifying, opposites. Hegel's importance for the British Idealist, then, is that he dispenses with the problem of epistemology and provides a metaphysic that is also a logic of the process and development of mind.[40]

William Mitchell's contribution to this volume was written when he was a young man, and still an undergraduate at Edinburgh University, taught by Campbell Fraser and Henry Calderwood. This article from *Mind*, submitted by Calderwood against Mitchell's wishes, illustrates the manner in which Scottish and British Idealists in general approached philosophical subjects. There is a good deal of historical reference, but also the setting up of a dualism between two positions in ethics, the subjective and objective, the opposition between which being overcome in a synthesis of the two. Mitchell contends that whether in criticism or in the creation of an ethical doctrine it is equally as imperative to discern the postulate from which to begin. What distinguished ethics from other forms of human action is moral obligation. The purpose of ethics is to elucidate our moral obligation. Ethical ends, he maintains, must be both subjective and objective. Subjective in that they must reflect my interests

[39] Jones, 'Idealism and Epistemology', p. 306.
[40] Henry Jones gives a detailed and critical account of the development of the epistemological dilemma through Hegelian eyes in his 'Idealism and Epistemology', *Mind*, n.s. II (1893), in two parts. Also see my 'Practical Hegelianism: Henry Jones's Lecture Tour of Australia', *Journal of the History of Ideas*, 51 (1990), pp. 429–32.

and desires as a condition of my accepting them as a law to myself. Objective in that it must present to me an interest external to my subjective desires before I can recognize it as a law at all.

Mitchell developed into an unorthodox Absolute Idealist emphasizing more strongly than most of them that thought should not be confounded with its object. He argued that objects do not become mental; nor are they altered in being felt, imagined or known. He argued that: 'words and their notions or meanings are only instruments and are never facts of what they denote and describe'.[41] He was accused of being too close to realism or materialism. However, more orthodox Absolute Idealists, such as Henry Jones and Bernard Bosanquet, conceded that things do not come into existence because we think about them, but maintained that they are nevertheless unintelligible, independent of thought. Like them, Mitchell thought that the idea of things in themselves was unintelligible. Things that are not perceived, and which are isolated from other things, are beyond comprehension. In rejecting materialism 'proper' he did not, however, think of the mind and its experiences as the brain and brain processes. Like Bradley, Mitchell accepted the idea of degrees of reality on the question of truth. The criterion of truth Mitchell posited, however, had a lot in common with that of the pragmatist. We have what Gadamer was later to call forestructures of meaning, or certain expectations or prophecies about the world, when if the expectations are not fulfilled the beliefs are thought to be false, and if fulfilled, they are thought true. Mitchell maintained that: 'We take and reject beliefs according as they are consistent with the system of beliefs that we happen to have formed, but what is the test of the system itself? How do we know that it is true to nature? The answer is . . . namely, it works'.[42] Mitchell's greatest influence was upon Brand Blanshard who confessed that he owed a 'large obligation' to *Structure and Growth of the Mind*.[43]

Idealism was a radical reforming philosophy that took social responsibility seriously. This entailed having strong views on the role of the state in distributive justice. The popularity of Herbert

---

[41]   William Mitchell papers, University of Adelaide, notebook, vol. 33,

[42]   William Mitchell, *Structure and Growth of the Mind* (London: Macmillan, 1907), p. 334.

[43]   Brand Blanshard, *The Nature of Thought* (London: Allen and Unwin, 1939), vol. 1, p. 97.

Spencer's *Man Versus the State* could not be ignored. It gave the case against state interference on two grounds. First that it was unnatural in that it impeded natural selection perpetuating strains in society that would ultimately weaken its tenacity and ability to adapt. He famously distinguished between the deserving and the undeserving poor and employed an entitlement theory of justice. Each person, in his view, was entitled to the consequences, both good and bad, of his or her labour. Only if destitution was the result, not of poor character, but of fortuitous circumstances that impair human effort, such as the invention of electricity bankrupting the candlemaker, should that person deserve charitable assistance.

The second reason to oppose state interference was that it was impracticable. Society was such a complex organism (with no central nervous system as T.H. Huxley complained) that any interference inevitably had unintended negative consequences. The example Spencer was fond of giving was the Metropolitan Housing Act which resulted in less rather than more houses being available for rent to the poorer classes. David George Ritchie proved to be the most formidable of opponents and his book *The Principles of State Interference* rivalled Spencer's both in worldwide sales and popularity. Ritchie argues that the Idealist need not, after rejecting hedonism, shy away from the utilitarian. On the practical side, he suggests, an ethical system like that of Green's is really J.S. Mill's Utilitarianism placed upon a firmer basis and end, offering a more effective criterion for discerning the different qualities of pleasures.

The debate between those who wanted to inhibit state interference and those who wanted to extend it, was characterized as 'Individualism' versus 'Socialism'. Typically Idealists took this to be a false dichotomy. At the end of the nineteenth and the beginning of the twentieth centuries the opposition between Individualism and Socialism was addressed by people of all ideological persuasions,[44] and the British Idealists, whose ethical concerns embroiled them in all the leading political controversies of the times, were naturally drawn towards this debate. Their predilection to resolve all contradictions predisposed them to conclude that the opposition between the two categories was false, and that each in

---

[44] See W.H. Greenleaf, *The British Political Tradition, vol. 2, The Ideological Heritage* (London: Methuen, 1983).

some way implied, or absorbed into itself, the other.[45] On the 'Individualism' side any increase in state activity was deemed to be an interference that diminished individual responsibility and impaired freedom of choice.

Ritchie, very like Green and Jones, did not think that substantive universal principles of state intervention could be established. There could be no *a priori* presumption for or against state intervention.[46] The limits of state socialism could not be determined by abstract principles. The test of any extension of state activity should always be the question of whether the individual personality was being empowered by being offered a wider opportunity to develop. Little is gained when any element of state action is proposed by asking whether it falls within its sphere or whether it encroaches on the sphere of the individual. These spheres cannot be determined in advance of experience, nor need they be mutually exclusive.[47] It cannot be predicted on what issues the state might profitably intervene. Each case must be taken on its merits and comply with the evolutionary utilitarian test of whether it is expedient, that is, whether it contributes to or detracts from the common good of society now and for future generations. What Ritchie is emphatic about is that evil conditions that are sources of misery must be eradicated, and we as members of a moral community have a collective responsibility to eradicate them.[48]

In the second selection from Ritchie he talks of animal rights, extending the argument of his book *Natural Rights*, in which he is critical of traditional conceptions of natural rights as somehow

[45] See for example, Edward Caird, *The Moral Aspect of the Economical Problem* (Glasgow: Maclehose, 1888) and *Individualism and Socialism* (Glasgow: Maclehose, 1897). For a summary of Caird's position see Henry Jones and John Henry Muirhead, *The Life and Philosophy of Edward Caird* (Glasgow: Maclehose, 1921), pp. 317–31. Also see David G. Ritchie, 'Law and Liberty: The Question of State Interference' (1891) reprinted in *Studies in Political and Social Ethics* (London, Swan Sonnenschein, 1902), pp. 43–65; and Bernard Bosanquet, 'The Antithesis between Individualism and Socialism Philosophically Considered', (1890), reprinted in *The Civilization of Christendom and other studies* (London, 1893).

[46] David G. Ritchie, 'Moral Function of the State', in *Collected Works of D.G. Ritchie*, ed. Peter Nicholson (Bristol: Thoemmes, 1998), vol. 6, p. 9.

[47] David Ritchie, *The Principles of State Interference* (London: Swan Sonnenschein, 1891), p. 107.

[48] Ritchie, 'Moral Function of the State', p. 5.

inhering in the individual in a pre-social condition and, through a social compact, brings them into society. On this view the purpose of the state is to protect individual rights. Ritchie's point is that rights are social and are recognized and sustained by the moral community. Animals have been at the centre of rights issues in recent years, most prominently in the writings of Peter Singer. He uses the analogy of blacks who argued against discrimination and fought to eliminate second-class status to suggest that animals should be regarded as equal in certain morally relevant respects. Singer's argument does not really constitute a defence of animal rights as such. He actually makes a case for a different kind of equality, the equal consideration of interests rather than the equal respect of rights.[49] To focus on animal interests is to acknowledge that our mistreatment of animals is morally wrong not because we have violated their rights, but because we have harmed them in some way. The issue is not one of egalitarian justice, as it was in the civil rights movement, but of unnecessary and unjustifiable cruelty to animals.[50] Ritchie suggests that an utilitarian argument for the rights of animals cannot be sustained. Sentience and the capacity to feel pain as the basis of equating human and animal rights requires criteria to determine different degrees of sentience and what rights may be assigned to them. Once a scale of this type is published it is logically difficult to resist gradations being applied within human society. If animal rights permit the humane treatment of the horse as a beast of burden, then the humane treatment of negro slaves may be equally as compatible with human rights.[51] Like Green, Ritchie believes that all rights depend upon membership of a community, and membership of a community entails being a moral agent. Animals are not moral agents and may be said to have rights only metaphorically, if we admit them with a sort of membership into our homes and families as quasi-persons. We are, in such circumstances, admitting of special claims on us to which we owe obligations, but this is not to concede animals the possession of legal or moral rights.

[49] Peter Singer, 'All Animals are Equal' in *Animal Rights and Human Obligations*, ed. Tom Reegan and Peter Singer (London: Prentice Hall: 2nd edn., 1989), p. 73.

[50] Carl Wellman, *The Proliferation of Rights* (Oxford: Westview Press, 1999), pp. 176–7.

[51] Ritchie, *Natural Rights*, p. 107.

The legal protection of animals from cruelty, and the classification of some as endangered, does not mean that they have rights, anymore than ancient monuments or works of art have rights because they are protected by law. Animals are the beneficiaries of obligations we have under the law, but it is stretching the concept of rights too far to suggest that animals possess rights, or to suggest that they are able to claim them. Pain, Ritchie argues, is an evil, not in any special moral sense, but in that it impedes the development of life and is instinctively avoided as best it can by every sentient being. Sympathetic and imaginative empathy with human and non-human animals who have been subjected to pain, have brought us to the view that it is a duty to prevent unnecessary and gratuitous pain. Animals, then, do not possess legal rights. In the case of moral rights, those rights that are acknowledged and enforced by society, animals may with greater justification be said to have rights. But even with moral rights Ritchie thinks it more accurate to say that *we* have duties of kindness towards animals: 'these duties being duties owed to human society and enforced, more or less, by it.'[52] In other words cruelty to animals is uncivilized and an affront to any decent society, but not a violation of the rights of animals as such.[53] Carl Wellman argues a similar case when he suggests that being a right-holder necessarily presupposes moral agency.[54] Non-human animals are not citizens, nor are they persons, and because they lack moral agency they are incapable of possessing either legal or moral rights.[55]

R.B. Haldane, as a prominent Liberal politician before and during the First World War, bore the brunt of public disapproval in popular newspapers and magazines for his admiration of German philosophy and the German education system.[56] Haldane was an enthusiastic defender of Hegelian Absolutism, and was therefore implicated in the criticism that in subordinating the individual to the state, and in making individuality an adjectival mode of being, the idealists gave credence to the all powerful totalitarian state in which the individual is an instrument to its

[52]   Ritchie, 'The Rights of Animals', p. 388.
[53]   Ritchie, *Natural Rights*, p. 111.
[54]   Carl Wellman, *Real Rights* (New York: Oxford University Press, 1995), pp. 105–77.
[55]   Wellman, *The Proliferation of Rights*, p. 175.
[56]   See Stephen E. Koss, *Lord Haldane: Scapegoat for Liberalism* (New York, Columbia University Press, 1969), chapters 3 and 6.

ends. This was an unjustifiable criticism, but it nevertheless persisted.[57]

The British Idealists, including the Scottish, were much more internationalist than is generally appreciated, and therefore diverge considerably from Hegel. Green and the British Hegelians in general were more forceful than Hegel in maintaining that the organization of sovereign states would be superseded by a gradual extension of the community within which a common will prevailed. Even in the most primitive communities, Green suggests, there is a consciousness of a good and of participators in it. Reason and the consciousness of the unfulfilled potential of a common rationality lead us to acknowledge wider and wider circles of people who have claims upon us and who are capable of participating in the common good. He contends that: 'It is not the sense of duty to a neighbour, but the practical answer to the question Who is my neighbour? that has varied.'[58] Furthermore, it is not the idea of a cosmopolitan humanity that needs to be explained, but the retreat from it by sectional interests and privileged classes who are prepared to lend their weight to any counter-theory that furthers their exclusive ends.[59]

There is no international moral tradition comparable with that sustained within a state, but their relations are nevertheless 'mitigated by humane conventions and usages'.[60] The existence of these conventions and usages functioning as and constituting a code of morality is emphasized much more prominently by Caird, Sorley, MacKenzie, MacCunn, Jones, Watson and Haldane. They value highly the fact that the constant interaction of nations, especially among Europeans, has given rise to a common morality. Morality, they maintain, does not require or rest upon legal enforcement, and the discharge of one's moral duty does not depend upon legal sanction. There is much in morality that falls outside the scope of law, such as compassion, decency

---

[57] David Boucher, 'British Idealism, the State and International Relations', *Journal of the History of Ideas*, 55 (1994), pp. 671–94, and David Boucher, 'British Idealist International Theory', *Hegel Society Bulletin*, 31 (1995), pp. 73–89.

[58] T. H. Green, *Prolegomena to Ethics* (Oxford: Clarendon Press, 1899), p. 247.

[59] *Ibid.*, p. 250.

[60] Bosanquet, 'Patriotism in a Perfect State', p. 149; Also see, *ibid.*, pp. 135, 137, and 150; Bosanquet, 'Function of the State in Promoting the Unity of Mankind', pp. 288, 192, 295 and 297.

and humaneness, the duties attaching to which do not depend upon enforced obedience. The classic statement of this point of view among British Hegelians is that of Lord Haldane's 'Higher Nationality: A Study in Law and Ethics'.[61] He argues that in addition to law there is a broader body of guidance quite different in character and distinctive in sanction. It is *Sittlichkeit*, defined as 'the system of habitual or customary conduct, ethical rather than legal, which embraces all those obligations of the citizen which it is "bad form" or "not the thing" to disregard'.[62] It is held in such high esteem that those who disregard it suffer the social sanctions of disapproval or of being slighted. It is not the ethics of conscience as such. Its standard is the example of respected decent people in their relations with members of the community to which they belong. Haldane suggests that, 'it is this instinctive sense of obligation that is the chief foundation of society'.[63]

---

[61] Reprinted in *Selected Addresses and Essays* (London: Murray, 1928), pp. 49–93. The essay was written in 1913.

[62] *Ibid.*, p. 68.

[63] *Ibid.*, p. 69.

One

Edward Caird

Edward Caird was born in Greenock on 23 March 1835, the fifth of seven sons of John Caird, a Greenock engineer who died in 1838, and Janet Roderick Young from Paisley. During his childhood Caird lived with his aunt Jane Caird, who was a devout Christian and determined to instil religion into Edward. He was educated at Greenock Academy and in 1850, at the age of fifteen, entered Glasgow University. He attended classes in the Faculties of Arts and Divinity, until illness forced him to move to St. Andrews and then to Errol in Perthshire where his elder brother John, later Principal of the University of Glasgow, was the parish minister. Edward went to Dresden to improve his German and study classical literature. He admired the work of Goethe and was inspired by reading Carlyle's poetic and philosophical idealism. In 1858 he returned to Glasgow University to study Divinity, but then went to Oxford where he met up with his old class friend John Nicol who founded the Old Mortality Society at Oxford. Its members included A.V. Dicey and T.H. Green. Caird was the only under-graduate invited to join. He was taught by Benjamin Jowett at Oxford, who was familiar with the writings of Hegel. Caird became friends with T. H. Green with whom he shared the same passion for politics and educational reform as well as a keen inter-est in German philosophy. In 1863 Caird graduated and became a fellow and tutor of Merton College. In 1866 he left Oxford to take up Adam Smith's old chair of moral philosophy at Glasgow. In 1893 he returned to Oxford to succeed Jowett as Master of Balliol College. Caird was married on 8 May 1867 to Caroline Wylie, the daughter of a Lanarkshire parish minister. They had no children. In 1907 Caird retired because of ill health after suffering a stroke in 1905. He passed away at home, 12 Bardwell Road, Oxford, on 1 November 1908. He was laid to rest next to Green and Jowett in St. Sepulchre's cemetery.

Caird exercised an immense influence on those he taught, among them Henry Jones, who was to succeed him at Glasgow, J.H. Muirhead and John Watson. Caird was passionate about pol-itics and social questions, and loved the company of students, especially females, often inviting them for walks during which he said very little. He was notoriously absent minded and was said to remark to his wife, who found him standing by the side of the bath, that he could not remember whether he was getting in or getting out. Like Green, he was always a strong advocate of uni-versity education for women and working men. He supported the establishment of Ruskin College, Oxford, for the higher educa-tion of working men, and actively extended education to the industrial areas of the South East of England by means of the Uni-versity Extension Scheme. He lectured in the East End of London, for example, on socialism. In Glasgow he was the leading light in establishing 'The Women's Protective and Provident League' whose objective was to improve by protective legislation the working conditions of women and children in industry. He was instrumental in setting up 'The University Settlement Associa-tion', modelled after Toynbee Hall in London. He also admired the Garibaldi rising of 1859 and the place of Abraham Lincoln in the American Civil War. He was a vociferous opponent of the

Boer War and strongly objected to Cecil Rhodes being honoured by Oxford University in 1899.

Caird was awarded honorary doctorates from the universities of St. Andrews (1883), Oxford (1891), Cambridge (1898) and Wales (1902). He was an original Fellow of the British Academy (1902) and a corresponding member of the French Académy des Sciences morales et politiques. He delivered the Gifford Lectures in St. Andrews, 1891–2, and in Glasgow, 1900.

Biographical

The Times, 3 Nov. 1908.

Glasgow Herald, 6 Nov. 1908.

'Caird, Edward (1835–1908), *Dictionary of National Biography*.

John Watson, 'Edward Caird as Teacher and Thinker', *Queen's Quarterly*, xvi (1908).

Bernard Bosanquet, 'Edward Caird 1835–1908', *Proceedings of the British Academy*, 3 (1907–8).

Sir Henry Jones and J.H. Muirhead, *The Life and Philosophy of Edward Caird* (Glasgow, Maclehose, 1921).

'Caird, Edward' in *Dictionary of Nineteenth Century British Philosophers*, ed. W.J. Mander and Alan P.F. Sell (Bristol: Thoemmes, 2002), pp. 179–85.

Colin Tyler, 'Biographical Appendices' in *The Collected Works of Edward Caird*, ed. Tyler (Bristol: Thoemmes, 1999), vol. 11, pp. xiii–xxxviii.

Principal Works

A Critical Account of the Philosophy of Kant (Glasgow: Maclehose, 1877).

Hegel (Edinburgh: Blackwood, 1883).

Essays on Literature and Philosophy, 2 vols. (Glasgow: Maclehose, 1892).

The Evolution of Religion (Glasgow: Maclehose, 1893).

The Collected Works of Edward Caird, ed. Colin Tyler (Bristol: Thoemmes, 1999).

READING I

THE PROBLEM OF PHILOSOPHY AT
THE PRESENT TIME[1]

In complying with the request which you have done me the honour to make, to deliver the introductory address to this Society, I think that, instead of treating of any special philosophical subject, it will be more profitable to make some general remarks on the nature and objects of the study to which the Society is devoted. I propose, therefore, to say something as to the general problem of philosophy, and the special forms which that problem has taken in recent times. In doing so, it will not be possible for me to avoid an appearance of dogmatism, as I must make some assertions which are much disputed, the objections to which I shall not have time to discuss. But instead of interpolating any cheap formulas of modesty, I venture simply to make this apology once for all, and to ask you to adopt, for the time, a point of view which may not be your own. Afterwards you can avenge yourselves for this temporary submission by subjecting my words to what criticism you think fit. A philosophic temper is shown, above all things, in the power of entering into the views of another, and taking them for the moment almost as if they were your own, without prejudice to the subsequent critical reaction, which will be effective just in proportion to the degree of your previous sympathetic appreciation of the ideas criticized.

What, then, is the task of philosophy? What is its task in general, and how is that task modified by the circumstances of the present time? To the first of these questions, I answer that, stated in very general terms, the task of philosophy is to gain, or rather perhaps to regain, such a view of things as shall reconcile us to the world and to ourselves. The need for philosophy arises out of the broken harmony of a spiritual life, in which the different elements or factors seem to be set in irreconcilable opposition to each other; in which, for example, the religious consciousness, the consciousness of the infinite, is at war with the secular consciousness, the consciousness of the finite; or again, the consciousness of the external world. It is easy to see this, if we reflect on the nature of the controversies which most trouble us at present. They all,

---

[1]   'The Problem of Philosophy at the Present Time' in *Essays on Literature and Philosophy*, Vol. 1 (Glasgow: Maclehose, 1892), pp. 190–229.

directly or indirectly, turn upon the difficulty of reconciling the three great terms of thought — the world, self and God: the difficulty of carrying out to their legitimate consequences what seem to be our most firmly based convictions as to any one of these factors in our intellectual life, without rejecting in whole or in part the claims of others.

Thus, for example, many writers in the present time find it impossible to admit the truth and solidity of the principles and methods of physical science in relation to the material world, without extending their application beyond that world. Yet, if we make this extension, and treat these methods and principles as universal, we inevitably reduce consciousness, thought and will, to the level of physical phenomena, and make even their existence an insoluble problem. Others, again, find it difficult to assert the truth, that the consciousness of self enters into all our experience, without reducing that experience to a series of states of the individual soul. And others, like Mr Spencer and Professor Huxley, poised between these two conflicting currents of thought, have adopted the odd, and we might even say irrational, expedient of telling us that we may regard the world *either* as a collection of the phenomena of mind, *or* as a collection of the phenomena of matter, but that we can never bring these two ways of looking at things together — a view which supposes man to be afflicted with a kind of intellectual *strabismus*, so that he can never see with one of his mental eyes without shutting the other. Again, looking beyond this conflict of materialism and subjective idealism, the intellectual unity of our life is disturbed by the opposition of the consciousness of the infinite to the consciousness of the finite. To many of our scientific men it seems axiomatic that all our real knowledge is of that which belongs to the context of a finite experience, and that all religious and metaphysical efforts to reach beyond the finite are attempts to think the unknown and unknowable. Yet such men often feel strongly the need, and, from their point of view, the extreme difficulty, of finding anything to give to the moral life of man that support which was once found in the belief that these dreams are realities. On the other hand, there are not a few men in our day — like the hero of that remarkable little book called *Mark Rutherford* — men whose very life is in religious ideas, yet who have imbibed from the literature of the time a conviction that such ideas must be illusory, and who therefore dwell, as it were, in a world of eclipse and paralysis, neither able to find a faith nor to do without one, sitting

> by the poisoned springs of life,
> Waiting for the morrow that shall free them from the strife.

Now, it is impossible, so long as our ultimate thought of the world is thus in discord with itself, that our lives should be what human lives have sometimes been — impossible that we should rise to that energy of undivided will and affection, that free play of concentrated intelligence, that sense of the infinite resources of the spirit that moves us, out of which the highest achievements of men at all times have sprung. Nor, after the unity of our first instinctive faith has been broken by difficulties such as those I have mentioned, is it possible entirely to recover it, except by some kind of philosophical reflection. Bacon said that in the last period of ancient civilization philosophy took the place of religion, and the same is to some extent true now. In face of the modern spirit of criticism, it is rarely possible for educated men, and for students of philosophy it is impossible, to rest for the entire support of their spiritual life upon the simple intuitions of faith. For them the age of unconsciousness is past, and they must call in the aid of reflection, if it were only to heal the wounds of reflection itself. As the builders of the second Temple had to work with arms by their side, so, in our day, those who seek either to maintain, or to replace, the old Christian synthesis of life, must provide themselves with the weapons of philosophy. It is not of our own choice that we have been born in an age of criticism; but being here, and being by our education brought face to face with all the prevalent currents of thought, we have only two alternatives before us; we must face our difficulties, or we must suppress them. Do we resolve to suppress them — we see often enough what kind of moral temper comes of *that* — the fevered fanatical spirit that founds its faith on the impossibility of knowing anything, and determines to believe, because it dare not do otherwise. Yet, if we are not content with such faith, we must seek the reconciliation of the contradictory elements of our consciousness in some new reflective synthesis, in other words, in philosophy.

The task of philosophy then, I repeat, is to rise to such a general view of things as shall reconcile us, or enable us to reconcile ourselves, to the world and to ourselves. This vague statement, however, might easily be admitted by many who will be startled and repelled when we draw out its meaning. For it means no less than this, that philosophy, by the very condition of its life, is forced to attempt what Comtists have called an 'objective', or what perhaps might more properly be termed an 'absolute' synthesis. It is true that many philosophers, and even great philosophers, have tried to evade this necessity, and to narrow the problem of philosophy within limits which made its solution seem easier. Especially in times of transition, when social bonds have become relaxed, and religious faith has been weakened or destroyed, philosophy also has generally lowered its claims, and has been content to abandon the great world to chaos, if only it could secure some little cosmos of its own. To these causes of diffidence in philosophy others in recent times have been added; for our very widening knowledge of the universe has thrown a shadow of suspicion upon the attempt to measure it, and has inclined us to narrow our views to a solution of the problem of human life, and to disconnect it from the problem of the unity of all things. Can we not, it is natural to ask, find a meaning in our own lives without spelling out the secret of the universe? Can we not build our fragile houses of mortality on something less than an eternal foundation? With the growth of our knowledge grows also the consciousness of our ignorance, and more and more the latter seems to reduce the former into something merely relative and transitional. Looking out upon the wide sea of knowledge, with some measure of appreciation of its extent, it seemed but reasonable for one like Comte to say, that an 'objective synthesis', a systematic view of the world as a whole, was beyond the reach of man; and that, if his life was to be brought into harmony with itself on a basis of knowledge, he must content himself with a 'subjective synthesis', a synthesis which leaves out all speculation in relation to the greater whole of the universe, and attempts only to gather knowledge to a focus in the interests of man.

In taking up this position, Comte, it has been urged by his followers, showed a true insight into our needs as rational beings, who must desire to bring our lives into harmony and unity upon an intelligent view of the facts of our condition; and he showed at the same time a right appreciation of the limits which are set around us as finite creatures, standing in the face of a universe,

the ultimate meaning of which is hidden from us by the weakness
of our mental capacity and the narrowness of our opportunities.

Comte's view of things is thus based upon two incontrovertible
facts — the limitation of man's powers and the imperative wants
of his moral being. The old aspiring religious and philosophical
synthesis, he argues, has been discredited forever by our knowledge of the immensity of the universe and of our own feebleness.
It is impossible for the creature of a day to see things *sub specie
aeternitatis* [under the aspect of eternity], for a finite mind to carry
back the infinity of the universe to its central principle, to view it
as a harmonious system, and, like God, to pronounce it 'very
good'. But yet there remains the inextinguishable requirement of
a rational and moral nature to rise above chance impulses and
energies, and to find some one guiding principle of thought and
action which shall make his life harmonious with itself. And this
principle, since we cannot find it in an Absolute, whom we do *not*
know, we must find in man — man individual or man social —
whom we *do* know. Renouncing, therefore, all questions as to the
system of the universe, even the question whether it *is* a system,
we can still draw back upon ourselves and find and produce system and harmony in our own lives. Or, if this is impossible for us
as regards the fragmentary existence of the individual, we may
yet detect in the history of the human race a tendency towards
unity and organization, to which all the great and good of the past
have contributed, and we may give value and completeness to
our individual lives by making them the instruments of this 'increasing purpose'.

The question which Comte thus brings home to us is, as I have
already indicated, not a new one. It is the question whether it is
possible to have a religion — *i.e.*, 'a free convergence of all man's
affections and energies' to one object, without a God; and a philosophy, *i.e.*, a synthesis or gathering to one focus of all knowledge, without an Absolute.[2] And this is a question that has been
raised more or less distinctly in every era of transition, when the
'native hue' of human resolution has been 'sicklied o'er with a
pale cast of thought', and when men have been fain to gather up
the fragments that remained in the shipwreck of their greater
faiths and hopes. The individualism of the Stoics, Epicureans and

---

[2]   Cf. *The Unity of Comte's Life and Doctrine*, by J.H. Bridges. London:
       Trübner & Co., 1866.

Sceptics, for example, corresponding as it did with the decay of ancient religion and social morality, was in great measure a result of such a temper of mind. As men gave up the hope of organizing their own social relations, and of understanding the world as an intelligible order, they fell back upon the idea of an inner life, which might maintain harmony with itself in the face even of an outward chaos. Philosophy, it began to be said, is needed, not to penetrate into the secret of the world, which is impenetrable, but to teach us our limits and to make us content with them. *Tecum habita et noris quam sit tibi curta supellex* [Live only with yourself, and you will realize how limited your household goods are]. Yet that *curta supellex* [those limited goods] is enough; the peace of inward unity may be attained, even if we know nothing and can do nothing in the world without. Sure of nothing else, the individual may be sure of himself, and in the strength of a mind centred and at rest in itself, may cease to concern himself with things that can only touch the outward life.

> *Si fractus illabatur orbis,*
> *Impavidum ferient ruinae.*
> [If the world should fall in on him,
> its ruins would strike him unafraid.]

Now, I need not dwell on the self-contradiction of this extreme of 'subjective' synthesis, in which all that is without is abandoned to chaos or uncertainty, in order that the integrity of the inner life may be preserved. It is a commonplace of philosophy that we cannot thus withdraw into ourselves and leave the world to wander its own wise or unwise way, inasmuch as the two terms thus separated by abstraction are essentially united, and our experience of the world *is* our experience of ourselves. The life of reason or consciousness is essentially a life that goes beyond itself, and in which the inward cannot be absolutely fenced off from the outward without itself ceasing to have any meaning or content. It is a life of *knowledge*, in which we can know ourselves, only as we know the universe of which, as individuals, we form a part. It is a life of *action*, in which we can realize ourselves, only by becoming the servants of an end which is being realized in the world. Concentrate consciousness entirely upon itself, and its unreflected light will cease to shine. The world without and the world within are not two separate worlds, but necessary counterparts of each other; and, just in the extent to which we succeed in withdrawing from the world without, we narrow the world within.

The attitude, therefore, of the Stoic or Sceptic who turns away from a world which he surrenders to chaos and unreason, or in which, at least, he gives up the hope of seeing or producing any rational order, and who seeks thus to find all truth and happiness within, is essentially irrational. He is striving to realize in isolation a life whose essential characteristic is community. He is seeking to save the life of the seed, which must be cast into the ground and die, that it may live, by keeping it shut up from all external influences. For the Christian law of self-sacrifice, 'he that would save his life must lose it', is nothing more than the transcription into terms of morality of that which is the general law of spiritual life — a life whose riches are always for the individual exactly measured by the extent to which he breaks down the limits of a self-centred individuality, to find himself again in the larger existence of the whole.

But if this be the case, and if it is impossible to solve the problem of the inner life without solving the apparently wiser problem of the outer life, or to base on a purely subjective synthesis a reconciliation of the spirit with itself, such as was formerly based on the objective synthesis of religion or philosophy, equally impossible is it to draw any other absolute line of division, such, for example, as that between the life of the nation and the life of humanity, or again, between the life of humanity and the course of nature. In every similar division we are separating elements so correlated that the meaning of each one of them begins to evaporate so soon as we realize what we have done in separating it from the rest. To make such an abstraction must introduce a fatal discord between the practical life of man, and the facts upon which we pretend to base it. And indeed, as I think can be shown in the case of Comte, such an attempt involves the self-deception of treating that as absolute and divine, which we at the same time admit to be uncertain and transitory.[3] How, for example, can we make a God out of humanity, if we think of mankind as a race of beings which is not really organic, but in which there is only a general tendency to organization, a tendency, which again is subjected to an immeasurable external contingency? Comte's attempt to escape the

[3]   I have attempted to show this in my book on *The Social Philosophy and Religion of Comte.*

great difficulties which confessedly beset an optimistic creed — the creed that in some way all things work together for good — by thus falling back from the assertion of system in the universe, to the assertion of system only in the life of man, like most compromises, unites all the difficulties of both extremes it would avoid; the difficulties of an absolute philosophy, which seems to go beyond the limits of human knowledge, and the difficulties of a scepticism, which leaves the moral and intellectual life of man without a principle of unity. The Stoic or Sceptic who bids us concentrate ourselves on our own soul, and the Positivist, who bids us worship humanity, are equally bidding us treat a part, which we can know and understand only as a part, as if it were the whole. They are attempting to break in one place only the indivisible unity of the intelligence and the intelligible world; but if that unity be broken in one place it is wholly destroyed. *Falsus in uno, falsus in omnibus* [faulty in one, faulty in all]. For it is a unity which is not like a particular hypothesis, that may be asserted or denied without detriment to the rest of our knowledge, but it is the hypothesis, if we may so call it, which is implied in all knowledge whatever, the hypothesis which constitutes our rational being. Hence Kant showed a true sense of the conditions of philosophical synthesis, when he said that, if it could be shown that there was one metaphysical problem with which his *Critique of Pure Reason* was incompetent to deal, it must be regarded as an entire failure. If philosophy is incapable of a universal synthesis, it cannot make any synthesis at all. If it admit any absolute division, whether between the ego and the non-ego, or between man and nature, or even between the finite and infinite, it is driven of necessity into scepticism. Unless it reconciles us with the universe, it cannot even reconcile us with ourselves. The present is a time in which there are many voices to welcome the well-known saying of Pope:

> Know well thyself, presume not God to scan,
> The proper study of mankind is man;

but the simple, yet demonstrable answer to such partial Agnosticism is, that if we cannot, in the sense I have indicated, know God, we cannot know anything.

But if this be so, if we cannot give up the idea of a universal synthesis, without practically giving up philosophy altogether, we must not hide from ourselves the enormous difficulties with which philosophy has to contend, difficulties which seem to grow every day with our increasing knowledge of man and of the world in which he lives. For all this knowledge seems to be making wider and wider the division between the individual and the universal, between the vision of short-sighted, changeable creatures such as men seem to be, and the all-embracing whole. These difficulties, however, though they by no means disappear, yet somewhat change their character, when we consider that the work of philosophy is not in the first instance constructive, but rather critical and reconstructive; that its business is not to seek for something transcendent, some hypothesis as to things hitherto unknown and alien to our experience, but rather to bring to light the hypothesis, if we choose to call it so, on which our rational being is founded. Philosophy must necessarily seem to be something extravagant and wildly ambitious to any one who does not discern that the problem it would solve is not one which arbitrarily, or as a matter merely of curiosity, we *choose* to solve, but one which we have in some way been solving, or of which we have been presupposing the solution, at every moment of our lives. To rise from the finite to the infinite would be impossible, if the consciousness of the infinite were not already involved in the consciousness of the finite, and developed along with it. Philosophy is not a first venture into a new field of thought, but the re-thinking of a secular and religious consciousness, which has been developed, in the main, independently of philosophy. It was the great work of Kant to show that experience itself is possible only through the necessity and universality of thought. But in thus proving the relativity of the finite objects of experience to the intelligence (which is not itself such an object), he really showed — though without himself being fully conscious of it, and almost, we might say, against his will — that we cannot admit the validity of the empirical consciousness without admitting the validity of the consciousness of that which, in the narrower sense of the word, is beyond experience.

Hence, to one who follows out the Kantian principles to their legitimate result, it becomes impossible to treat the objective synthesis of religion as the illusion of a finite mind trying to stretch itself beyond its proper limits. The religious takes its place beside the secular consciousness, the consciousness of the infinite beside consciousness of a real object, or rather of the ultimate reality upon which everything else rests. And philosophy, in dealing with the one as with the other, is discharged from the absurd and impossible feat of finding its way into a transcendent region beyond all consciousness and experience. In both cases, in relation to the infinite as in relation to the finite world, the work of philosophy goes beyond the primary unreflected consciousness of man only in this aspect, that it brings that consciousness to a deeper understanding of itself. In both we have a right to begin our task of criticism and reconstruction with a faith in the great work achieved in and by the spirit of man in the past; and we ought to begin it with the consciousness that *our* criticism and reconstruction can have value only as a continuation of that work. For it is this consciousness that alone can justifiably raise us above the feeling of our own weakness for the task which is laid upon philosophy in our time, and can save us from the intruding suspicion, that in his religions and his philosophies man has been perpetually renewing the history of Babel – attempting to build a tower that shall reach to heaven, only to find that work again and again stopped by the confusion of languages among the builders. If, therefore, philosophy may be described as a critical reconstruction of belief, we must recollect that this reconstruction, from a higher point of view, is merely development; or, to put it more simply, we must remember that, in philosophy as in other things, the hope of mankind for the future must be a vain illusion, unless it can reasonably be based on a deep reverence for the past.

In the 'Faust' of Goethe, the poet who of all others has most deeply fathomed and expressed the conflict of the modern spirit with itself — though it may perhaps be said that, like a physician strong in diagnosis but not in therapeutics, he often stops at the description of the disease, and finds his own poetic deliverance from it simply in this describing it[4] — we find some words that may be applied to the work of philosophy. When Faust utters all his despair of life in that comprehensive curse in which he disowns every faith, and even every illusion that has hitherto supported mankind, the chorus of spirits breaks in with a song, in

---

[4] 'Physician of the iron age, / Goethe has done his pilgrimage. / He took the suffering human race, / He read each wound, each weakness clear, / And struck his finger on the place, / And said: '*Thou ailest here, and here!*' *Arnold's Poems, Memorial Verses*, April 1850.

which lament over what has been lost is mingled with a far-off
hint of the only possible restoration:

> Woe, woe, thou hast destroyed it,
> The beautiful world,
> With mighty blow;
> It trembles it falls to ruins.
> A Demigod hath broken it down.
> We bear away the ruins into nothingness,
> And lament over the lost beauty.

And then the song goes on:

> Mighty One
> Of the sons of earth,
> With greater majesty
> Build it up,
> In thine own soul build it up again;
> A new course of life
> Begin,
> With fresh unclouded sense,
> And let new songs rise
> In place of those that are silenced.

'In thine own soul build it up again' — this is the ever-repeated
call to philosophy at all times, such as the present, when the first
unity of faith and reason is disturbed. But the task has become, if
in some respects a harder, yet in other respects a more hopeful one
in modern times. That this is so may be shown by a short comparison of the form in which the problem presented itself to Plato and
Aristotle, with the form in which it presents itself to us. In Plato's
Republic, we find an attempt to 'build up again in the soul' of the
philosopher the falling edifice of Greek civilization, to restore its
religious and political life, by going back to the ideal principle on
which it rested. But the difficulty of such restoration lay in this,
that the first intuitive synthesis of Greece was a synthesis of the
imagination, in which that which was essentially limited and
national was treated as unlimited and universal. Greek morality
did not look beyond the boundary of the nation, seldom even
beyond the boundary of the civic state. Greek religion, as it was an
apotheosis of the special gifts of Greek genius, was in some measure a consecration of the national spirit of exclusion. Hence, neither religion nor morality could offer an effective resistance to the
disintegrating power of reflection. As it was mainly the poetic
imagination which had peopled Olympus with the fair humani-

ties of the gods, the power of Greek religion disappeared almost as soon as the people became capable of distinguishing poetry from prose. And as, in the ethical life of the Greek state, the local and temporal was rather confused than reconciled with that which is universal, it fell an easy prey to the casuistry of the Sophists. On the other hand the scepticism of the Sophists remained superficial and rhetorical, just because it found so little power of resistance in the institutions which it attacked. When, therefore, philosophy in Plato and Aristotle set itself to the task of reconstructing the synthesis upon which the moral and intellectual life of Greece was founded, and restoring the broken harmony of faith and reason, its reconciliation was necessarily imperfect, because of the imperfection of the positive and negative elements which it sought to reconcile. It tried to combine the freedom of thought, which had shown itself in the Sophistic movement, with the substantial contents of Greek life, morality and religion, which Sophistry had rejected. But the freedom and universality of thought was in essential conflict with the limited character of the contents; and even to Plato himself a merely imaginative religion could not be more than a 'noble lie', *i.e.*, a truth veiled under an inadequate sensuous form. The element of philosophy in which the reconciliation was attempted, was itself fatal to the reconciliation aimed at. Hence already in Plato we find the beginning of that withdrawal into the inner life from an unideal world, which was carried out in subsequent philosophy, and which of necessity ended in the self-contradiction of scepticism.

The modern movement from faith to reason bears a striking analogy to the movement of ancient thought. Yet there are important differences, which make the struggle of tendencies in modern times harder and more obstinate, but which also for that very reason enable us to anticipate a more satisfactory result. Here, too, we have system of religion apprehended by the intuitive consciousness of faith, and manifesting itself in definite forms of intellectual and social life. Here, too, we have the spirit of reflection after a time awakening and subjecting the whole religious system, as well as all the institutions founded upon it, to a searching, and often a destructive criticism. And here, too, we find philosophy attempting to restore the broken harmony of man's consciousness of himself and the world, by separating the permanent from the transitory elements of his earlier faith. But, beneath this general similarity of development there are many points of contrast: which we may roughly sum up by saying that the first synthesis of Christendom took the form of a religion which was not national but universal, and that the negative movement against it has been not merely analytic and sophistic, but also scientific, and, therefore, within certain limits, constructive. Hence, also, just because of the deeper spiritual meaning and fuller development of the two seemingly opposed powers that divide our life, we have some reason to think that it may be possible to combine what is good in both, and to attain to a philosophical synthesis, which may be not merely provisional but of permanent value for mankind. Let me say a few more words on each of these points.

The religion of Greece was, as I have said, national, not universal, and for that very reason it was essentially a religion of the artistic imagination; for it is the imagination which lifts the part into a whole, and makes a particular into a substitute for the universal. It has been called an anthropomorphic religion; but, as Hegel has remarked, in the higher sense it was not anthropomorphic enough — it lifted some human qualities into the divine, but not humanity itself as such. Its gods were ideal figures, humanized rather than human, fixed like statues in the eternal repose of beauty, and lifted above all the narrowing conditions of human life. Christianity, on the other hand, brought down the divine into the form of an individual life lived under those conditions, struggling with the wants and pains of mortality and the opposition of fellow mortals, and undergoing and accepting the common lot of renunciation, sorrow and death. It thus idealized, not choice specimens of intelligence and valour, but humanity itself, in its simplest and humblest form of life. It taught the world not to regard the ideal as something which a few elect spirits might reach, by escaping from the commonplace itself; to make the limits of mortality the means of freedom, and to turn pain, death and even evil into forms of the manifestation of good. Now this optimism on the very basis of pessimism, whose Christ has 'descended into hell', this idealization of ordinary reality as it stands without selection or change, just because it was *this*, was no religion of phantasy, of art, of the poetic imagination merely. It did not flinch from the facts of life, however dark and threatening, or seek to turn its eyes to some earthly paradise lifted above the clouds and the winds.

Art in it was secondary, not primary; in its poetry truth was bursting through the sensuous veil. And from this it necessarily follows that it is not a dream that vanishes with a waking of the prosaic consciousness in either of its shapes, either as the distinct common-sense apprehension of fact, or as the reflective analysis of thought. Whatever changes of form, therefore, it has been, and may yet be subjected to (and I do not say that these will be small), the Christian view of the world in its essence is based upon such a simple acknowledgment of the truth and reality of things, that it need not fear overthrow, even from our widening knowledge of the facts of life, or from the deeper self-consciousness to which reflection is gradually bringing us. In the midst even of apparent rejection, its ideals have maintained and increased their hold over the emancipated intelligence of Europe, and its fundamental conception of life penetrates and moulds the social and religious speculations of those who, like Comte, seem to have most thoroughly renounced it.

On the other hand, if the first intuitional basis of modern life is thus strong in itself, strong too, it must be acknowledged, are the powers that assail it. The sophistic culture that undermined the old beliefs of Greece, and the morality founded upon them, was but a feeble solvent, compared with the disintegrating force of negative reflection and scientific criticism, to which *our* faiths are subjected. The boldness of the ancient sceptic was chilled by a sense of the weakness of his own position. He might set the human against the divine, the individual against the State, the finite and relative against the infinite and absolute; but he was paralysed by the negative character of his own teaching, by the consciousness that his emancipation of the intellect was a process whereby it was emptied of all contents, and that his liberation of the individual from limited social bonds could lead to nothing better than anarchy. In modern times, on the other hand, it has ceased to be so. The world of finite interests and objects has rounded itself, as it were, into a separate whole, within which the mind of man can fortify itself, and live *securus adversus deos*, in independence of the infinite. In the sphere of *thought*, there has been forming itself an ever-increasing body of science, which, tracing out the relation of finite things to finite things, never finds it necessary to seek for a beginning or an end to its infinite series of phenomena, and which meets the claims of theology with the saying of the astronomer, 'I do not need that hypothesis'. In the sphere of *action*, again, the complexity of modern life presents a thousand isolated interests, crossing each other in ways too subtle to trace out — interest commercial, social and political — in pursuing one or other of which the individual may find ample occupation for his existence, without ever feeling the need of any return upon himself, or seeing any reason to ask himself whether this endless striving has any meaning or object beyond itself. Nor need we wonder that the prevailing school of philosophy is one that renounces all such questions as vain, and bids us be content to know that we can know nothing. The very wealth of modern life and science, both because it makes the ultimate synthesis more difficult, and because it supplies us with such a fullness of interests independent of that synthesis tends to drive us back to the old simple Agnostic philosophy of the Persian poet, Omar Khayyam:

> Myself when young did eagerly frequent
> Doctor and sage, and heard great argument
> About it and about, but evermore
> Came out by the same door that in I went.

> With them the seed of wisdom did I sow,
> And with mine own hand wrought to make it grow;
> And this was all the harvest that I reaped;
> I came like water, and like wind I go.

> There was a door to which I found no key,
> There was a veil through which I could not see.
> Some little talk awhile of Me and Thee
> There was: and then no more of Thee and Me.

The Agnosticism and Secularism of these latter days, however, has a far deeper meaning than that which we can attribute to the verses of Omar Khayyam, or to any similar phase of opinion in past time. It is like in expression — as, indeed, in the first aspect of them, all negations seem to be much alike. But, just as the ordinary commonplaces about the sorrows and trials of life have a greater significance when they fall from the lips of age and experience, than when they are merely the utterance of the first dawning thoughtfulness of youth; so our modern Agnosticism implies a deeper consciousness of the problem of human existence than could possibly have been attained by Omar Khayyam. For it is based, not on a mere Epicurean concentration upon the individual life, nor on the materialism of passion, but on our knowledge of the greatness of the universe, and on the complexity of finite interests, both practical and scientific, which seem to stand on their own merits, and to need no reference to anything higher, in order to recommend them as sufficient objects of our lives.

A consideration of these two main elements of modern thought enables us to understand why the struggle of positive and negative tendencies — of the consciousness of the infinite with the consciousness of the finite, of the religious with the secular spirit — should be so much more violent and protracted than the analogous conflict in earlier times. A religion which is universal and not merely imaginative, and a reflection which is scientific, and not merely analytic or destructive, are each of them charged with interests vital to man; and, so long as they are opposed as enemies, they are necessarily involved in a contest which is incapable of being decided by any final victory on one side or the other. Man, as he has an understanding, cannot but acknowledge the facts of his finite life, and in view of them he must sooner or later withdraw his allegiance from every ideal that does not prove itself to be real, and renounce every belief which is found inconsistent with the laws of thought or the nature of experience. Yet, on the other hand, as he is a self-conscious being, who knows the world in relation to the self, and who therefore cannot but realize more or less distinctly the unity of all things with each other and with the mind that knows them, he must equally reject any attempt to confine him to the finite world. Nor, however he may seek, in accordance with imperfect theories of knowledge, to limit himself to that world, can he ever really succeed in confining his thoughts within it. All our knowledge of the things of time is, so to speak, on the background of eternity itself. The scientific impulse itself presupposes the presence in our own minds of an idea of truth as the ultimate unity of being and knowing, which in all our inquiries into the laws of the universe we can only develop and verify. For it is just because we are obscurely conscious, even from the beginning, of this unity that we regard every apparent discord of things with each other as a mystery and a problem, and so are continually seeking law and unity — in other words, seeking *thought*, in things, with the confidence that ultimately it must be found there.

In like manner the practical impulse, whenever it goes beyond, as in every conscious being it must somewhat go beyond, a craving for the satisfaction of immediate sensuous wants, implies the presence in our minds of an idea of absolute good, which is at once the realization of the self and of a divine purpose in the world. What, indeed, could we possibly hope from our feeble efforts after a good, which is only gradually defining itself before us as we advance, if we did not believe that they unite themselves with the great stream of tendency which is independent of us? How could we think to attain our 'being's end and aim', if we did not regard it ultimately identical with the 'divine event to which the whole creation moves'? Hence a sober philosophy, admitting to the full all that can be said by the Agnostic about the feebleness of the powers of men as individuals, and greatness of the universe, can yet reject the Agnostic conclusion from these premises, and can maintain that an absolute or objective synthesis is no mere dream of the childhood of the human race, when the distinction between the possible and the impossible had not yet been made, but rather that it is a task which is forced upon us by our rational nature, and which, as rational beings, we cannot but attempt to fulfil.

All thought and action, all moral and intellectual life, presupposes in us the power of looking at things, not from the point of view of our own individuality, but *in ordine ad universum* [the universal order of things]; and whatever presumption there is in the idea of a universal synthesis is already involved in our existence as rational or self conscious beings. Philosophy may therefore begin its work by a vindication of the religious consciousness — the consciousness of the infinite — as presupposed in that very consciousness of the finite, which at present often claims to exclude it altogether, or to reduce it to an empty apotheosis of the unknown and unknowable. And having thus taught us to regard the consciousness of the infinite as no mere illusion, but as the consciousness of a real object, an Absolute, a God, who has been revealing himself in and to man in all ages, philosophy must go on to consider the history of religion, and indeed the whole history of man as founded on religion, as the progressive development of this consciousness. Nor can it fail to discover that the idea on which the higher life of man is founded — the idea of the unity of man as spiritual with an absolute Spirit — has in Christianity been brought to light and made, in a manner apprehensible by all. Whatever, therefore, may be the change of form to which this idea may have to submit in being applied to our ever-widening knowledge of nature and man, and whatever developments of it may be necessary ere it can solve the difficulties suggested by this increasing knowledge, we have good reason to be confident that we have in it a principle of universal synthesis which is adequate to the task.

On the other side, while this is true, it is also true that philosophy cannot conclusively meet the attacks of scientific criticism, except by coming into closer relation with the work of finite science than it has ever hitherto done; for the only true answer to such attacks is to show that the facts and laws, upon which they rest, are capable of a higher interpretation than that which has been drawn from them by those who have attended to these facts and laws alone. Philosophy, therefore, in face of the increasing complexity of modern life, has a harder task laid upon it than ever was laid upon it before. It must emerge from the region of abstract principles and show itself able to deal with the manifold results of empirical science, giving to each of them its proper place and value. If it ever could sit 'upon a hill remote' to reason of 'fate, free-will, foreknowledge absolute', it may not do so now. Within, as without, the special province of philosophy, the times are past when, to give spiritual help to men, it was sufficient to have a deep intuitive apprehension of a few great principles of spiritual life, and to denounce the representatives of empirical knowledge and finite interests, as sophists, 'apostles of the dismal science', and 'apes of the Dead Sea'. We may be thankful to our Carlyles and Ruskins, as we are thankful in higher measure to the great men of their type in an earlier time — men who utter in powerful language the primary truths of morality and religion — even when they express these truths in a one-sided and intolerant way, refusing to pay due regard to the achievements of finite science, and treating with contempt every improvement that does not involve a fundamental change of man's moral being. But it is, after all, a mark of weakness to address the modern world with the unguarded utterances of an ancient prophet. To repeat against men like Mill and Darwin the old watchwords with which Plato attacked the Sophists is, to say the least of it, an anachronism; for it is to refuse to recognize how far such men are from being Sophists, and how much of the spirit of Plato they have imbibed. And it is to forget on the other hand that philosophy has a different task from that which it had in the days of Plato, that it has abandoned the Greek dualism of form and matter, and thereby accepted the task of idealizing interests and objects from which Plato might have been excused for turning away. He who would further the philosophical work of the future must renounce once for all this questionable luxury of contempt, which in this, as indeed in almost all cases, is the mortal enemy of insight. For the speculative labour of the future is one that requires the patient consideration of every partial truth, and the persistent effort to give it its due place in the whole, as well as a firm apprehension of the principles that underlie all truth. And the practical labour of the future is, not merely by a shock to awaken men to the reality of spiritual things, but to follow out the spiritual principle in its application to all the details of our physical, economical and social condition, till we have seen how the life of each human being, and every part of that life, may be made worth living for itself. Plato speaks of an 'old quarrel between the poet and the philosopher', which is to be reconciled only if poetry can be shown to be truth, or truth, in its highest aspect, to be poetry. In like manner we may say of this almost equally 'old quarrel' between the prophet and the man of science, that it can be healed only by carrying back our scattered knowledge of the facts and laws of nature to the principle upon which they rest, and, on the other hand, by developing that principle so as to fill all the details of knowledge with a significance which they cannot have in themselves, but only as seen *sub specie aeternitatis*.

Two

William Paton Ker

William Paton Ker (1855–1923) was born in Glasgow on 30 August 1855. His father William was a merchant, and his mother was Caroline Agnes Paton. W.P. Ker attended Glasgow Academy and Glasgow University where he won the Snell Exhibition to Balliol College, Oxford in 1874. He was taught philosophy by Edward Caird at Glasgow and T.H. Green at Oxford. During 1878–83 he was also the recipient of the Taylorian scholarship and Assistant to the professor of Humanity, William Young Sellar, at Edinburgh University. In 1879 he was elected to a fellowship at All Souls College, which, because he never married, he retained until his death on the Pizzo Bianco in Italy, 17 July 1923. He is buried in the churchyard of Macugnaga in the Italian Alps.

Ker's position was unique in that he kept rooms in All Souls, staying there most weekends, and played an active part in its business, while living in Gower Street, London and fulfilling his professorial obligations, which were often onerous, in University College, London.

Ker was one of the many Scottish Idealists who began their careers in Wales. In 1883, at the age of twenty-eight, Ker was appointed professor of English Literature and History at University College of South Wales and Monmouthshire. In 1889 he went to University College London to take up the Quain Chair of English Language and Literature, where he transformed the curriculum and was the pioneer of Icelandic studies, becoming the University's first director of the department of Scandanavian Studies (1917–23). Ker had already taught Icelandic to his students for many years, and as well as being proficient in German, French, Italian and Spanish, he was believed to be proficient in every dialect from Lapland to Provence. In 1920 Ker was elected to the Chair of Poetry at Oxford and his lectures were published in 1923 under the title *The Art of Poetry*.

Ker is an exemplar of how in Scotland, but not in England, Idealism as a philosophy was integrally connected with poetry and literature. His first published work was the essay he contributed on 'The Philosophy of Art' to *Essays on Philosophical Criticism* in 1883. His output was mainly literary, and he did valuable editorial work on the writings of John Dryden and Froissart's *Chronicles*, as well as influential studies of the literature of the Dark Ages and the Medieval period. He addressed the philosophical issues of interpretation and drew out the relationship between philosophy, literature and history in an address he gave to the University of Glasgow Historical Society in 1909, entitled 'On the Philosophy of History'.

Biographical

Obituaries and appreciations in *The Times*, 20, 21, 23, 25, July 1923.

R.W. Chambers (with the assistance of John McCunn and J.W. Mackail, 'W.P. Kerr 1855–1923', *Proceedings of the British Academy*, xi (1924–5).

A.D. Godley, 'W.P. Kerr', *The Alpine Journal*, November 1923.

R.W. Chambers, 'Philologists at University College, London. Arthur Platt, A.E. Houseman and W.P. Ker' in R.W. Chambers, *Man's Unconquerable Mind: Studies in English Writers, from Bede to A.E. Houseman and W.P. Ker* (London, Jonathan Cape, 1939), pp. 359–406.

Andrew Tate, 'Ker, William Paton (1855–1923)' in *Dictionary of Nineteenth Century British Philosophers*, ed. W.J. Mander and Alan P.F. Sell (Bristol: Thoemmes, 2002), pp. 631–2.

Principal Works

'The Philosophy of Art' in *Essays in Philosophical Criticism*, ed. Andrew Seth and R.B. Haldane (London: Longmans Green, 1883), pp. 159–86.

Epic and Romance: Essays on Medieval Literature (London: Macmillan, 1897).

The Dark Ages (Edinburgh: Blackwood, 1904)

'On The Philosophy of History: An Address Delivered to the Historical Society, University of Glasgow, January 8, 1909' (Glasgow: Maclehose, 1909).

English Literature: Medieval (London: Butterworth, 1912).

The Art of Poetry: seven lectures, 1920–22 (Oxford: Clarendon Press, 1923).

Collected Essays of W.P. Kerr, ed. Charles Whibley (London: Macmillan, 1925).

Form and Style in Poetry, ed. R.W. Chambers (London: Macmillan, 1928).

READING II

ON THE PHILOSOPHY OF ART[1]

Plato in the 'Protagoras' makes Socrates say that conversation about poetry and the meaning of poetry should be left to people who have not completed their education and are not able to converse freely. The vulgar like to dispute about the interpretation of the sayings of poets, who cannot come into the company to answer for themselves; men who have been well schooled prefer, in their conversation, to go on without the help or the distraction of poetry, 'each one in the company taking his turn to speak and listen in due order, even though they be drinking deep'. To turn conversation into a wrangle about the interpretation of poetical passages is hardly less a sign of want of education than to bring in flute-players in order to save the banqueters from the sound of their own voices. Socrates, before making this contemptuous speech, had criticized and explained a passage of Simonides in a way that shows how possible it is for a critic to maintain his freedom and speak his own mind while professing to draw out the hidden meaning of his author; how the sermon may be made a different thing from the text. The whole passage is characteristic of an age which has grown too old for poetry, which is determined to work out its own problems with its own understanding, not expecting much help nor fearing much hindrance from the wisdom of bygone ages. The belief that is the centre of all Plato's theories of art is expressed here. Stated rudely, the belief is this, that art has lost its authority, that the poets and their followers are well-meaning men who would have today rule itself by yesterday's wisdom, whereas today has its own light to which yesterday's light is an impertinence. Enlightened men speak the thoughts that are in them, free from bondage to the letter of

---

[1]   'The Philosophy of Art' in A. Seth and R.B. Haldane, eds. *Essays in Philosophical Criticism* (London: Longmans, Green, 1883), pp. 159–86.

ancient wisdom; the philosopher knows clearly what the poets knew vaguely and confusedly. Plato's various theories of art are all expansions of this speech in the 'Protagoras'. At the worst, art is a false semblance; at the best it is an education. The philosopher knows what beauty is better than they do who listen to the singers in the market-place. There cannot but be a quarrel between poetry and philosophy; poetry is weak, imperfect and ignorant, pretends to be strong and all-seeing. Philosophy secures its own position by showing how poetry in its proper place may be the servant of truth, and how dangerous to truth it may be in its light-minded pretence of omniscience.

This dissatisfaction with art is not mere puritanic bitterness, not the caprice of a sectarian who sets himself against the common belief of the world. Plato is speaking for his age, not against it. He has no innate spite against art, he has the sincerest reverence for it, yet he cannot choose but bring it down from its height, because the age for which he is speaking knows that there are results to be gained which cannot be gained in the old ways, that the philosophers are working towards new ends of which the poets and imagemakers have never dreamt. This is the way in which the attitude of Plato towards art becomes intelligible. It seemed to him that art with all its excellences was not enough for the needs of a new age, and that it should not be allowed to claim more than its fair share of respect from men who were in search of truth, who were minded to try what they could make out for themselves, without superstition or bondage to idols. Yet no one more than Plato recognized the value of poetry, of imagination, in the progress of the mind towards pure truth. He did not contradict himself in so doing. He denied that poetry was the whole of wisdom; he did not deny that it was the beginning of wisdom. It is the positive side of his theorizing about art which has been best remembered. The polemic against the teaching of the poets was forgotten. The belief that the beauty of sensible things is in some way the image of an unseen beauty remained as an element of many later philosophies, the creed of not a few poets. There is something in it which wins an assent that is not altogether founded on a critical investigation. The theory that the youth are to dwell in a place of pleasant sights and sounds, and to grow up unconsciously into the image of reason, that when reason comes they may welcome it as not alien — all this is heard at first as a story which ought to be true, which overcomes prejudice at the outset. The difficulty is to fix the details of the story. The listener wants to know more about the beauty and more about the reason, and to know where, if anywhere, there is anything like this progress from the half-conscious life among beautiful things to the awakened life in reason.

This theory in the 'Republic', and the similar theories in the 'Symposium' and the 'Phœdrus', are the first attempts at a philosophy of beauty. They describe in dark language a relation of the manifold beautiful things to the one unchangeable idea of beauty, and describe the progress of the soul from the beauty of the manifold of things of sense to the unity of reason or of the idea of beauty. If there be such a progress, it is obviously in it that the secret of beauty lies. But how are we to conceive this progress? What is the idea in which it ends? The education which begins in art and ends in philosophy, how does this resemble or differ from other progresses of mind; for example, the progress of any mind, however ill educated or uneducated, from the unreal world of childhood to the more or less real world of common sense, or the historical progress of nations from myths to rationalism? Everyone knows that there are some progresses in which the mind rejects old fancies for new truths, turning in revolt against its old self; are there others, like this one of the 'Republic' or this one of the 'Symposium', in which the old unreal things which are passed by are not falsehoods but images of the truth? And supposing that art stands in some such relation as this to philosophy, will it not be of some importance to know what is to become of the images when the reality is attained to, of the pleasant places of art when philosophy is perfected, of the manifold shapes of beauty when the one idea of beauty is revealed? Are they to be rejected as Socrates rejected the wisdom of the elder moralists, as Plato rejected the art which was an imitation? Plato's own attitude towards art is a continual wavering between two opinions, which are both based on the one sure opinion that the poets do not at any rate contain all wisdom. Admitting this sure opinion, there are still two alternatives to Plato; sometimes he is for expelling the poets altogether; sometimes he speaks more gently of them, as servants of the Divine Wisdom, who say more than they know, more than sane men are able to say. The difficulty which he finds in explaining art, and the poet's character, and the beauty of sensible things, arises from his opposition to them. He is the first philosopher to attempt to make a philosophy of art, and the sum of that philosophy is that art and philosophy are different. It is the imperfection of art, the imperfection of visible beauty, which he emphasizes. To be content with art is a fatal mistake; it is to prefer opinion to knowledge. Thus Plato's philosophy of art was almost wholly negative. It could not help being negative to begin with, could not help asserting its superiority as critic over the matter criticized. The first thing of importance to be said about art is that there is a science which goes beyond it; and Plato said this, and described in many ways the movement of the mind from the scattered things of sense to the unity which they reflect. But he never succeeded in teaching anyone that science of unity; what he taught was that science of the unity was to be sought after. And so long as this science was unattained, the unity, the universal, was simply an abstraction of which the only thing that could be said was that it is a negation of the many, of the particulars — including them in some way, but in some undefined, unknown way — including them as a limit outside of them. Plato recognized that the relation of the many to the one was not explained simply by being stated; he recognized that the many were not a mere negation of the one — that wrong opinion was possible — that knowledge of the inexact line and the inexact circle have their place in the world for those who wish to find their road home [*pros to anthropenesthai, Philebus,* 62 B]. He apprehended that the ideal was not always the truth. The criticism of Simonides in the 'Protagoras' succeeds in showing that the ideal is often much respected by bad men who find their actual circumstances irksome: that the duty of a man often compels him to leave the ideal alone and be loyal to his kinsfolk, *accepting* the particular circumstances in which he is placed. This apprehension of the value of particular things is never elaborated by Plato into part of the science of the universal; so that at the end there is little more said than that there is one idea, and that there is a progress of the mind from particulars to this universal through successive stages of subordinate universals. So the end of his philosophy of art is that there is one idea of beauty, eternal, the same with itself, not in any likeness of anything in heaven or earth, and that the earthly beauty is a stage on the way to this. That is the end, that is the philosophy of earthly beauty — that it is nothing in comparison with the one idea of beauty, that it passes away as the thought goes beyond it to reach the idea of beauty.

Plato praises art, regarding it as a step on the way to true knowledge, and blames it, regarding it as without life in itself, as without any principle in it which can give it permanency or authority; but whether he praise it or blame it his view of it is always this, that it is valueless in comparison with philosophy. At its best it is a makeshift, at its worst it is a makeshift pretending to be the chief good. This theory of art is unsatisfactory because of its meagreness, its abstraction, but it is necessarily the first philosophy of art. The first point in the creation of a philosophy of art is the separation of art and philosophy — the hostility of philosophy to art. Philosophy comes in a time succeeding the time of the flourishing of art, and to justify its own existence has to prove that art is not the whole of wisdom, not the summit of man's history. Philosophies of art, to begin with, are either puritanic *elenchoi* [critical examination] of art, proving that art is vanity, or theories of the fitness of things according to which fitness art leads the way to true knowledge, to enlightenment. The view of art as an education is the natural one for enlightenment to adopt. It has an appearance of justice, because it admits the value of art, and it does justice to enlightenment itself by making it the end to which art is an instrument. There is and must be an enmity of philosophy towards art, because it is in opposition to the past, which art represents, that philosophy arises. Criticism is enmity, to begin with. The first step towards reconciliation of this enmity is to show that the matter criticized is not really hostile, but really exists for the sake of the critic. It is this step which is taken by any theory which regards art as an education — as existing for the sake of something higher, namely enlightenment, accurate and self-conscious insight. This reconciliation is imperfect because art, the subject criticized, the instrument existing for the sake of the end, which is enlightenment, maintains its separate existence in spite of the critic, pursues its own ends without regard to the existence of any enmity against itself, or to any disputing in the Schools about the end of art.

Ella s' è beata e ciò non ode [she is happy and does not hear it].

The theory that art is an education does not make art much easier to be understood. That art exists for the sake of something else may be a fact about it, but does not reveal anything of the laws of art itself, of the end which it realizes for those unfortunate people who have not yet passed beyond the stage of art. That is to say, that however true it may be that art is an education, or a step to something higher, it is still impossible to explain art fully by reference to the something higher, because for the artist art is not this education, not this step, but an end in itself. And it is a reasonable claim that art should be considered as an end in itself — as an activity following its own laws. If it be not this, then the opinion is wrong. But wrong opinion is not nothing. Wrong opinion is as complicated as right opinion, is as much a *positive* fact as right opinion. So in this case, art, as it is for the artist, is not explained by the statement that art is not the goal of the mind, that it is not an end in itself. If art be an education leading to philosophy, and the philosophy to which it leads be worth anything, then it ought to be possible for philosophy to regard art not merely as an incident in the development of philosophy, but as a form of activity with its own laws and its own history. Art may be a king to whom it has been given to be the nursing father of philosophy, but in his own kingdom that title is not ascribed to the king openly, and it is in no case the whole truth of the kingship.

The theory that art is an education is of very doubtful value if taken by itself. Art is certainly an education for the artist: with other men it is less certainly an education. And it is seldom an education whose pupils can boast that they have done with it. It is true that there are cases of great artists withdrawing themselves for a time from art into the sphere of pure thought, making art for a time external to them in place of being the spirit of their life and work. But these periods of abstraction lead not always to a renunciation of art, and sometimes lead to a higher kind of art, to perfection in art, so that regarding the lives of individual artists it is impossible to arrive at any certain formula. Sometimes it seems that art is the porch of philosophy, sometimes that philosophy is for the individual artist only a passing phase in his life, a centre of indifference, not fruitless, but leading to the production of different beauty, from the incorporeal beauty which Plato wrote of in the 'Symposium'.

Dante describes a change in his life which is like that which Plato related of the favoured children of his 'Republic'. Dante tells in the 'Convito' how, after the death of Beatrice, when the fantastic world of his youth was broken in pieces, he went to philosophy (in Boethius and others) for consolation. There, he says, seeking silver he found gold; he found not only remedy for his grief, but clear knowledge, whereas his mind before has seen many things but only as in dreams, which things were written of in the 'Vita Nuova'.[2] This confession of Dante about himself and the way in which he came to the knowledge of philosophy is of some value. It describes a progress of the mind in a way which may enable us to understand what is meant by saying that those who are brought up among fair sights and sounds will find when reason comes to them that it is no unfamiliar thing. But the parallel does not hold absolutely. It is dangerous to force the resemblance between the prophetic utterance of Plato and the actual life of the man who was not suffered to become a guardian of his earthly city. The world of imagination in which Dante spent his youth was a world in which poetry was not a natural growth, but in great part philosophy disguised — idealism and symbolism which owed a good deal to the Schools. And the progress of Dante did not end with his entry into the Schools. The clear vision in which Dante ended his progress was not a vision of abstract ideas, or not of them only. The 'Vita Nuova' is more removed from actual life than the 'Paradiso': the vision of the Highest is at the same time the vision of the narrow streets where the unrighteous dwell, the Monna Berta and Ser Martino who pass infallible judgment upon sinners. Dante at one time, he tells, read till he grew nearly blind, trying to unravel the mystery of First Matter; but he did not end in these abstractions. He gathers together into one vision all things and all men that he had ever seen or heard of, and in the vision of them he finds his wisdom — of them and of the unseen ruler, in whose mind all things are determined, the meanest chances of earth no less than the highest self-proven truths. Such art as this is not to be explained by the ready formula that fair sights and sounds are good for weak minds that have hope of becoming stronger. We can understand how the youth of Dante was educated by the world of symbolism and mysticism in which he lived, by the pure enthusiasm of the poets: we can understand how this corresponds in some measure to the place of beauty in which Plato's fosterlings were to be trained. We can understand how the abstractions of philosophy were welcomed as expressing what had before been dreamt of. We can understand also in part how

---

[2] *Convito*, II. 13. '*Per lo quale ingegno molte cose quasi come sognando già vedea*' [his mind has already seen many things, as though he was dreaming].

the abstractions were discovered to be abstractions — how the memory of visible things and the knowledge of them in their particularity, as having value of their own, became the end of his philosophy. We can see that however true it may be that art is an education, it does not necessarily mean that it is an education for some end different from art. All artists are educated in this way, in this half-conscious apprehension of beauty. The history of almost every great artist tells how his life begins in vague enjoyment of beautiful surroundings: he lives in a world of beauty, of which he is part and which he only half understands. He conforms to the fashion of the world in which he lives: his early works are no better than those of his fellows, not at least in the opinion of his own age. As he grows older he asserts his freedom: he works no longer as a mere natural outgrowth from his nation and his time, but as a free man walking his own way in the world, seeing things as they are, valuing them for himself, not as others have valued them before. Chaucer in his later life is not merely part of the pageantry of the English court: he is a spectator, not merely a singing man in the show. He is *more immediately* part of the life of the time when he is with the English army in France, learning to rhyme fashionably about cruelty and pity. He has made his place for himself, gained for himself his freedom, when he sets down his own view of his age in the prologue to the Canterbury Tales. He is not less but more an Englishman of the fourteenth century because he belongs to his age, not simply as the trees grew and blossomed according to the fashion of these years, but as a free man who, while not ashamed of being a child of time, does not hold that 'thought's the slave of life, and life time's fool'. He is not the less the brother of the Englishmen his contemporaries because he in a manner withdrew from them for a time, and set down their outward appearance in his book. But he did withdraw from them, he did refuse to be bound by laws of art which were not true for him, to see things with other men's eyes. In this refusal is the end of his apprenticeship.

The creative memory of the artist is as different as abstract philosophy from ordinary experience which grows unconsciously. There is a difference between the unconscious manner in which beauty of art or nature influences the mind of the pupil, and the manner in which the prefect artist works in full consciousness of the end at which he is aiming and the means by which he is to attain it, if not always with perfect consciousness or developed curiosity concerning the sources of his power.

The problem for the philosophy of art is thus not merely 'how is philosophy to indicate its claim to supersede art, as being perfect science of that which art feels after blindly?' but 'what is the kind of end which the artist attains? how are we to analyse the relation of works of art to the mind?'.

Art and science are very much alike at the beginning. Science does not know anything *about* things at the beginning; it simply perceives things — or rather, simple perception, to perceive things clearly, is the ideal which early science aims at — which it does not always attain. It is here that art begins its services to mankind. The bone knives found in the caves of the Dordogne show that the artists who engraved them saw reindeer clearly, and were ingenuously interested in them, having reached a stage of civilization and wealth in which they were not simply ravenous for reindeer, but could afford to contemplate them with self-restraint, like gentlemen. Their contemplative leisure employed the keen eyesight, no longer that of a beast of prey, and the interest, no longer of the stomach, in engraving a clear outline of the interesting animal on the handles of their hunting knives. Other early engravings show how the mammoth might be made, by untrembling hands, into a lasting ornament. The idols that stand in the porch of the British Museum show that some long-forgotten dwellers in the Easter Islands grew one day to be *securi adversus deos* [free from fear of the gods], and employed their security in making images of the beings they worshipped, in order to know what sort of beings they were. When it is said that the makers of such images had reached a certain degree of civilization, it is not meant merely that they had attained some technical skill in shaping materials, but that they had so far raised themselves above the level of the beasts, so far withdrawn themselves from sensation and appetite, as to be able to make permanent for themselves the objects of their interest and their worship. This defining of the perceived or imagined object is the great triumph of early art, and it is at the same time the beginning of science, of clear knowledge. Thus early art is sometimes extremely realistic, and seems to accompany wonderful powers of perception — of combining various particulars in one intuition. The Esquimaux, who draw the things they see with some skill, are said sometimes to show a talent for remembering locality, the relative positions of places, so as to be able to make fairly accurate charts of a coast after a short acquaintance with it. The artistic faculty of clear apprehension of details here has to do duty for science.

How does completed science differ from completed art? For science the particular visible object is unimportant, or important only as an example of a general law, or as material for an experiment to lead to the knowledge of a general law, or as a member of a species, interesting and intelligible, not in itself but as a member of the species — the species itself being interesting and intelligible only as having a definite place in the universe, as standing in a definite relation to other things. Things are interesting to science not for what they *are*, but for what they *are not*, that is, for the other things to which they are related, or still more, for the relation — for the general formula of relations which sums up the truth about the particular things. Science is thus an endless process. It is perpetually busied with certain things of the outward world, but interested in them only as they point to other things. The particular things with which science deals are instruments, not ends in themselves. The particular members of a species is of little more importance to science than the particular chalk triangle drawn on a particular slate. The triangle is merely a perceptible repetition of one type, the truth about which type is quite independent of the particular chalk triangle. The particular member of a species has no importance, unless it has some individual peculiarities which make it different from its species, in which case it may be important as one of a new species. But in no case has it any importance in itself. It has importance either as being an example of a species in which the characteristic of the species may be known and demonstrated; or as a link in a chain of causation, and it is the chain, not the link, which is important. Even individuals, having from one point of view value in and for themselves, may for science be simply instruments and specimens to demonstrate the working of a law, or particular phenomena, whose importance is not in themselves but in their causes or effects. Mahomet or Columbus may be considered by scientific history not as individuals interesting in themselves, but as single terms in a series. History is not interested in any single event, or in any individual man, but in the *relations* of men and of events.

In art the case is altogether different. There the particular thing exists with a being of its own, as a thing which can suffer nothing else to stand in the place of it, as something which cannot be exhausted by any formula or expressed in words, as something whose relation to other things, to causes or effects or laws, is altogether a subordinate matter — not the true essence, but an accident which not even inadequately can express the nature of the thing. Both art and science have for their end to make things clear to the mind. But science makes things clear by perpetual reference to other things. Its activity is an endless process; its kingdom of light is rounded by the darkness of the unknown on which it encroaches, but which it can never conquer. Art does not make things clear to the understanding which asks the reasons of things and their connection with other things. Its creations do not prove anything; they have no reference to things beyond themselves, they add nothing to knowledge, they do not throw light upon the natures of things, they are themselves clear and definite objects, that is all. The things which art makes are interesting to the mind with an interest quite different from that which belongs to the demonstrations of science. Science throws light on a portion of the object world; clearing it up, showing the secret of it, the unapparent law of its being; using particular perceptible things as instruments to demonstrate the law. Art makes a thing which is not an instrument by which to demonstrate the general law of a class of objects, but is free, serving no law but its own, revealing itself, and nothing but itself, to the mind. Science is face to face with an object world, which is a system of related classes of things, and explains certain classes of those things, regarding each thing as an example of a class, and each class as explicable by formulas more or less fixed. Art makes new things, whose value is that they explain themselves in a way with which science is unacquainted. Art satisfies the mind not by affording it new examples for experiment, from which to arrive at new truths of the objective world, but by presenting to it objects which have that freedom from dependence on other things and other laws, that unity in themselves, which is wanting in all the objects of science — in the object world which for science is never a whole complete in all its parts, and is *one* world only *ex hypothesi*. The work of art is an object which is only partially or accidentally subject to the laws of the object world; which is in the world but not of it. A statue is a perceived object, a particular thing in the object world, but it is not to be explained scientifically, like other objects, like natural things, as a member of a species, as standing in particular relations to the universe. It is not to be explained by reference to other things; its nature is that it explains itself. It is not a problem to be solved; or rather it is both problem and solution, both the secret and the revelation of the secret. This does not mean that works of art are exempt from the law by which the universe is one and all the parts of it correlated; this is not to say that there can be no science of art things, or that they can be *understood* apart from their history. But all histories or explanations are inadequate — not as in other cases because the relations of any one thing to the rest of the universe are inexhaustible — but because they regard works of art *only* as phenomena to be explained, and forget the main point, that they are phenomena which explain themselves.

The work of art is separate from the world in which it exists. It is a contradiction to any theory which would regard each thing as a point in an endless series of relations. The work of art is a thing which will not be explained, like other things, by a natural history or a statement of its relations to other things. It is in one sense finite, because it has had a history, because it stands in relation to other things that are finite. In another sense it is not a finite thing, because its nature will not yield itself to analysis; it cannot be dissected. There is a point at which its history ceases, and *only then* does it exist; before that it is not. It is a commonplace that the beauty of things adds nothing to the matter of knowledge. Works of art add nothing to knowledge except in themselves. It is their essence that they should be known. The mind which perceives them apprehends them not as new phenomena which are to have their place assigned them, after due consideration, in relation to other objects in the complicated world. The mind apprehends them at once as things which have no other nature than to be apprehended. They are not things which are to be brought into harmony with the mind by having their relation with other things and the universe explained. They are things which have no necessary relation except to the mind; which are from the first akin to the mind and formed for it, so that being seen they are intelligible. They are not any more intelligible in themselves for any trouble that science may take to get beyond them and inside them, to find out the machinery and the secret of them. Science and history may discover a great deal about them, but they remain intelligible in their own way, indifferent to science and history. Their way of being intelligible is not altered by science; science may, indeed, modify the individual's appreciation of works of art or of art effect, but it does not put its explanation in place of the works of art. The student of the science of art hears his lecture (from the Pythagoreans or others), and does not forget his lecture when listening to music; but however the lecture may improve or interfere with his individual appreciation of the music, it does not alter the *mode* in which the music is apprehended by him. The value of the music to the hearer, be it great or small, is a different thing from its value to the student of physics. And its being heard — its being apprehended in this way — is the whole history, the whole life of the piece of music. The things of the object world, the things with which science is busied, have histories of their own, and make a demand upon science that their histories shall be discovered and made clear to the understanding; that something shall be predicated of them. The work of art makes no such demand. It declares of itself what it is, and refuses to be compared with other things; refuses to have anything predicated of it which can imply that it is different from what it appears. It is above the world of movement. The one relation which is necessary to it is the relation to the mind that apprehends it.

The relations of objective things can never be summed up. The progress of science is an endless progress. Works of art as things of the objective world are not exempt from this law; it is impossible to know everything about them, as it is impossible to know everything about anything. But considered in themselves they are exempt from this law, because at the first view of them they are apprehended, not as appearances with an unknown reality behind them, but as appearances whose reality is in their appearance; not as problematic things, but as the solution of a problem; not as the starting-points of an inquiry, but as unities whose freedom is unimpaired by external or accidental relations.

From one point of view they are unreal and dead, because they have no share in the give and take of the universe. They are removed from all possibility of change, except the change of material decay and the passing into oblivion. This is one aspect of works of art. In another aspect this apparent deadness becomes a life higher than any life of natural things. The changelessness of the works of art is not death. They are unchanging because they are worlds in themselves, their various parts correspond to the various stages of existence in the object world, and the parts of the work of art are apprehended at once in the apprehension of the completed work, as the various stages of existence would be apprehended if the endless progress of science were to come to an end, and the universe be grasped in one intuition. The work of art is *formally* a solution of this contradiction between the abstract unity of science and the endless process towards it — it does not really do anything to make this contradiction less of a contradiction in the objective world, but it gives an example to show that it is not a contradiction in which the mind is in all cases forced to lose itself. The work of art is a proof that completed knowledge — knowledge which does not imply an endless process — is possible to the mind. The freedom gained by art is an earnest of freedom; a proof that freedom is not a mere ideal.

In all knowledge of the objective world there is a contradiction between the two elements of knowledge, the particular and the universal. The particular thing, with its differences, is known only in relation to that which is permanent and unchangeable, and one. At first neither of the sides has much meaning, but with the progress of knowledge both sides increase in meaning; the manifold is seen to be an ordered world, the unity is not an abstraction but the regulating principle in the manifold. The progress of science is, however, subject to this contradiction, which for science is insuperable, that as it is impossible to exhaust the manifold of the object world, it is impossible ever to attain complete knowledge of the unity as it is shown in the manifold. Science has to go on accomplishing its impossibilities, increasing the sum of knowledge, without drawing any nearer the end of the unknown. Art is the first attempt to find a cure for this. It is a mode in which the mind can make part of the objective world intelligible to itself without being troubled by continual reference to other parts of the objective world beyond the limits it has chosen. It is a return of the mind to itself from seeking fact after fact and law after law in the objective world; a recognition that the mind itself is an end to itself, and its own law.

A moral act is analogous to a creation of art in this way, that it is a denial of the necessity which belongs to the objective world and its laws. It differs from the creation of art in this way, that it has to lose itself apparently in the objective world again. It is an act done to carry out principles that are universally true, but as a *matter of fact* its importance is limited. It is a phenomenon whose true nature is not wholly apparent. The freedom asserted is the freedom of the individual, and that freedom is inward. The freedom gained in the work of art is apparent and universal, it remains to be beheld by all men. The moral act, like the work of art, is individual; nothing else can be put in its place, and in that particular phenomenon the universal reason expresses itself. But not, as in the work of art, for the sake of the expression, for the sake of contemplation, not in order to raise the particular phenomenon, the particular matter, above the complication of the outward necessity, but in obedience to an inner law which does not outwardly contradict the necessity. A moral act, like any other event, is subject to the laws of objective relation, to the necessities of time, of cause and effect. It is outwardly finite and passes away disregarded. Only in the character of the man who does the act is it that the act acquires its freedom, only he knows the value of it. Morality progresses, like science, not by withdrawing itself from the necessity of the objective world, but by accepting that necessity in order to conquer it point by point. The man who is working out his moral freedom has to accept all the shocks of events that come upon him in the form of necessity, in order to give them their moral meaning; and the acts by which he asserts his moral freedom have the appearance of natural events. Hence his progress is endless, because the objective world with which he connects himself is an endless series; hence he has to be content to be free without appearing free. His acts are not done for the sake of appearance but for the sake of reality. They differ from the ordinary events of the objective world in that they are not to be understood by reference to the external events with which they are connected. Their true meaning is in themselves, and in this they resemble works of art. They differ from works of art in that their appearance is not their reality. They appear to be nothing but events in a necessary sequence of causes and effects, but their true meaning is not to be exhausted by exhausting all external influences inside or outside the body of the man who has done the acts. Their true meaning can be gained only by knowledge of the character which is the author of them. The moral character cannot express itself otherwise than in particular acts, as the artist's ideal beauty cannot appear except in particular creations. But the particular acts that express the moral character do not fully express it; no moral act is wholly free; whereas the particular beautiful creations which exist only for the sake of appearance do fully express what they are.

The world of morality is the same world as that of science — the world of finite things and particular events — and morality like science is in opposition to it. The opinion with which science begins is that truth is not apparent; that things as perceived are known only partially, that the relations of things to one another and to the universe are secret, and have to be discovered. Science is in opposition to the apparent universe — the disconnected world of particular things — and its progress is to bring to light more and more the real connection of things. But it can never accomplish its progress. It goes on in faith that nowhere will anything be found to contradict its conception of the unity of the universe, but it can never succeed in proving this in detail, in showing the place of each thing in the universe. Morality also begins in a contradiction between reality and appearance, but the progress of morality is not, like that of science, to start from the appearance and reach the hidden reality. It starts from reality, from the self which is reality to itself, but which at first has no connection with the objective world except the pure negative consciousness of freedom from subjection to the objective world. The progress of morality is to make that apparent which is real, to live in the objective world a life whose law is not discoverable among the laws of the objective world, but only in the self which is a law to itself. Morality begins in pure theory. It is pure self-consciousness and nothing more, the negation of all that is outward — the pure negative 'I am not subject to necessity'. But this inward unity which is proof against all the shocks of time, which is not subject to the objective necessity of particular finite events, is so far in contradiction with itself that it is merely inward and therefore finite, limited by those very finite events whose value it theoretically denies. The self-consciousness would believe itself to be absolute in itself, but it finds that it is absolute only so long as it does nothing. Its freedom is not freedom to do anything, it is mere negation. Then begins the endless progress of morality; it is forced outward into the objective world to make that freedom *apparent* which to the self-conscious subject is the reality of realities. The presupposition of morality is that there is a freedom superior to the incomprehensible necessity of events, and that that freedom must make itself the law of outward things, taking up into itself the necessity of outward things, and becoming the only true explanation of actions which apparently are subject to the ordinary necessities of the objective world. Like science morality conquers point by point, and like science its progress is endless. The nature of its conquest is this, that the particular acts which are called moral are not to be explained simply by reference to other particular events in an objective world, which is *one* world *ex hypothesi*, but must be explained by reference to a unity which is not hypothetical, namely the free individual whose conscious self is not an event nor a particular link in the chain of causation.

There is this resemblance between science and morality, that in both cases reality remains reality, behind the appearance, and appearance remains appearance, hiding the reality. The ordinary perception of things remains one thing, and the scientific explanation of things another. The moral act does not outwardly show its real nature, it appears simply as an event. The moral value of an act cannot be proved to a man who is content with discovering an apparent motive of self-interest.

Art resembles both science and morality in that it is a conquest of nature. It differs from them both, first, because it is not an endless process; secondly, because its product is the unity of reality and appearance. The freedom that it gains is complete because it has not to refer to anything beyond itself, to any horizon beyond which all is unknown, or any ought-to-be which is not yet realized. In art the opposition between the one and the many, between the law and its manifestation, between the subject and the object, is overcome. It is overcome not by simple abolition of the distinction between them, but by so uniting them that each receives the meaning of the other. In art the subject does not express itself in its limitation, in its abstraction, asserting abstractly its superiority to nature and to natural conditions. This assertion of freedom is pure emptiness, a beginning of movement, a point, not a universe. In art the subject goes out into the objective world, and redeems part of that world from bondage to natural laws, makes it the revelation of freedom. The subject is no longer a self-conscious atom separated from the world, anxiously craving for increase in its knowledge of an inexhaustible manifold universe; it has learned from morality that the unity of the universe is not to be sought in the objective world and its laws, because the self is higher than those laws. Neither is it bound by the prejudices of morality which would place the completion of freedom in an unapproachable future. Art is the vindication of present freedom. Moral freedom may be always limited on its phenomenal side by particular contingencies; there is always an apparent contradiction between what a man appears and what he ought to be; his best actions 'are not done without a motive', or 'are not unmixed good', or 'are exceedingly well intended'. But the works of art are perfect, they express what they are intended to express. They are not simply the acts of an individual, which may be interpreted as good or bad according to the intention of the individual. They are not particular things with an unknown essence behind them. They are particular things which are to be interpreted or apprehended for what they are. They are particular things whose meaning is universal, yet whose meaning is nothing apart from the particularity. Existing in the world of finitude they have nothing to do with it. They exist only for the mind. They are things which are not things, because in them particularity does not mean separation of reality and appearance, as it does with all other things.

Art is not to be explained by the categories which are applicable to finite things. Art is not to be explained, *e.g.*, by any physiological or psychological inquiries about the physical conditions of aesthetic perception. All such inquiries, however successful, can only result in what, as far as art is concerned, is meaningless abstraction, because they explain something which is totally different from the work of art, namely its conditions — things which have to be *before* the world of art can be apprehended. But they can tell nothing about the work of art as apprehended, because of this self-sufficingness of art which will not allow any analysis to explain its works without making them something different from what they really are.

Art is not to be explained by including it in the subject matter of ethics, by treating it as a stage in the education of the individual, or as the storehouse of the ideas of virtue, because the moral worth of art is accidental to it, it is not the servant of practical life, no pedagogue to show men the way to a better life; it stands beyond morality, has overcome the contradiction which morality is overcoming.

Then is art not to be explained in any way? to be left untroubled in its own kingdom? Perhaps not if there be other methods of explanation than the methods of natural history or physical science. The works of art are to be left to be appreciated one by one, simply to fulfil their own end without question, only if the unity and the freedom which belong to art are the highest attainable by the mind. But there is a finitude in the works of art which is a challenge to the reason, though not the same finitude as that of the natural things which science explains. Its finitude is not that it is an unexplained thing, but that it is an insufficient explanation, a partial revelation. It is infinite because it is raised above the flux of things, free from the darkness and incomprehensibility which is the curse of finite things considered in themselves; free from the infinite multiplicity of reference to all other atoms in the universe which is characteristic of the particular things of the outward world. It is finite because the mind goes beyond it, because it is not the highest mode in which thought reveals itself to itself. Art is subject not to the criticisms of science, but to the thought which has thought itself for an object, which criticizes the methods of science as it criticizes sensation and perception, and morality, and all the ways in which mind exerts itself.

Art is higher than science in this way, that it is not limited by an objective world which is superior to it, which defines efforts to exhaust it. Art can boast of conquests which are absolute, can point to finished work which it is impossible to mend, which contains *in itself* no seed of decay.

It conquers by taking that very particularity which forms the limitation of science and making it universal, making it a thing of infinite value, a thing which the mind accepts as in itself intelligible. Any account of the world which rests satisfied with the mechanical categories of science thus shatters itself against the creation of art and is condemned by them as inadequate. But this conquest of art over the limitations of science is purchased at some cost; the particularity of the work of art, which is quite different from the particularity of natural things, still remains as a limitation. It is a limit beyond which lies, not the objective world, but the intellectual world to which the work of art belongs. The science of that world is not an endless process, but the activity of thought which has come to know that the unity which is the pre-supposition of science is thought, that the moral ideal of freedom is thought, and that it is thought which in the work of art finds its own image.

The philosophy of art must necessarily be less abstract than pure metaphysics or ethics, because it is not like them a criticism of a statement of universal conditions; it does not simply state what is true of all art, as metaphysics or ethics state what is true of all experience and of all morality. The philosophy of art cannot speak, or not for long, of the sublime and the beautiful in the abstract. It must recognize what is particular and apparently con-tingent and inexplicable in the creations of art. It must recognize that they are necessarily connected each with its own particular time. Metaphysics and ethics may look on experience and moral-ity abstractly, apart from any reference to the history of man, con-sidering the elements in them that are one and the same in all minds. The philosophy of art must be a philosophy of history as well. Its end is not to state abstractly what the elements in art cre-ation or aesthetic apprehension are, which are the same in all cases. It recognizes that what is important in creations of art is not their identity but their difference, their individuality, not their conformity to any type or standard. Part of their individuality is their relation to particular times and seasons in the actual history of the world. The problem of the philosophy of art is to make the history of art intelligible — not simply a series of biographies or catalogues, of artists or their works, but a history of showing the place of art in the development of the human reason. It is not a light task, but it is not an impossibility. It is simply a working out of the problem which finds many occasions to present itself nowa-days. 'What is meant by saying that the art of a people or a century enables us to understand the people or the century?' What is there in art which makes it a kind of explanation of things apparently so different from itself? Is it anything but an amiable illusion to sup-pose that Greek art has more than an external relation to Greek history? or that anything can be inferred from the history of art about the progress of humanity as a whole? The philosophy of art will have to show whether the creations of art are to be regarded as fortuitous appearances, inexplicable — as they certainly are — by any of the ordinary methods of science, or whether they are to find their place in the history, not of events, but of the achievements of reason in this actual world. If it is possible to show that all the changes in man's ways of regarding the universe are not accidental, but necessities of thought, then there will be a philosophy of art. All the various kinds of art, and all the artists, and all the works of art will then become intelligible — not as phenomena in relation to other phenomena (in which case they are unintelligible), but as comprehended in a system of knowledge, which is not the science of an objective world, but the science of all that the mind knows about itself. This science would include not only abstract metaphysics and ethics, as sciences of what is necessary in knowledge and morality, but also a philosophy of the progress of thought in time. Part of this philosophy will be the philosophy of art, for art has made good its right to be considered as belonging to the world of thought, not to the natural world, and yet its connection with particular periods in history is something which cannot be abstracted from. If the science of thought is to be purely abstract, then there is no place for the philosophy of art. But neither will there be room for the consideration of religion, or of the history of philosophy or of political science, because all these things imply reference to the concrete facts of time. This science of the development of thought will not be empirical, but *a priori* (if there be any meaning in *a priori*) because it begins not like ordinary science with a suspicion that there is unity somewhere, an unexplained presupposition that the universe which it explains is one universe, but with the clear knowledge that thought is the unity of the universe, and that the apparent going out of thought to an object apparently external to thought is only appearance.

Such a philosophy of art will get rid of some annoying questions. It will get rid of the question about the relation of art to morality. It will show that art has not to do either with the furthering or the hindering of the individual's moral progress. There are at least three possible cases in which art may appear to have an immoral influence. Two of these are clearly cases where it is ignorance of art that really is the misleading power. Art brings with it the possibility of bad art: but this can hardly be made a ground of accusation against it; in any case, ignorance or contempt of art will not make bad art less harmful. Or works of art which are pure and great in themselves may be turned to evil, because art as an image of human life includes the element of evil in it — it represents evil on the stage, or in poems. But any bad influence it may exert in this way is plainly accidental — not to be considered except by the pathologist of human nature. Or, thirdly, art though served with unselfishness and sincerity may be unfitted to be the sole end of any one man's life. It may be that the practical life is not sacrificed to the theoretic or the artistic life without retribution. This is not a simple question, but whatever ethics, or casuistry, or any other science may say to it, it is certain that art itself, and the philosophy of art, will make no claim on anyone to become less than other men before he can become an artist. What is it that makes a man moral? Not his actions, but his habitual view of things and events, and men, and himself — his living memory which makes him true to himself and to all his neighbours. The selfish man's memory is one to which the artistic or imaginative representation of things is utterly repugnant. He remembers only what has served or what has baffled him, and values the particulars of his experience only in reference to his own selfish ends. The unselfish memory remembers things and men as the artist remembers them. It values the things of experience according as they are good or bad; that is, according as they fulfil their proper end or not — not using any abstract standard of good or bad, but Plato's science of inexact things, which enables a man to find his way home, using imagination, for which each particular thing has an interest of its own, apart from any question of its use, apart from all abstract preconceptions of what ought to be. Art is the wide world's memory of things, and any man may make his own memory a sharer in its wisdom on one condition — that he shall not hate or love anything that is revealed to him there according as it thwarts or furthers his selfish purposes, but according to its own virtues or vices. The artistic imagination is part of the highest morality, because it gets rid of the last selfishness of all — the Stoic selfishness which is proud of its superiority to external things.

The philosophy of art has no other aim than to bring together as far as possible into one view all that there is in the world's memory — to make a history in which the characters shall speak for themselves, become themselves the interpreters of the history. It will regard the artists as helping to create the mind of the ages in which they live — the mind is only what it knows and worships, and the artists are the means by which the different nations and ages come to have characters of their own.

The philosophy of art finds periods of ambition, of achievement, of criticism and barrenness, just as the biographer of any one artist distinguishes the periods in his life — the periods of youth and imitation, of manhood and originality, or the period of inspiration and the period of faultlessness, or otherwise. Only to the biographer the succession of phases in the life of his hero is more or less a matter of contingency — the philosophy of art finds the periods succeeding one another according to the necessity of thought. It does this because it has room enough to work in. The biographer finds his labour ended by the death of the man he is writing about, or perhaps the decay of his powers; but where it is the art of the world which is studied there is less of such interruption to inquiry. Decay of art can be explained because it is seen what succeeds it — what new form of intelligence takes the place of art, as Greek philosophy grew strong when Greek art began to decline from its supremacy. It can compare Greek art and Christian art, not as two independent phenomena, but as two different forms of judgment, where the first form is necessarily first and progress toward the second is inevitable.

To do this it has to consider not only art but religion and the history of philosophy, and show how the art of an age is related to the other forms of intellectual activity in that age, and how all even in their opposition are expressions of one spirit. The history of Greek philosophy notes, as the characteristic of Greek philosophy, that it does not centre on the conception of the self with his consciousness and knowledge, opposed to an external real world, that it accepts at first the unity of thought and being and confuses clear conceptions with science. Greek art and Greek religion are found to be also on this level of thought. The gods are to be worshipped; there is no disputing about the evidences of their existence; they are accepted because they are beautiful, more beautiful than an actual thing: the thought of the worshipper is satisfied with the mere idea of the god: he does not ask for any proofs of the being of Apollo or Athena. Greek art is the most perfect of all art, because it appeals least of all to the understanding which looks for the meaning of things. Greek sculpture is not symbolic of anything. It sets up the god before the worshipper — for his contemplation, not to excite his curiosity. The Greek gods in sculpture are beautiful as they are: they do not show their power in any matter-of-fact way. That they are benefactors of mankind in any way is kept in the background, and is in no case a necessary part of their character. They are revered not as helpers, but as impersonations of what is most admirable in man. They are most strong and most beautiful, but they take little part in the earthly contests of men. Greek art is a progress from this high ideal of pure beauty to less pure, more complicated forms. The tragedy is an effort to solve the contradiction implicit in sculpture — namely the contradiction between the Olympian *power* and the Olympian *weakness*, between the freedom of the ideal and its incapacity to influence action. The drama shows the gods and heroes retaining their worshipfulness, their divinity, and their heroism even in the entanglement of circumstances. The end of tragedy comes when it is no longer the spectacle of the action as a whole that claims the attention, but the feelings or the inner life of the hero. Then the passions are not purified as they were by the tragic pity and terror that had no weakness in them. The pathetic tragedy against which Plato wrote is part of the same movement of thought with the rise of the sophistic teaching. It is the return of the mind into itself, making a universe for itself out of its own accidents. The true remedy for this comedy, which is a revolt against pathos, and also a reaction against the elder tragedy because it finds that anything may be true of the gods and heroes to a mind robust enough of imagination. Comedy is not the private fantasy of a mind which would like to upset the universe. It is unsparing laughter at everything, even at itself. It confesses that it is not its business to preserve the heroic aspect of heroes or the divine aspect of the gods. It cannot keep anything in order. But it will waken up the sleepers who were too fond of their own dreams; it will show them all the baseness and meanness they had shut their eyes to, and at the same time the beauty of a new heaven, with the clouds in it, and the deathless race of birds, and of a new earth with cool green places in it, and the voice of frogs to reprove the faint-hearted. Aristophanes is not the destroyer: he is the maker of a new world of art. Sculpture had made gods who were beautiful but motionless, ineffectual. Tragedy made the gods and heroes act in their proper characters, and gradually came to forget the unity of the drama and to make interesting the sorrows — not the misfortunes, but the lamentations — of the hero. Then comedy found work to do. The pathetic tragedy had destroyed the old world of tragedy. Comedy could not bring back the simple manner of regarding things, but it could show at least that there were other things in the world than weeping heroes. It showed that there were all sorts of things in the world and pointed them out, pretending not to know anything about the way they should be arranged, and finding nothing surprising in the co-existence of beauty and infamy. The progress of Greek art is a progress from contemplation, like that of Xenophanes when he found the secret of the universe by looking into the open heaven, to dramatic interest. It is a progress from simplicity to complication, from rest to movement, from the sameness of the statue to the contradiction of comedy. In one sense it was a decline of art. The statue is a pure work of art; the drama cannot avoid raising more questions than it can answer. But in another way it was progress. It was the invention of a new beauty; the beauty of movement, of action. Thought could not rest without trying to include all things in art. The progress was from the pure beauty of the ideal, in sculpture, to the perplexed beauty of the actual world as it appears, all in confusion, in Aristophanes. It is the movement from abstract to positive thought in the sphere of art.

There is an analogous progress in all art: a progress from the art which is akin to religion to the art which is akin to science. Icelandic poetry begins with cosmogonies and theogonies. When the character of the gods is becoming settled they are represented in action and adventure. Worship of the gods is not in itself a full satisfaction of the mind: it must see characters in movement: circumstance and chance must try their utmost against the hero. Then the god and the hero are found to be not very different from ordinary men: to have no different kind of courage from ordinary men. Then it is the actual life of men that is interesting, and with an interest far exceeding that of the stories of the gods. In this kind of art all things are interesting that are true — the horses and the ships and the hay-fields, and the children that play at being men, as well as the wisdom of Njal or the high courage of Gunnar.

In the Christian art of Europe there is the same progress, only there is this difference, that the religious art which comes first is not like that of Greece or Scandinavia. The Greek poets and sculptors made the gods they worshipped, because what was clearly seen was reckoned true. Christianity belongs to a new age which has learned some things from the Stoics and Sceptics — the difference between reality and appearance, and the opposition of the thinking subject to the objective world. The distinguishing mark of Christianity is that it is true in the strict historic sense. It is not a matter of imagination but of evidence. Hegel says that there could be no battle between Christ and the old gods, because they belonged to quite different spheres of thought. The Greek gods were nowhere but in the imagination. This makes a difference between Christian and Greek art from the outset. Art was all-important to Greek religion, for the god who was not clearly imagined was nothing. In the art of Christianity there is no need, no possibility that the image should accurately represent the reality. They are incommensurate from the first. The Byzantine image is not the god to be worshipped, but a symbol. Religion goes beyond art and remains beyond it, a different kind of life forever. The progress of Christian art is as in Greek art towards a complete conquest of the universe — to find beauty not in gods and heroes only, but in all levels of existence. It does this, however, always with the consciousness that its effort is doomed to fail, that it is less than the reality, that it is in the unseen and the spiritual that the chief beauty dwells, inexpressible by art. This very sense of deficiency, however, leads it to be persevering beyond all Greek art in presentation of reality, and of any atom of reality that can be made to have any artistic interest at all. And the 'soothfastness' of a story comes to be part of its charm and its claim to immortality, as the Scottish poet thought.[3] So Giotto painted fewer pictures for devotion and more for the intelligence, setting down things in their reality. So Dante portrayed each man he met in Hell, Purgatory or Paradise without regard to anything but the nature of the man before him: not being interested in anything more than in the true nature of the man, to whom the doom passed on him is an external thing. There was a separation imminent between religion and art when it was possible to treat calmly of low human things unblinded by the light of theology. There was no disappearance of religion. The Norse religion grew weak in proportion as Norse culture and art and knowledge of humanity grew. But the Christian religion was stronger than this: it could not pass away into art. There was a separation for a time of spiritual religion from art, as there was a separation of philosophy from both. Art was left to go its own way. It ceased, as philosophy ceased, to be merely the

---

[3]   Barbour, *Bruce*, at the beginning.

interpreter of Christian tradition. It expressed in its own way, as philosophy expressed in its own way, the idea of Christianity, that it is the individual subject which is of infinite value. The music which is the creation of the modern world expresses that which is inexpressible in all other arts — the mind's freedom from the contingency of the outward world and obedience to its own law.

Three

Andrew Seth Pringle-Pattison

Andrew Seth Pringle-Pattison was born Andrew Seth on 20 December 1856, in Edinburgh. His father, Smith Kinmont Seth, the son of a farmer from Fife, was a bank clerk in the head office of the Commercial Bank of Scotland. His mother, Margaret, was the daughter of Andrew Little a farmer from Berwickshire. Seth's elder brother died in infancy, and his younger brother James Seth, an idealist theologian of Kantian rather than Hegelian persuasion, was his colleague at Edinburgh University from 1898 to 1919.

Seth was educated at the Royal High School, Edinburgh before going on to the University in 1873. He was influenced by Alexander Campbell Fraser, who he later succeeded, and was a contemporary of D.G. Ritchie, W.R. Sorley, and R.B. Haldane, with whom he became a life-long friend. Campbell Fraser imparted a form of Berkeleian theism, which was tempered in Seth's mind by the German Idealism of James Hutchison Stirling, the author of the infamous *The Secret of Hegel*.

Seth graduated with first class honours in classics and philosophy in 1878, and was awarded a Hibbert travel scholarship to study for two years in Berlin, Jena and Göttingen. Among his teachers in Germany were R.H. Lotze, to whom he frequently refers in his writings. In 1880 Seth became class assistant to Campbell Fraser, succeeding W.R. Sorley, during which time he also wrote for *The Scotsman* and in 1883 he was appointed professor of logic and philosophy at the University College of South Wales and Monmouthshire at Cardiff. From there he took up the chair of logic, rhetoric and metaphysics at St Andrews University and in 1891 the chair of logic and metaphysics at Edinburgh. He was awarded honorary degrees by St Andrews University (1892), Princeton (1898), Durham (1902), and Edinburgh (1919). He was elected a Fellow of the British Academy in 1904, and delivered the Gifford Lectures at Aberdeen (1912–13) and Edinburgh (1921–3). He retired in 1919.

In 1884 Seth was married in Berlin where he had taught his future wife Eva Stropp of Borgislavitz, Silesia, as a student. They had five children, four sons and a daughter. The youngest son was killed in action on the Somme in 1916, and the eldest daughter died in infancy. In 1898, on the death of Mrs Pringle-Pattison, Seth became a beneficiary of her will on the grounds that he was a promising young man distantly related to her husband. Seth inherited the family fortune and estate of The Haining, Selkirk, in the Scottish Borders. The condition was that he had to adopt her surname, a distinction he shares with another famous idealist John McTaggart Ellis McTaggart, who was born in London and adopted the name as a condition of a bequest. Andrew Seth Pringle-Pattison died at The Haining on 1 September 1931, and is buried in Edinburgh.

Seth's importance in Idealism is that he co-edited *Essays in Philosophical Criticism* with R.B. Haldane, in which the future programme of philosophy along Kantian and Hegelian lines was set out. Only four years after its publication Seth began to question the Absolute Idealism of Hegel and many of his British followers, including Edward Caird, Bernard Bosanquet and Henry Jones. Andrew Seth Pringle-Pattison in Britain and Rudolph Eucken on the continent rescued personality from being submerged in the Absolute. Personal Idealism defended the metaphysical autonomy of personality against both naturalism, which made personality the outcome of nature, and Absolute Idealism, which made personality an 'adjective' of the Absolute itself.

Biographical

The Times, 2 September 1931.

The Scotsman, 2 September 1931.

John Laird, 'Pattison, Andrew Seth Pringle (1856–1931)', *Dictionary of National Biography 1931–41*.

E.N. Merrington, 'A Scottish Thinker: Andrew Seth Pringle–Pattison', *The Australasian Journal of Psychology and Philosophy*, ix (1931).

J.B. Baillie, 'Pringle-Pattison as Philosopher', *Proceedings of the British Academy* (1931).

A. Seth Pringle-Pattison, *Balfour Lectures on Realism: with a Memoir by G.F. Barbour* (Edinburgh: Blackwood, 1933).

W.J. Mander, 'Pringle-Pattison, Andrew Seth' in *Dictionary of Nineteenth Century British Philosophers*, ed. W.J. Mander and Alan P.F. Sell (Bristol: Thoemmes, 2002), pp. 922–7.

Principal Works

The Development from Kant to Hegel (London: Williams and Norgate, 1882).

Scottish Philosophy (Edinburgh: Blackwood, 1885).

Hegelianism and Personality (Edinburgh: Blackwood, 1887).

Man's Place in the Cosmos (Edinburgh: Blackwood, 1897).

Studies in the Philosophy of Religion (Oxford: Clarendon Press, 1930).

The Balfour Lectures on Realism (Edinburgh: Blackwood, 1933).

READING III

HEGELIANISM AS AN ABSOLUTE SYSTEM[1]

J endeavoured in the preceding Lecture to point out two lines of thought in Hegel. The one starts from the idea of God, which is Neo-Platonically constructed as Trinity in unity, but which is simply the idea of knowledge as such, treated as a real being. There is no passage from this hypostatized conception to the facts of the finite world. The second line of thought starts with these facts, and treats the historical development of humanity as the process in which the Absolute comes to itself. These two lines of thought, I argued, are not successfully brought together by Hegel, and the attempt to bring them together involves a violation of the true notion of development. One of these views was bound to give way to the other; and it was only natural that the strength which the second view derived from its contact with reality should enable it to triumph over the first. This is observable in Hegel himself, and still more in the history of the school. In spite of a certain mystic or Platonic vein, there never lived a man more wedded to hard fact than Hegel; and he had an instinctive aversion to seeking the Divine in some ideal beyond the confines of the world that now is. God must be found here, he argued, or not at all. Hence he came more and more strongly to insist upon the fact that the revelation and the reality of the Divine existence is contained in history. He undoubtedly insists in this connection on much that is true; but when the position is transformed by some of his ablest followers into a frank identification of the Absolute with man, we are face to face with a consequence of the Hegelian argument to which attention has not yet been called.

This is, that if we identify the Absolute with the subject of the development, we are unable to rise higher than man's actual achievement, and are therefore inevitably led to put man in the place of God. God or the Absolute is represented in the system as the last term of a development into which we have a perfect insight; we ourselves, indeed, as absolute philosophers, are equally the last term of the development. It is impossible, therefore, to discriminate in the account given between the absolute

---

[1]   'Hegelianism As an Absolute System' and 'Conclusion' in *Hegelianism and Personality* (Edinburgh and London: Blackwood, 1887), pp. 185–230.

philosopher and God. The philosopher's knowledge is God's knowledge of himself; and, with some reservations as to particularity and contingency, this knowledge is apparently put forward as perfectly adequate. No provision is made, no room seemingly is left, for any further knowledge of himself on God's part. The Philosophy of Law, of History, of Aesthetics, of Religion, and the History of Philosophy itself, all conclude in the same style. The Absolute is attained in each of these spheres, being simply man's record and ultimate attainment along these various lines. 'God is not a Spirit beyond the stars', says Hegel. 'He is Spirit in all spirits'[2] — a true thought finely expressed. But if the system leaves us without any self-conscious existence in the universe beyond that realized in the self-consciousness of individual philosophers, the saying means that God, in any ordinary acceptation of the word, is eliminated from our philosophy altogether. Thus translated, it is no longer fine and no longer true. The same tendency is observable throughout the 'Philosophy of Religion', where we should naturally expect to meet it least. The self-existence of God, if I may so speak, seems to disappear; God is begotten, and has His only reality in the consciousness of the worshipping community. Evidently this is to renounce the idea of anything like a separate personality or self-consciousness in the Divine Being. Whether Hegel had himself explicitly renounced the idea, it is perhaps impossible to say with certainty. Many students from his own day till now have refused to draw this conclusion from his writings, finding in them, as I am far from denying, numerous passages which seem to support their view. But to me most of these utterances have a doubtful ring. The drift of Hegel's mind appears to me, on the whole, to be in the opposite direction; and the religious or theological form into which he often throws his thought I cannot regard as other than a metaphorical expression of positions which, in themselves, have no affinity with the dogmas in question. In a notable passage in the 'Philosophy of Religion', he frankly compares his own treatment of the Christian dogmas to the procedure of the Neo-Platonists in infusing a philosophic meaning into the popular mythology which preceding thinkers of a rationalistic turn had altogether cast aside.[3] But whatever may have been Hegel's personal position in the matter, the negative view taken by most dar-

[2]   *Werke*, xi. p. 24.
[3]   *Werke*, xi. p. 95.

ing and perhaps his ablest followers — the Hegelians of the Left, as they were called — would appear to be the only one for which, in consistency, the system has room. For as water cannot rise higher than its source, so the development cannot go further than the philosopher himself. As long as we claim to have an absolute philosophy in the Hegelian sense, so long must we identify our own thought with the divine, and treat the Absolute as a mere expression for human achievement in its different spheres.

This consequence was frankly avowed by the Hegelians of the Left. The Absolute realizes itself, they declared, only in the human individual. Behind or beside the individuals, there exists only the logical Idea, in which we are asked to recognize the ultimate self-sustaining reality of the universe.[4] The Absolute, accordingly, is not a complete and eternally existent self-consciousness, but an impersonal system of thought. This is the only thing permanent in phenomena; from it the phenomenal world arises, and into it it returns. In man this impersonal Absolute — this eternal system of abstract thoughts — comes to consciousness of itself. Human persons are, as it were, the foci in which the impersonal life of thought momentarily concentrates itself, in order to take stock of its own contents. These foci appear only to disappear in the perpetual process of this realzsation.

The independent existence here attributed to abstract thought or categories makes this result one of the most remarkable theories on record. The categories not only exist of themselves, but they creatively give rise to the phenomenal world of men and things. In comparison with this apotheosis of logic, materialism itself seems mildly reasonable. Yet these Hegelians of the Left — men like Feurbach, Ruge, Strauss, Bruno Bauer, and others — were only taking literally Hegel's own statements about the Logic, and abolishing that supreme Spirit, for whom, so long as the Absolute is identified with the subject of the process, there is really no room in the system. Indeed we may go further, and say that this is the natural outcome of a theory which endeavours to construct reality out of the logical Idea. What other result could we expect than that both God and man, as real beings, would van-

---

[4]   Hegel himself, it may be remarked, had spoken of the logical Idea as 'the realm of truth as it is without hull or wrapping in and for itself' — 'the exposition of God as he is in his eternal essence, before the creation of nature or any finite spirit' — *Ibid.*, iii. p. 36.

ish back into their source, leaving us with the logical Idea itself as
the sole reality? This is asserted in so many words of God. Man, of
course, as a phenomenal existence, is in evidence, and cannot be
simply denied; but he, too, is robbed of all true personality, and
appears only as the vanishing centre of a system of knowledge,
and exemplification of the form of consciousness in general. The
Idea is all in all. Truly, as Dr Stirling says, the Idea so conceived is
'a blind, dumb, invisible idol', and the theory is 'the most hopeless
theory that has ever been offered to humanity'.[5] And it is instruc-
tive to notice how the most absolute Idealism and Rationalism
historically transformed itself into its diametrical opposite — into
the most thoroughgoing Materialism and Sensualism. The process may be traced in Feuerbach, Strauss and others. For if the
Idea realizes itself in man alone, then man, as this sensuous individual, is the only reality which in any wise concerns us. The metaphorical priority assigned to the logical system pales before the
imperative reality of the senses. 'The new philosophy', says
Feuerbach, laying down the lines of the 'Philosophie der
Zukunft', 'has for its subject not the Ego, not absolute, that is,
abstract, Spirit, in short not Reason *in abstracto*, but the actual and
whole essence of man. The reality, the subject of reason, is only
man. Man thinks, not the Ego, not Reason. The new philosophy
rests therefore on the divinity (Gottheit), that is, the truth of the
whole man. If the old philosophy said, "Only the rational is the
true and the real", the new philosophy says, on the other hand,
only the human is the true and the real; for only the human is the
rational. Man is the measure of reason'.[6] A personal God to this
philosophy is no more than man's projection of his own image
upon the screen of his imagination. Immortality is likewise a delusion; to the individual belongs only the sensuous present. As
Idealism does not recognize the distinction of popular philosophy between the body and the soul, the reality of man is thus,
practically, identified with his bodily existence, and we pass to a
consistent Sensationalism and an essentially materialistic view of
the universe.[7] A similar transition to Materialism, or something

---

[5] Schwegler, pp. 474 and 435.

[6] *Philosophie der Zukunft*, §51, quoted by Harms.

[7] A logical Idealism of the Hegelian stamp lies, in truth, in some respects
     very near to Materialism. The categories, it is no doubt asserted, form the
     immanent reality of the material universe; and therefore, when man

indistinguishable from it, achieved itself more slowly in Strauss. Strauss began his career as one of the ablest and clearest of Hegel's followers. His last book, 'The Old Faith and the New' — a very interesting personal record — is to all intents and purposes a confession of Materialism. But, indeed, what is the difference between Idealism and Materialism, if in the one case human existence is the outcome of an unconscious system of logical conceptions, and in the other the outcome of unconscious matter? In the latter case, man is the chance result of mechanical laws; in the former, the process is said to be controlled by a logical necessity. But in both cases the evolution is for us — and for us alone it exists — in a true sense aimless. It is a spectacle constantly repeated, but it discards and tramples under foot those conscious ends which alone are to be deemed worthy of attainment. If we take away from Idealism personality, and the ideals that belong to personality, it ceases to be Idealism in the historic sense of that word. To call it so is merely confusing the issues, for it has joined hands with the enemy, and fights on the other side of the field.

A very simple reflection, however, suffices to deliver us from these results. We have only to remember that to speak of the self-existence of thoughts, without a thinker whose they are, is to use words without a meaning; and the whole fabric of this Hegelianism of the Left collapses. Nevertheless, as has been contended, it has the consistency of the system on its side, so long as we identify the Absolute with our knowledge of the Absolute, and take the process of human development as in very truth the evolution of God. Hegel's determination to have one process and one subject was the original fountain of error. This identification, therefore, is what we must begin by denying. The development we can trace is not the development of God, but of man's thoughts about God — a development, therefore, which does not affect the existence of their object. In the history of philosophy, for example, who can believe that we have the successive stages by which God arrived at a knowledge of Himself, complete knowledge being dated from the beginning of the present century? What we really have is the history of man's repeated efforts to solve the problem of the universe — a history which, even from this point of view,

arises out of Nature, it is as if thought came to itself. But the frank derivation of man from Nature holds its own, while the unsubstantial basis of categories falls altogether into the background.

we might not unreasonably expect to show marks of progress and increasing insight; though even at the end, if we are honest with ourselves, the insight is so dim that the title of absolute knowledge applied to it has the sound of Mephistophelian mockery. It is, if possible, even more plainly so in the case of religion. What is religion, if not an attitude of the subjective spirit of man? We are here altogether on human ground. And the same is true of art, and of history itself — the history of civilization, of states and empires. Is it not effrontery to narrow down the Spirit of the universe to a series of events upon this planet? Can we believe, as Lotze puts it, 'that the creative cause of the universe issued from its darkness into the light of manifestation only by the narrow path of earthy nature, and after having formed man and human life again retreated into infinity, as if with all its ends accomplished? For this dialectical idyll we must substitute an outlook into the boundlessness of other worlds, not with the vain effort to know the unknowable, but with the view of letting the boundlessness of this background mark out the narrow limits of the realm of existence actually knowable by us'.[8] It seems strange, he adds, in the 'Metaphysic', that these Idealists, though fully aware of the Copernican discoveries and living under their influence 'should yet be able to persuade themselves that the spiritual development of their Absolute was confined to the shores of the Mediterranean'.[9] Surely the explicit statement of such results is sufficient to discredit them. Only under cover of an ambiguous phrase can they have been believed.

It is perhaps in ethics and politics, which are essentially sciences of the ideal — the ought-to-be — that the malign influences of Hegel's attitude are most clearly seen. I am fully aware while saying this, that it is precisely in these spheres that some of Hegel's best work was done. But while recognizing the solidity and strength of his writing on these subjects, it is impossible to shut our eyes to the assumption of finality made here as elsewhere. And it is natural that in this more concrete sphere the assumption should appear more grossly at variance with the facts of the case. There are few more constantly recurring polemics in Hegel than that which he carries on against Fichte's *Sollen*, the attempt, that is, to interpret the universe entirely through the

[8]   Lotze, *Microcosmos I.* p. 458 (English translation).
[9]   *Metaphysic*, p. 379 (Clarendon Press).

notion of duty, something that is not, but is to be. As against this conception Hegel repeatedly tells us that 'the Idea is not so feeble as merely to have a right or an obligation to exist without actually existing'.[10] And he is fond of justifying his position by reference to the religious consciousness. 'The religious mind', he says, 'views the world as ruled by Divine Providence, and therefore as corresponding with what it ought to be'; or in more technical language, the Will must return to the point of view of Intelligence or cognition, which 'apprehends the world as the notion actual'.[11] 'It is easier', he says in the 'Philosophy of History', 'to discover a deficiency in individuals, in states, and in Providence, than to see their real import. This subjective fault-finding is easy ... Age generally makes men more tolerant; youth is always discontented ... The insight, then, to which philosophy is to lead us is, that the real world is as it ought to be'.[12]

Now there is no difficulty in admitting that when we try speculatively to comprehend all existence within our view, it is impossible to rest in Fichte's position. This has been already urged in a former lecture, and it was eventually admitted by Fichte himself in the emphasis which he laid in his later writings upon the actuality of God as distinct from the process of becoming. Both this later position of Fichte's, therefore, and the religious point of view to which Hegel appeals, affirm the reality of the Ideal; but there seems to be a not unimportant difference between the sense in which they do so and that in which Hegel asserts it. Hegel's invocation of 'the religious mind' here is perhaps hardly fair. It is quite true that the religious man views the world as ruled by Divine Providence, but this view is surely to be interpreted as a faith or belief — a faith which he clings to, may one not say, often with a species of desperation in the face of anomalies and difficulties which he cannot pretend to solve. This faith is his last refuge against complete moral scepticism; but he does not profess to *see* the plan of the Divine government. Still less does he make any assertion of the perfection of the actual world, such as Hegel puts in his mouth. On the contrary, the religious man is almost always found painting the present state of things in the darkest colours; and, if his religion be real, this is the source of his energy as a prac-

[10] Wallace, p. 9.
[11] *Ibid.*, pp. 322, 323.
[12] English translation, p. 38.

tical reformer. Hegel's position is essentially different. His whole
theory leads him up to the assertion that here too, just as in knowledge, the circle is closed, finality is attained; the ideal is real, and
we see that it is so.

This position is most clearly expressed in the 'Philosophie des
Rechts' [Philosophy of Right], published in 1820. But the acceptance, nay, the worship, of mere fact which it consistently
involves is so destructive of all ethical ideals, and the air of almost
brutal Actualism so fatal to further progress, that, when Hegel
slipped into the unqualified assertion of it in the Preface to this
work, the utterance roused something like a storm of obloquy. It
is here that the famous saying occurs — 'What is rational is real,
and what is real is rational'; and it is followed by other passages
equally strong. 'This treatise is intended to be nothing else than an
attempt to comprehend and to exhibit the State as an existence
essentially rational. As a philosophical work, it must most carefully avoid all construction of a State as it ought to be. The instruc-
tion which it may contain does not lie in instructing the State as to
the form in which it ought to be, but simply in teaching how the
State, the moral universe, is to be cognized. The task of philosophy is to understand the "what is", for "what is" is reason'.[13] Thus
on his reconstruction or transcript of man's creation, Hegel ech-
oes the verdict of the Divine Workman, when He saw everything
He had made, and, behold, it was very good. The resemblance is
striking, and was dictated by the whole tenor of his philosophy.
But such praise applied to the Prussian State in the year 1820
seems to have almost too strong an infusion of the tolerance of age
which he commends as the insight of true philosophy. We can
scarcely wonder that his enemies attributed such utterances to no
loftier source than the optimistic conservatism of the man with
whom the world has dealt liberally and who sees his own life-
purpose achieved. Hegel was branded as a reactionary, as the 'official' philosopher of the Prussian State, whose business it was to
rehabilitate the actual by decking it out in the trappings of rational
necessity. In this his enemies were certainly unjust. The statements in question are not insincere opportunisms; they are the
genuine outcome of one whole side of Hegel's thought. That side
was uppermost when he wrote the 'Philosophy of Law', and they

---

[13] *Werke*, viii. p. 18.

seem to have slipped from him almost unconsciously in this strong and unqualified form.

The clamour, however, to which this Preface gave rise, roused Hegel to a sense of his imprudence, and to an acknowledgement that his statements were not to be taken in their frank literal meaning. In the Introduction to the 'Encyclopaedia'[14] he expressly replied to his critics in a passage which reads very like a palinode. He begins by sheltering himself behind the religious doctrine already referred to, and then proceeds as follows: 'Existence is in part mere appearance, and only in part reality. In common life, any freak or error, evil and everything of the nature of evil, as well as every miserable and transient existence whatever, gets in a careless way, and as it were by accident, the name of reality. But even our ordinary feelings are enough to forbid an accidental existence getting the emphatic name of a reality. When I spoke of the real, it might have been understood in what sense I used the term, seeing that in a detailed Logic I had treated among other things of Reality, and had accurately distinguished it not only from the contingent, which, after all, has also existence, but even from the ordinary categories of mere existence (*Dasien, Existenz undandern Bestimmungen*)'. 'The understanding prides itself', he proceeds, 'upon its "Ought", which it takes especial pleasure in prescribing on the field of politics . . . for who is not acute enough to see a great deal in his own surroundings which is really far from being what it ought to be? But such acuteness is mistaken in the conceit that when it examines these objects, and pronounces what they ought to be, it is dealing with the interests of philosophical science. Philosophy has to do only with the Idea — with a reality, therefore, of which those objects, institutions, and conditions represent only the outward and superficial side'.[15]

The preface does not mean, therefore, that 'whatever is is right'. Not the real in the ordinary sense of that word is the rational, but only the truly real — that which reason justifies as such. The Idea realizes itself, but still the external fabric cannot be taken as its complete or even consistent realization. In short, the real, so far as it is rational, is rational; the rest we leave out of account. We deny the term real of that which is not rational. Surely this is to reduce the position to an empty tautology.

---

[14]   A second edition of the 'Encyclopaedia' appeared in 1827, a third in 1830.
[15]   *Werke*, vi. pp. 10, 11; Wallace, pp. 8, 9.

This equivocation between 'the real' and 'the truly real' is more, however, than an isolated quibble on Hegel's part to extricate himself from an uncomfortable position. It is not a piece of conscious insincerity; for we can hardly impute to him the stony-hearted optimism and the peculiarly gross empiricism which a literal rendering of his words would imply. He probably meant to say substantially what he afterwards explained that he had meant — namely, that *on the whole* a purpose of reason is visible in the social and legal structures of mankind. Philosophy, working on the great scale, can afford to neglect exceptions, misgrowths, positive evils. In itself, this is perhaps an intelligible and justifiable position, but is it one which is open to an absolute philosophy? The old difficulty of the contingent, of reality as such, is upon us again, and again Hegel tries to wave it contemptuously aside. The embarrassing facts are not 'truly real', or, more concisely still, they are not 'true'. Hegel's use of this constantly recurring term is little more than an index to the difficulty in question. In the 'Logic' every higher category is looked upon as the 'truth' of the lower, and the Absolute Idea is the full truth of which all the preceding forms of thought were imperfect expressions. Used thus of categories or abstract definitions, the term is sufficiently in place, and might be rendered by a phrase like 'adequate expression'. But it receives from Hegel a much wider extension, being applied to existences as well as to conceptions. Here the ambiguity begins, for an existence is properly said to have 'reality', truth being a term properly applicable to conceptions alone, and signifying their correspondence with reality. We have, however, the advantage of an express declaration by Hegel as to the sense to be attached to the term in this new connection. He distinguishes 'truth' in his usage from mere correctness or 'formal truth', as he calls it. 'Truth in the deeper sense consists in the identity between objectivity and notion. It is in this deeper sense that truth is understood when we speak of a true State or a true work of art. These objects are true, if they are as they ought to be — *i.e.,* if their reality corresponds to their notion. When thus viewed, *to be untrue means much the same as to be bad*. A bad man is an untrue man, one who does not behave as his notion or vocation requires of him'.[16] Hegel has the grace to say in another place that 'when the term untrue

---

[16] Wallace, p. 306.

occurs in a philosophical discussion, it does not signify that the thing to which it is applied does not exist. A bad State or a sick body may certainly exist; but these objects are untrue, because their notion and their reality are out of harmony'.[17] Nevertheless, he seems to say, such existences do not count; we may exclude them from our reckoning altogether. Would that we could believe this comfortable saying! That these facts have no place in an absolute system — that they 'ought not' to be there — is plain enough. They are the standing refutation of its claims. But dismissed in this fashion they cannot be.

The distinction which Hegel here attempts to draw marks the reappearance of the other line of thought which runs through the system. This Platonising strain, as it has been aptly named,[18] predominates in the 'Logic', and appears more or less in other works, but is markedly absent in the 'Philosophy of Law'. Under its influence, as we have seen, Hegel, like Plato, seeks reality not in the actual world, but in the eternal realm of an absolute and self-guaranteeing thought. The world of timeless forms is the real world, not the world of existing things and persons. To this latter world Hegel (when following out this train of thought) accords, like Plato, only as it were a *quasi*-reality. He even speaks, as we have seen, of the whole course of finite development as a species of illusion — 'only a hull or wrapping under which the notion lies concealed'. But, on the other hand, the identity of the real and the ideal is to an absolute system the very breath of its life. 'The real is rational' is the necessary complement of 'the rational is real'. Hence Hegel's apparent rebound from his Platonising strain to the opposite extreme of Empiricism or Actualism. His philosophy can justify itself only as the union of its Platonism with its Empiricism, or as the exhibition of the one in the other. Divorced from the world of facts, the Platonism or Idealism is all in the air. The reality of the rational is ultimately the proof of its rationality; for unless it asserts itself in existence, the circle of the system is not closed. Just so far indeed as the real does *not* correspond to the rational, the system itself falls into the ground, and its statements as to the nature of the rational take the character of undemon-

---

[17] *Ibid.*, p. 211.
[18] By Haym in his *Hegel und seine Zeit*, a book a good deal marred by its rhetorical strain and a semi-popular looseness of treatment, but often containing suggestive criticisms.

strated assertions. Sweeping, therefore, though the statements in the 'Philosophy of Law' and the 'Philosophy of History' are, they seem to me to represent the attitude which an absolute philosophy must necessarily assume so long as it is animated by a confident belief in itself. Strictly speaking, we can have no standing-ground in a system like Hegel's from which to criticize the actual. None the less, however, is this attitude one which will not bear examination. It only requires to be openly avowed, as here by Hegel, and it is at once seen to be untenable. The explanations or apologies to which Hegel has recourse do but acknowledge with a bad grace that the brave words formerly used will not bear to be pressed. The real and the ideal do not coincide or interpenetrate, and the two sides of the system are therefore not really brought together. Nature or existence, says Hegel, is the home of Contingency, and so it fails of truth — fails, that is, to body forth the notion. Necessity, says Plato, is mingled with Reason in the origin of the world, and Reason cannot quite subdue Necessity to itself. The very form of words is almost the same, in which the two thinkers record their own failure in the attempt to conceal it.

If we turn to the 'Philosophy of Law', it will be found that, in spite of Hegel's subsequent attempts to guard his meaning, the descriptions of it in the Preface were essentially correct. It is a transcript of what is — of existing institutions and customs, and of the existent State. There is throughout the book none of the enthusiasm of moral progress which meets us, for example, in Kant and Fichte. Indeed the inner side of actions — that which constitutes their whole *moral* significance — is hurriedly passed over, in order to arrive at a consideration of those bonds of social observance which keep the individual right, as it were, without his thinking about it.[19] The conscientious or self-questioning habit of mind is studiously depreciated, and no higher standard is set up than that of the society in which a man lives. Do as others do; perform the duties of your station; be a good father and a good citizen, and get rid of windy enthusiasms. Such is the temper of the book from first to last. It is, as it were, the externalization of morality. For the inner fact of duty there is substituted an automatic adoption to an external mechanism of observance and respect-

---

[19] It need hardly be pointed out that though the title of the book is the *Philosophy of Law* (*Philosophie des Rechts* [commonly translated *Philosophy of Right*]), it is a complete treatise on Hegelian ethics.

ability. Unquestionably there is a great deal of massive common-sense in all this; and Hegel is never happier than when adminis-tering a slap in the face to some superfine feeling. But it is also true that it is the justification of the existing standard. It is the mood of satisfied acquiescence in things as they are, which the years bring to the man of the world — a mood as far removed as possible from the atmosphere of moral endeavour. There is in it no impulse onwards, no impulse upwards. It is an atmosphere fatal to moral progress, and ultimately fatal to morality itself. Green is not slow to point out that the habit of conscientiousness — of moral self-interrogation — is the very mainspring of morality, essential even for preventing the deterioration of moral practice, much more so for the elevation of the existing standard. 'The standard of respectability', he says, 'could never have been attained, if the temper which acquiesces in it had been universal — if no one had been lifted above that acquiescence — in the past. It has been reached through the action of men who, each in his time and turn, have refused to accept the way of living which they found about them.'[20] Hence when he comes to treat of ethics, Green is forced to desert the Hegelian Absolutism, and to insist upon 'an ideal of virtue' as 'the spring from which morality perpetually renews its life'. He philosophizes here more in the spirit of Kant and Fichte than of Hegel. Fichte is in a manner the typical moralist; for the moral man can never tell himself that he has already attained. In the character of logical necessity which he imparts to the histori-cal process, and in his contention that the goal *is* reached and the long march of the Spirit ended, Hegel's attitude is as typically non-ethical.

This attitude of attainment and finality is also curiously observ-able in the 'Philosophy of History'. As Haym observes, the Hegelian philosophy of history has no future. From youth in Greece and manhood in Rome, Spirit has advanced in the German or Teutonic world to the stadium of old age. It is true, Hegel adds that while the old age of nature is weakness that of Spirit is its per-fect maturity and strength; but he fully accepts the finality of the comparison.[21] Yet, as the same writer acutely points out, this would-be absolute and final philosophy naively supplies us with its own condemnation. All readers of Hegel will remember the

[20] *Prolegomena to Ethics*, p. 324.
[21] *Philosophy of History*, p. 115 (English translation).

finely inspired passage in which he compares philosophy to the
owl of Minerva. It forms the conclusion of the Preface to the 'Philosophy of Law', and breathes at its outset the same spirit as the
passage formerly quoted: 'If it were the purpose of philosophy to
reform and improve the existing state of things, it comes a little
too late for such a task. It is only when the actual world has
reached its full fruition that the ideal rises to confront the reality,
and builds up, in the shape of an intellectual realm, that same
world grasped in its substantial being. When philosophy paints
its grey in grey, some one shape of life has meanwhile grown old:
and grey in grey, though it brings it into knowledge, cannot make
it young again. The owl of Minerva does not start upon its flight
until the evening twilight has begun to fall'. 'Just as each individual', he says a little before, 'is the son of his own time, so philosophy is *its own time formulated or reduced to thought (in Gedanken
erfasst)*; it is as foolish to imagine that a philosophy can go beyond
the world present to it, as that an individual can overleap his own
time'.[22] This is an idea deeply rooted in Hegel, and it forms the sta-
ple of most Hegelian histories of philosophy. But how are we to
reconcile this acknowledgement of thoroughgoing relativity with
the absolute claims made for his own philosophy? Is the future to
be an absolute monotony, bringing us no new lessons, and yield-
ing us no deeper insight? Not for a moment can we entertain such
an idea.[23] The 'horologue of the universe' did not run down and
come to a standstill with the dawn of the nineteenth century. In
truth, this golden age of philosophy, with its absolute knowledge
and its rational state, strikes at last upon the spirit with a sense of

---

[22] *Werke*, viii. p. 18. Cf. the emphatic assertion of the same position in the
       Philosophy of History — 'Each individual is the son of his nation and of his
       age. None remains behind it, still less advances before it' (English
       Translation, p. 55).
[23] The idea, however, is naturally suggested to the student who has lived
       himself into the Hegelian system, and it was not uncommon among
       Hegel's earlier and more confident followers. '*Jenes Pathos und jene
       Ueberzeugtheit der Hegelianer vom Jahre 1830 muss man sich vergegen-
       wärtigen, welche im vollen bitteren Ernste die Frage ventilirten, was wohl den
       ferneren Inhalt der Welteschicte bilden werde, nachdem doch in der Hegel'schen
       Philosophie der Weltgeist an sein Ziel, an das Wissen seiner selbst hindurch-
       gedrungen sei*'. Haym, p. 5. (English translation: 'One has to imagine the
       pathos and conviction of the Hegelians of 1830 who in deadly earnest
       aired the question of what would constitute the subsequent course of
       World History once — according to Hegel's philosophy — the World
       Spirit had finally attained its goal: Self-knowledge'.)

intolerable *ennui*. We feel instinctively with Lessing that the search for truth is a nobler thing, and better for our spirits' health, than the truth here offered for our acceptance. It might be otherwise if *the truth* were really ours, but that, we may well believe, is reserved for God alone. The perfect knowledge and the perfect State of Hegelianism ring alike hollow, when brought face to face with the riddle of the painful earth — with the always solemn and often terrible mystery that environs us. Let us be honest with ourselves, and let us be shy of demonstrations which prove too much. We are men and not gods; the ultimate synthesis is not ours. The universe is *not* plain to us, save by a supreme effort of faith — of faith in reason and faith in goodness. It is the splendid faith of Hegel in reason which gives such massive proportions to his thought, and makes it like the opening up of a new world to him who enters upon it. But if this faith be reduced to system, and put forward as a demonstration, I feel equally certain that the effect is as harmful as it was at first beneficial. It saps the springs both of speculative interest and of moral endeavour. No, we may rest assured that finality is not for the race of man; we cannot lift ourselves out of the stream of ever-flowing time in which our lives are passed. Hegelianism is one more great attempt satisfactorily to name the Whole, and to find room within it for all the different sides of existence. But Time is still the god who devours his own children, and the Hegelian system will be no exception. It will remain as the system of Aristotle or as the system of Spinoza remains, and men will draw from its rich materials for their own intellectual structures. They will draw inspiration and guidance from its successes; they will take warning by its mistakes.

Conclusion

If any justification be needed of this prolonged criticism of Hegel, it must be found in the considerations which I adduced at the outset. The truth of the Hegelian system, or of some essentially similar scheme, is presupposed in the doctrine of English Neo-Kantians or Neo-Hegelians as to the universal Self and its relation to the world. There may be no mention of Hegel in their writings, and the doctrine itself may be explicitly derived by them from a development and criticism of the Kantian philosophy; but the nerve of such development and criticism is supplied by Hegel's professed exhibition of existence as the process of such a Self. Hegel also exemplifies on a great scale the same mode of reasoning which was animadverted upon in the first lecture as the fallacy of Neo-Kantianism; and a study of his system enables us, better than anything else, to see the results to which this line of thought conducts us.

The radical error both of Hegelianism and of the allied English doctrine I take to be identification of the human and the divine self-consciousness, or, to put it more broadly, the unification of consciousness in a single Self. The exposure of this may be said to have been, in a manner, the thesis of these lectures. This identification or unification depends throughout, it has been argued, upon the tendency to take a mere form for a real being — to take an identity of type for a unity of existence. Each of us is a Self: that is to say, in the technical language of recent philosophy, we exist *for* ourselves or are objects to ourselves. We are not mere objects existing only for others, but, as it were, subject and object in one. Selfhood may also be said to imply that, in one aspect of my existence, I am universal, seeing that I distinguish my individual existence from that of other beings, while embracing both within a common world. Irrespective of metaphysical theory, every Self is universal in this sense, and by all means let this characteristic be embodied in the definition of the Self. If a mere individual, as we are often told, would be a being without consciousness of its own limitations — a being, therefore, which could not know itself as an individual — then no Self is a mere individual. We may even safely say that the mere individual is a fiction of philosophical thought. There could be no interaction between individuals, unless they were all embraced within one Reality; still less could there be any knowledge by one individual of others, if they did not all form parts of one system of things. But it is a great step further to say that this universal attitude of the Self, as such, is due to the fact that it is one universal Self that thinks in all so-called thinkers. This is, to say the least, an extremely unfortunate way of stating the necessities of the case. For though selfhood, as was seen in the earlier lectures, involves a duality in unity, and is describable as subject–object, it is none the less true that each Self is a unique existence, which is perfectly *impervious*, if I may so speak, to other selves — impervious in a fashion of which the impenetrability of matter is a faint analogue. The self, accordingly, resists invasion; in its character of self it refuses to admit another self within itself, and thus be made, as it were, a mere retainer of something else. The unity of things (which is not denied) cannot be properly expressed by making it depend upon a unity of the Self in all thinkers; for the very characteristic of a self is this exclusiveness. So far from a principle of union in the sense desired, the self is in truth the very apex of separation and differentiation. It is none the less true, of course, that only through selfhood am I able to recognize the unity of the world and my own union with the source at all, and this is the incentive to the metaphysical use of the idea of a universal Self which I am criticizing. But though the self is thus, in knowledge, a principle of unification, it is, in existence or metaphysically, a principle of isolation. And the unification which proceeds in the one case is, to the end, without prejudice to the exclusive self-assertion in the other. There is no deliverance of consciousness which is more unequivocal than that which testifies to this independence and exclusiveness. I have a centre of my own — a will of my own — which no one shares with me or can share — a centre which I maintain even in my dealings with God Himself. For it is eminently false to say that I put off, or can put off, my personality here. The religious consciousness lends no countenance whatever to the representation of the human soul as a mere mode or efflux of the divine. On the contrary, only in a person, in a relatively independent or self-centred being is religious approach to God possible. Religion is the self-surrender of the human will to the divine. 'Our wills are ours to make them Thine'. But this is a *self*-surrender, a surrender which only self, only will, can make.

The doctrine of the universal Self is reached by a process of reasoning which I have already compared to the procedure of Scholastic Realism in dealing with individuals and 'universals'. Realism also treated the individual as merely the vehicle of a universal form. It took the species as a real existence apart from its individuals; more real than they, and prior to them, for they are regarded as in effect its creatures. The individual man stands in this secondary and dependent relation to the species 'Humanitas', and that universal inheres in turn in a higher genus, till we reach the ultimate abstraction of a universal Being or substance of which all existing things are accidents. For the ultimate goal of Realism is a thorough-going Pantheism. Any student of the scholastic period may see that only inconsistent reservations and the compromises necessitated by their churchly position restrained the realists from this conclusion. It was widely drawn, however, in the heresies of the time, and the greater the speculative ability and consistency of the Realistic thinker, the nearer he approached it. And beyond the pale of Christendom altogether, in the system of Averroes, the typical infidel of the middle ages, the same Realism meets us in the doctrine of the identity of the human intellect in all individual men — identity not in the sense of essential similarity, but of existential unity. Though this universal intellect is regarded by Averroes as an inferior emanation of the Divine Being, and not as immediately identical with the divine intellect, the striking similarity of the doctrine to the Neo-Kantian theory of the universal Self cannot fail to be remarked. It does not affect the character of realism whether the universal is actually separated from the individuals and assigned a transcendental existence, or whether it is said to exist only in the individuals. This difference between the so-called Platonic and Aristotelian forms of Realism does not touch the fundamental doctrine common to both — the doctrine of the species as an entity in the individuals common to all and identical in each, an entity to which individual differences adhere as accidents. As against this view we may set Cousin's rendering of Abelard's doctrine — 'Only individuals exist, and in the individual nothing but the individual'. Similarity of essence or nature is one thing, existence is another. When existence is in question, it is in the individual, not the universal, that is real; and the real individual is not a composite of species and accidents, but is individual to the inmost fibre of his being.

In the last resort this realistic fallacy, whether in the Schoolmen or in Hegel and the Neo-Kantians, may be traced, as I suggested in the end of the first lecture, to a confusion between logic or epistemology and metaphysic or ontology. The imaginary subject (*Bewusstsein überhaupt*) of the theory of knowledge is hypostatized by the Neo-Kantians as the one ultimately real Thinker. Hegel's metaphysical logic may be taken without injustice as the culmination of this tendency. Kant ridiculed Fichte's system (not unnaturally, but as we have seen, not quite fairly) as an attempt to extract existence from mere logic, and said it looked to him like a kind of ghost.[24] This criticism would have been more applicable to Hegel's attempt to construct the universe out of mere universals. And even if we decline to take such Hegelian statements literally, the vice of the position still clings to the system; for the existence of things, however explained, is still regarded as serving only for the exemplification of these abstract notions. This holds true of the whole course of development, even in the case of spirit. If we examine Hegel's statements as the nature of spirit, they are all cast in the same mould. Spirit is that which has returned out of otherness to be at home with itself; spirit is that which restores itself; it is not an immediate but a mediated or restored unity; it is an identity which is not blank but constitutes the negation of the negation. Such are the constantly recurring phrases that meet us, and they all express the same thing — namely, that unity in duplicity (or trinity in unity, as Hegel might have called it) which characterizes self-conscious life. They give us simply that abstract scheme of intelligence which Fichte constructs for us in the 'Wissenschaftslehre'. But there is no virtue in this abstract form as such, and if the goal of the development is represented as the realization of the mere form of knowledge, it ceases to be anything of real value. It is this idealism of logical formulae with its sacrifice of the true goods of the spirit, which Lotze censures so severely in the Hegelian system.

My contention throughout these lectures has been that the attempt of the Hegelian and Neo-Hegelian schools to unify the divine and the human subject is ultimately destructive of the reality of both. If, as has been argued above,[25] the theory deprives man of his proper self, by reducing him, as it were, to an object of a universal Thinker, it leaves this universal Thinker also without any true personality. We cannot rightly conceive either the divine or the human Self in this impossible union, nor is this wonderful, seeing that they are merely two inseparable aspects of our own conscious life isolated and hypostatized. As for the divine Self, if *per impossibile* we figure this abstraction to ourselves as the permanent counterpart or sustainer of an objective world, such a purely objective consciousness is not in any true sense of the word a Self; it is no more than an imaginary focus into which an objective system of relations returns. We have learned — and this is well — to

[24] *Wie eine Art Gespenst:* in a letter dated April 1798 (*Werke*, viii. p. 812).
[25] Cf., for example, pp. 62–64 [of *Hegelianism and Personality*].

be chary of attributing to the Divine Spirit a subjectivity like our own. But it must not be forgotten that if we are to keep the name God at all, or any equivalent term, subjectivity — an existence of God for Himself, analogous to our own personal existence, though doubtless transcending it infinitely in innumerable ways — is an essential element in the conception. If it is said that this is abstract thinking, and illegitimately separates God's being from His manifestation or working in the universe, the charge does not appear to be borne out by the logical doctrine of Essence as we know it in its application to man. A man may be said to be for others what his acts and words are; and if we know these, we rightly say that we know the man. Similarly we may be said to know God as manifested in nature and history. Knowledge of the manifestation is in both cases knowledge of the essence; it does not cut us off from knowledge of the essence, as the Relativists would have us believe. But just as the man has a centre of his own, which we cannot occupy, and from which he looks, as it were, upon the inner side of his acts and words (as well as upon a private world of thoughts and feelings, many of which do not take shape in the common or general world at all), so, if we speak of God at all, there must be a divine centre of thought, activity and enjoyment, to which no mortal can penetrate. In this sense every man's being is different for himself from what it is as exhibited to others, and God's being may infinitely transcend His manifestation as known by us.

Moreover, the admission of a real self-consciousness in God seems demanded of us if we are not to be unfaithful to the fundamental principle of the theory of knowledge — interpretation by means of the highest category within our reach. The self-conscious life is that highest, and we should be false to ourselves if we denied in God what we recognize as the source of dignity and worth in ourselves. Only, as was said in a previous lecture, though we must be anthropomorphic, our anthropomorphism must be critical. Just as we do not read our full selves into life of lower forms, so — or rather much more so — must we avoid transferring to God all the features of our own self-consciousness. God may, nay must, be infinitely more — we are at least certain that He cannot be less — than we know ourselves to be.

The Hegelian system is as ambiguous on the question of man's immortality as on that of the personality of God, and for precisely the same reason — namely, because the Self of which assertions are made in the theory is not a real but a logical self. Hence, although passages may be quoted which seem direct assertions of immortality, they are found, on closer examination, to resolve themselves into statements about the Absolute Ego, or the unity of self-consciousness as such. Thus, we are told, Time is but a form of the Ego's own life — a form in which it knows objects — but the Subject itself is not bound by time-determinations. It is present to all the moments of time alike, being, in fact, the bond which ignites the several moments in one time. The Ego, it is argued, is, in a strict sense, timeless or out of time, and it becomes absurd, therefore, to apply time-predicates to it and to speak of its origin or decease.[26] As applied to the immortality of the individual self, however, this argument proves nothing. It only proves that the Ego must have co-existed with, or been present to, all its experience in the past; it does not prove that that experience may not come to an end, and the Ego along with it. Or again, we are told that the Ego is the absolutely necessary presupposition of thought and existence. We cannot strip off the Self; we cannot even conceive our own annihilation. But this is one of the demonstrations which prove too much. It applies as much to the times before our birth as to the times after our death. If we think at all, we cannot abstract from self-consciousness. But if, as Lucretius says, the future is to be of no more import to us than the days of old when the Pœni flocked together to battle, and the empire of the world was at stake, then surely the immortality thus guaranteed can be of no concrete concern to us. It rests, indeed, again, upon the conversion of a logical necessity into a metaphysical existence. This logical necessity under which we lie is said to be due to the presence in each of us of an unoriginated and unending Self. Even if we take the argument at its own valuation, therefore, it is the immortality of this Absolute Self which it proves. In like manner Aristotle maintained the eternity of the Active Reason,[27] and

---

[26] This argument involves, it may be remarked, the subtle confusion between the logical and the metaphysical criticized in a former lecture. Only an abstraction can properly be spoken of as out of time; so far as the Ego is real, it is not out of time, but abides or persists through time. Even in speaking of the Divine Being, that is the only sense which the term 'eternal' can bear to us.

[27] Aristotle's theory of the Active reason has directly been compared to the doctrine of the universal Self. The history of the Peripatetic school, it

Averroes the immortality of the intellect identical in all men. Spinoza, too, spoke of the *pars æterna nostri* [our eternal parts]. In no other sense does Hegel speak of the immortality of 'man as spirit' — an immortality or eternity which he is at pains to designate as a 'present quality', an actual possession.[28] Hegel's utterances on this subject are all pervaded, to my mind, by this *double entendre*, and virtually amount to a shelving of the question. For it has been abundantly seen that the Absolute Ego or the Active Reason is in itself a pure abstraction; and to be told that we survive in that form is no whit more consoling than to be told that the chemical elements of our body will survive in new transformations.

The two positions — the divine personality and human dignity and immortality — are two complementary sides of the same view of existence. If we can believe, with the Hegelians of the Left, that there is no permanent Intelligence and Will at the heart of things, then the self-conscious life is degraded from its central position, and becomes merely an incident in the universe. In that case we may well believe that human self-consciousness is but like a spark struck in the dark to die away presently upon the darkness whence it has arisen. For, according to this theory, the universe consists essentially in the evolution and reabsorption of transitory forms — forms that are filled with knowledge and shaped by experience, only to be emptied and broken by death. But it is a mockery to speak as if the universe had any real or worthy End, if it is merely the eternal repetition of this Danaid labour. And an account which contradicts our best-founded standards of value, and fails to satisfy our deepest needs, stands condemned as inherently unreasonable and incredible. I do not think that immortality can be demonstrated by philosophy; but certainly to a philosophy founding upon self-consciousness, and especially upon the moral consciousness, it must seem incredible that the successive generations should be used up and cast aside — as if character were not the only lasting product and the only valuable result of time. It may be said that morality is independent of the belief in immortality — that its true foundation is goodness for the sake of goodness, virtue for vir-

---

may be added, forms an interesting parallel to the development of the Hegelian school as indicated in the sixth lecture. The Active Reason speedily disappeared in the purely naturalistic system of Strato of Lampsacus.

[28] *Werke*, xii. p. 219.

tue's sake — and I willingly admit the nobility of temper that often underlies this representation. As against the theory which would base morality upon selfish rewards and punishments in a future state, it is profoundly true. But immortality is claimed by our moral instincts in no sense as a reward, but simply as 'the wages of going on and not to die'. And the denial of immortality seems so much at variance with our notions of the moral reasonableness of the world, that I believe it must ultimately act as a corrosive scepticism upon morality itself.

> Gone for ever! Ever? No; for since our dying race began, Ever, ever, and for ever was the leading light of man.
> Those that in barbarian burials killed the slave and slew the wife,
> Felt within themselves the sacred passion of the second life.
> Truth for truth, and good for good! The Good, the True, the Pure, the Just,
> Take the charm 'for ever' for them, and they crumble into dust.[29]

One word by way of conclusion and epilogue. It is possible that to some these lectures may appear to contain only unmitigated condemnation of Hegel and his system. That is an impression which I should much regret. I should regret it, not only because of my own great personal obligations to Hegel, which would make such a condemnation savour of ingratitude, but also on account of the great debt which philosophy in general owes to Hegel, and the speculative outlook which is got by studying him. I would dissuade no one from the study of Hegel. His aim is so great that the mere effort to keep pace with him strengthens the thews of the mind. Moreover, there is much in Hegel of the highest philosophical importance and truth. His services to the phenomenology or philosophical history of consciousness in all its forms have been simply immense. His 'Logic', looked at as a criticism of categories, with its insistence on self-consciousness as the ultimate principle of explanation, is also an imperishable gift. I have already defended his anthropomorphism in this respect, and am ready to do battle for it again. Nothing can be more unphilosophical than the attempt to crush man's spirit by thrusting upon it the immensities of the material universe. In this respect, Hegel's superb contempt for nature as nature has a justification of its own. In fact, we

---

[29] 'Locksley Hall: Sixty Years After'.

might adopt Fichte's strong expression, and say, that if matter alone existed, it would be equivalent to saying that nothing existed at all. In all this, Hegel is the protagonist of Idealism in the historic sense of that word, and champions the best interests of humanity. It is Hegelianism as a system, and not Hegel, that I have attacked. The point of my criticism has been that in its execution the system breaks down, and ultimately sacrifices these very interests to a logical abstraction styled the Idea, in which both God and man disappear. Nor are these interests better conserved by the Neo-Kantianism or Neo-Hegelianism, which erects into a god the mere form of self-consciousness in general.

Four

Henry Jones

Henry Jones was born 30 November 1852 at Llangernyw, Denbighshire, Wales and, on his own account, was born again when he entered the lecture hall of Edward Caird. Jones' family was strongly Calvinistic Methodist. He was the third son of Elias Jones, a shoemaker, and Elizabeth Williams. Jones followed in his father's footsteps when at the age of twelve he became apprenticed. He was, however, persuaded to continue his education while working, having to exist on only four hours sleep per night. He won a scholarship to Bangor Normal teacher training college in 1870, and became the headmaster of the Ironworks School at Brynammam, South Wales, in 1873. During his two years there Jones more than doubled the enrolment. He was a lay preacher and a registered Calvinistic Minister which inspired him to further his studies in theology. In 1875 he went on a scholarship to study at Glasgow University where he encountered Edward Caird and John Nicol. They persuaded him that his true aptitude was for philosophy. He followed their advice, but in practice Idealism became his religion and he preached its gospel from lecture halls all over the world. Like Caird, he saw no useful distinction to be made between philosophy, religion and poetry.

As undergraduates Jones, with James Lambie and Mungo Mac-Callum founded a philosophical society called 'The Witenagemonte', of which Jones was the first secretary. It met in a pub in Park Road, Hillhead, and exercised a strong influence on the study of philosophy at Glasgow for many years. After graduating with first class honours, Jones won the Clark fellowship which enabled him to study for four more years, in Germany and Oxford, but the bulk of which were spent in Glasgow as Caird's assistant. In 1882 he married Annie Walker, a shareholder in Glasgow City Bank, and the eldest sister of his friend, Hugh Walker.

Jones left Glasgow with great reluctance when he was appointed to a lectureship at University College, Aberystwyth, in 1883. In 1884 he became professor of philosophy and political economy in the newly established University College of North Wales, Bangor. Intellectually, however, he felt much more at home in Scotland, to which he returned in 1891 to take up the chair of logic, rhetoric and metaphysics at St Andrews which Andrew Seth had vacated to replace Campbell Fraser at Edinburgh. In 1894 Jones, much to John Watson's chagrin, succeeded to Caird's chair of moral philosophy at Glasgow. David George Ritchie was also in the competition and went on to succeed Jones in S. Andrews. In the last year of his life he secured the appointment of Bernard Bosanquet to the chair of moral philosophy.

Jones had strong Liberal leanings, reflecting his Welsh nonconformism, and was a close friend of David Lloyd George. He strongly held the view that university professors had a moral duty to provide leadership and guidance to the general community, and enter into debates and campaign on issues that affected the lives of ordinary people. He was influential in establishing and supporting the University Settlement in Glasgow. In good Idealist fashion he believed that opposing views should be aired and mutually understood, and established the Glasgow Civic Society devoted to the task. He committed to forging links between the University and business, and of getting businessmen to acknowledge their responsibilities to the broader community. Every workshop, he believed, should become a school of virtue. He was a champion of educational reform in both Wales and Scotland. He campaigned for Intermediary Schools in Wales, university education for women, and served on Haldane's Royal Commission of 1916–17 into the University of Wales. He was a member of the Universities Mission to America in 1918. He was extremely patriotic and believed in Home Rule for the separate nations in the United Kingdom, joined within the Empire. During the war he campaigned on behalf of the Parliamentary Recruitment Committee throughout Wales in an attempt to circumvent syndicalist opposition from miners in Merthyr and North Wales slate quarrymen.

He received honorary doctorates from the University of St Andrews and the University of Wales. In 1904 he was elected a Fellow of the British Academy. He was knighted in 1912, an honour he was reluctant to accept, and became a Companion of Honour in 1922. He was Hibbert lecturer at Manchester College, Oxford, for many years and, at the invitation of Mungo MacCallum, in 1908 delivered a series of lectures at Sydney University that were published as *Idealism as a Practical Creed*. He was the Gifford Lecturer at Glasgow University in 1920 and 1921.

Jones's life was filled with personal tragedy, but his faith in God made him an eternal optimist. Two of his six children died early, and a third was taken prisoner of war in Turkey. A fourth was killed in France during the War. After a prolonged and painful battle against mouth cancer he died 4 February 1922 and is buried in the churchyard at Kilbride, the Isle of Bute.

Biographical

Henry Jones, *Old Memories*, ed. Thomas Jones (London: Hodder and Stoughton, 1922).

J.H. Muirhead, 'Sir Henry Jones', *Proceedings of the British Academy*, (1921-3).

H.J.W. Hetherington, *The Life and Letters of Sir Henry Jones* (London: Hodder and Stoughton, 1924).

H.J.W. Hetherington, 'Jones, Henry 1852–1922', *Dictionary of National Biography 1921–1931*.

The Times, Feb. 6, 1922; *John O'London's Weekly*, March 11, 1922; *Western Mail*, Feb. 6, 1922.

Leonard Russell, 'Sir Henry Jones', *Mind*, xxxi (1922).

David Boucher and Andrew Vincent, *A Radical Hegelian* (Cardiff and New York: Wales University Press, and St. Martin's Press, 1993–4).

Principal Works

Browning as a Philosophical and Religions Teacher (Glasgow: Maclehose, 1891).
The Philosophy of Lotze (Glasgow: Maclehose, 1895).
Idealism as a Practical Creed (Glasgow: Maclehose, 1909).
The Working Faith of the Social Reformer (London: Macmillan, 1910).
The Principles of Citizenship (London: Macmillan, 1919).
A Faith That Enquires (London: Macmillan, 1922).

READING IV

IDEALISM AND EPISTEMOLOGY[1]

Jt can scarcely be maintained that the prevailing characteristic of recent English speculation is its 'Cheap and Easy Monism'. The 'Hegelians' and 'Neo-Hegelians' who are always referred to as deepest in this error (though they are not identified by their critics) are less in evidence than the Lotzians and Neo-Lotzians. And these latter are anything rather than Monists. Monism, if we may judge by them, is giving way to more or less thinly disguised Dualisms, or even Pluralisms; and philosophy is putting on motley. The tendency of 'the young bloods', if I may quote the phrase of a young philosopher, is critical rather than constructive. They evolve no systems. They suggest that system-making is not consistent with sobriety of thought, and they confine themselves to analysis, the exposition of difficulties and polemic. They will admit, I do not doubt, that 'the desire to comprehend the Universe as a revelation of a single principle is the genuine impulse of philosophy'. But, so far as I can see, they do not give way to any such impulse. The speculative duty of the day seems to them to be that of dividing Philosophy into special departments. Besides Psychology, which is manifestly a special science, there are other disciplines different from each other but falling within Philosophy. Before we can attempt to construct a Metaphysic there are 'manifestly preliminary' problems to be solved. We must *first* have Psychology to deal with the inside of

---

[1] 'Idealism and Epistemology' in *Mind* n.s. II (1893), in two parts.

the individual's consciousness; then Epistemology to deal with the relation of the inside and the outside; then Ontology to deal with the nature of what is both inside and outside; and, I presume, Logic to deal with the processes of that 'hypothetical' existence, 'thought in general'. There may, indeed, be some way of bringing these departments of philosophy together, either under one of their own number, or under some fifth. But, as yet, that way has not been revealed to us. For the time being it has seemed sufficient to the new school of critics to expose the difficulties and errors which have sprung from the confusion of the categories and problems of these different and distinct disciplines by the 'Hegelians' and 'Neo-Hegelians'.

Now this critical endeavour is capable of being very useful labour, although a mere *distinguo* [distinction] solves no problem. And the most faithful adherent of Idealism may well admit that no philosophic system stands in greater need of articulation. He would also fain believe that no system would gain so much by that process. A fresh application of its main principles to new data would not only enrich and substantiate but also modify them, and lead the way to a more complete and true view of the world. But criticism, if it is to claim the attention of philosophers, must itself be philosophical, that is, it must itself derive its impulse and guidance from some intelligible single principle. The difficulties urged against a philosophy should have some higher source than the commonplace empiricism of ordinary consciousness. The duty to criticise must be based on a right to criticize, and that right can only be derived from some consecutive and ultimately constructive theory of existence. I do not wish to imply that ordinary experience and the ruling convictions of unsophisticated mankind have no claim upon the philosopher's adherence; nor even to deny that philosophy may find its whole task in the systematic reconstruction of ordinary experience. But it is one thing to pay regard to the facts of such experience, and quite another thing to regard its own theories of these facts as the touchstone of philosophic truth. Philosophy is bracing itself to its most difficult and most productive task in attempting the former; it is denying its own right to exist in adopting the latter. Why should it toil if there lies ready to hand the cheapest and easiest of all methods, namely, that of simply accepting and re-wording the unconscious theories of traditional opinion?

Now, so long as the critics of Idealism produce no evidence that their criticism is itself construction disguised, they are liable to the charge of this lower appeal to 'common-sense'. Their recoil against Monism may seem to be a recoil against philosophical method; and, in the words of a recent writer, ' their sympathy with the German reaction' may appear merely to 'restore the rule of traditions which we are just beginning to lay aside'. No doubt they cut themselves free from such uncritical traditions by claiming to rest their polemic on the basis of the Idealism which they examine. They profess an Ontology that is all-comprehensive. They will even admit, at *times,* as Lotze does, that the Supreme Subject, which used to be called the Absolute, is 'the only reality'. But their Ontology is, so far, a name and nothing more; and their supreme 'Subject' is only an Honorary President who hypothetically acquiesces in the activities of his subordinate 'manifestations'. In virtue of that office the Subject holds things together somehow or other, and even unites thought and being. Professor Seth assures us that 'the chasm' (*i.e.,* between thought and reality) 'is not an absolute one, otherwise knowledge would be for ever impossible'. And, in my opinion, this is self-evident. But in the previous sentence he tells us that 'Ontologically, or as a matter of existence, they remain distinct — the one here and the other there — and nothing avails to bridge the chasm'. And these two consecutive sentences, if we are not to forget one in reading the other, leave the relation between knowledge and reality in a very obscure state. The relation exists, but it is not ontological. Knowledge, we are told, is entirely within the subjective consciousness, while reality is not within it; and yet the former is connected with the latter, though it is not connected really but ideally — or, shall we say, unreally? I think it fair to urge that the unity of knowledge and reality, which prevents 'the chasm which nothing can avail to bridge from being "absolute" ', needs further explanation. But no explanation is given. Attention is concentrated on the opposing terms. We are presented with a series of exclusive alternatives. Feeling is set over against knowledge, simple apprehension against reasoning, the 'given' against our thought, perception against conception, particulars against the universal, the subjective against the 'trans-subjective', the ego against its experience, consciousness against its phenomena. Idealism, which has sought to bring these differences together as manifestations of a single principle, is regarded as having merely obscured their distinctions. Its obedience to the 'genuine impulse' of philosophy seems to its critics to have issued only in a theory of the 'altogetherness of everything'. Now, I willingly admit that to obliterate differences is not to explain them. But to insist on differences to the exclusion of their unity is equally futile. And it is obvious that no criticism of idealism can be effective or just if it does not seize upon its 'single principle', its colligating hypothesis, and show either that that principle is altogether untrue, or that its application to particulars is inadequate. But the critics attempt neither of these tasks. The idealistic Ontology which they profess is quite otiose. They dwell on the various aspects of the opposition of knowledge and reality as if, after the manner of the sceptics, they would fain make it absolute. They save themselves from the sceptical position by occasional hints at a 'faith' which is to do service when reason fails, or at a feeling which is to give evidence of matters of which we cannot be conscious. And in all these respects they seem to me to occupy the attitude of ordinary consciousness, except that critically they are better equipped. In other words, they are more fully conscious of the different aspects of experience which philosophy has to reconcile, if it has any task or function at all, but they make no attempt to effect that reconciliation; they put forward the problem of philosophy in the place of its solution; they criticize Idealism from a dualistic point of view.

It is in this dualistic spirit that they explain Kant, under whose broad ægis [patronage] every writer on modern philosophy seeks refuge. For they certainly have gone 'back to Kant', and, I believe, much further, even to Dr Thomas Reid. They are proceeding to give us 'the authentic Kantian philosophy'; for who cannot find his own creed in Kant? And that 'authentic' or expurgated Kantian philosophy is, as they believe, a philosophy from which the 'many idealisms' could not have sprung except by the confusion of obviously different things, namely, knowledge and things known. Kant, it seems, held that knowledge was all inside, that all our perceptions are subjective phenomena and nothing more; and in this respect occupied 'practically the same ground as Berkeley'. He differed from Berkeley mainly in that he did more justice to the *a priori* elements in our purely subjective perceptions, and held consistently to things-in-themselves. This means, if I rightly understand, that Kant opposed ideas and things after the manner of Locke.

The hints given to us of the positive theory which lies behind this criticism of Idealism and this reconstruction of Kant point to the same dualism. That theory is to be a combination of Epistemological Realism with Ontological Idealism. It shall show (1) that knowledge is not the reality known; (2) that knowledge is nevertheless *of* reality; (3) that the universe is 'essentially related to intelligence' and not 'a brute fact existing outside the divine life and its intelligent ends'. I am not aware that any idealist would be prepared to dispute any one of these conclusions. No 'Hegelian', 'Neo-Hegelian', or 'Neo-Kantian' would hold that his ideas are the things which they represent. No one, except an absolute Sceptic, would deny that knowledge is '*of*' reality, though every philosopher would like to explain that '*of*'. And we are now, thanks mainly to Kant, all convinced that reality is 'essentially related to intelligence'; though some of us would like to understand that intelligence and that reality in such a way as to make their relation intelligible. If it is sufficient to occupy these positions one after the other, or combine them externally into an epistemologico-realistico-ontologico Idealism, then we may all assume, equally with our critics, that proud title.

But philosophy cannot be satisfied with 'the cheap and easy method' of solving difficulties by a *distinguo* [distinction]. It seeks a principle of unity *in* the differences; and that principle is scarcely brought to the surface by a theory which combines the dogmatism of·Reid with the ontology of Hegel; for this seems to be the plain English of Epistemologico-realistico-ontologico Idealism. Dualism, which is philosophic failure, is too thinly disguised by this mixture of such heterogeneous elements as the absolute philosophy and unsophisticated popular opinion. And those who advance it, if they are not, as Mr Bosanquet says, 'fatally deficient in philosophic thoroughness', will be obliged to abandon either the one or the other of these elements. Nor is it difficult to see which element they will have to abandon. They are really objecting to the theory of Hegel from the point of view of Reid. Their Hegelian or idealistic Ontology is, as yet, not operative. Their active convictions are that man's knowledge is not the objects which it represents and that Hegelians say that it is; that books on philosophy, even if that philosophy be absolute, are not

the Universe, and that Hegelians say that they are. The fundamental vice of the 'Hegelians' and 'Neo-Hegelians' is confusion.
They have confused many things. They have mistaken a theory of
knowledge for a theory of being, the facts of their own consciousness for the real things which they represent; they have identified
their own ego with a logical category, and themselves with God.
The claim of the critics to a hearing rests on their efforts to disentangle these confusions and set the elements apart. But before
attempting their tasks the critics may justly be required (1) to be
quite sure that Idealists have confused these elements; (2) to bear
in mind that the real task of philosophy begins only with the
attempt to bring these elements together again as manifestations
of a 'single principle'.

Now, I would be loath to assert that Idealists have at no time
given colour to the charge that they have confused the distinction
between knowledge and reality in one or other of its various
aspects. But I would maintain, at the same time, that the Idealists
have not identified their own ideas of things with the things
which the ideas mean, or regarded the books of Hegel as the Universe. And I shall try to prove that to insist as *against* Idealism that
knowledge is not that which is known springs from a fundamental misapprehension of the idealistic point of view.

I regard Idealism — to put the matter as plainly as I can — as a
theory which represents the Universe as a thinking activity, an
activity which reaches its highest form in this world in man. The
critics accuse Idealists of saying that the Universe consists of *ideas*
or thoughts, hanging together in a kind of system. Such a 'world
of ideas' they, quite naturally, find to be very unreal, lacking all
stability and substantiality — a mere cloudland. It is, they hold,
only a subjective world, inside the 'consciousness' of individuals;
and they would, therefore, attach it at both ends to realities — at
one end, to individual thinkers who produce thoughts, and, at the
other end, to 'trans-subjective' facts which the thoughts represent. They thus get three sciences, or three departments of philosophy, namely, Epistemology to deal with our thoughts 'of'
reality, Psychology to deal with the thinkers, and Ontology to
deal with the nature of things, including thinkers. In consistency
with this view they accuse Hegel and his followers of 'swamping
Epistemology in Metaphysics', as well as of the opposite error of
swamping Metaphysics in Logic. This means, I presume, that

Hegelians succeed in both making the world of realities swallow the world of ideas, and the world of ideas swallow the world of realities — like the conjurer's two snakes, each of which disappeared inside the other. Or, to speak without the violent metaphors of 'swamping' and 'swallowing', the opposition of thoughts and things has been obliterated by the Hegelians, old and new; and their critics are bent on holding the opposites apart, and on giving a theory of each of them and a theory of their relation. This, I believe, is the precise point on which most of the critics of Idealism base their attack; and on this rests their own constructive endeavour. In other words, they contend for the need and possibility of a science of the relation between ideas, 'the subjective states, which are plainly our data', and 'transsubjective realities', or the things meant by these ideas.

Now any theory of the relation of these opposed terms implies that both of them exist. The critics thus rest their case on the existence of a world of ideas (or of as many worlds of ideas as there are individual thinkers), and on its difference from and relation to a single world of real objects. The Epistemology which is to clear the way for Metaphysics is to give a systematic account of the relation of these inner and outer worlds; and the fundamental error of Hegelianism is that it has rushed straight on Metaphysics, without distinguishing the sphere of thoughts from the sphere of things, the categories of Epistemology from those of Metaphysics.

But 'Hegelians' are, in my opinion, exposed to a still more fundamental charge. They not only have no Epistemology, but they deny that such a science is possible. They do not recognize the existence of a sphere of ideas requiring to be related to a sphere of thoughts. And it is evident that before a science of the relation of two worlds, one subjective and the other objective, can be justly demanded *from* them, they must be convinced that both of these worlds exist. Idealism, as I should like to call the theory of Hegel and his followers, leaves room for Psychology, as it does for Botany or Physics or any other special science that deals, under its own appropriate hypothesis, with definite facts or special elements of the real world of objects. But its own proper task is throughout metaphysical; it is to investigate the nature of a single real principle and to trace its activity both in outer facts and in thinking individuals. Of a 'world of ideas' — whether in individual thinkers, or hanging in mid-air, so to speak, between individual thinkers and the things they think about — it is obstinately ignorant. And, consequently, they do not oppose the world of ideas 'with its imperturbable repose and clearness', as Lotze says, to the world of things with its innumerable activities. The opposition is to them meaningless. They cannot confuse therefore its terms, nor feel the need of an Epistemology to expound their relation.

The first task of the critics of Idealism is, therefore, to prove that a 'world of ideas' exists, either in thinkers or between them and the world they know. But of this I have seen no proof; and I think that no proof is possible. So far as my experience goes — and these critics of Idealism lay great store on the experience of any individual — ideas form no world, but each of them exists as long as it is being produced, and no longer. They are evanescent products of an intelligent activity which vanish when the process that brings them forth stops. It is not Idealism but Associationism that regards ideas as capable of hanging on to one another like a swarm of bees, or of arranging themselves in a system 'imperturbable in its repose'. And it is not Idealism but Associationism that can demand and seek to establish a science to relate these subjective systems of ideas to the outer world. One might expect that Mr Bradley's criticism of this view had given it its final quietus, but a little experience of philosophers should cure the youthful error of being sanguine. May I repeat, then, that ideas seem to me to occur in sequence; that they follow one another, so far as they are distinct presentations, in a serial order; that not one of them persists in existence; that having once perished it is never revived; and that, for each and all of these reasons, a world of ideas 'imperturbable in its repose' is impossible?

This is a very simple matter, it seems to me, but the consequences of ignoring it are so numerous and important that I am tempted to dwell a little upon it. These consequences may be more fully realized if we consider a possible and even probable objection to our view. We speak of an inheritance of knowledge capable of being hoarded by one generation and handed down to its successors. And surely, it may be urged, there are systems of knowledge, symbolized in books and otherwise, which have a universal meaning and a permanent value for mankind. Such bodies of knowledge are to be confounded neither with the fleeting psychical presentations in the minds of their authors, nor with the realities which they represent. The ideas of Plato and Newton, in the sense of their psychological presentations, perished as they arose, one after the other. They were never in the minds of their authors, all at once. They are now all perished with their authors. Nevertheless, it seems little less than wilful perversity to deny that these men left behind them in their works systems of knowledge — what are not inappropriately called 'worlds of ideas' as an inheritance for all thinkers. Is it not undeniable that of certain parts of the earth we obtain information only from books of Geography; that there are ideas in those books for all who can understand them; and that these ideas are neither the psychological presentations in the minds of the writers of those books nor the actual parts of the earth? Ideas, then, it may be urged, perish as psychical events, but as having meaning they are capable of being permanent and of forming systems.

This distinction is also applicable to the ideas of an individual. We speak of the growth of a man's knowledge, a growth which implies both the accumulation and systematization of his ideas. And, apparently, we can be as sure that this growth takes place as we can of any other fact of experience. Such knowledge cannot be identified with the evanescent psychical events in his consciousness; for these latter are serial and fleeting, and can, therefore, be neither accumulated nor systematized. To confuse this distinction is to confuse an idea as a psychological datum, which is as subjective, incommunicable and transient as the pain of toothache is, with an idea as having objective, and therefore universal and permanent meaning.

Now, it may be urged, while it is evident that Epistemology as a science of subjective phenomena is impossible, Epistemology as a science which explains the objective reference or universal meaning of these ideas may be both possible and necessary. But it is in the latter sense *only* that the critics of Idealism regard Epistemology. Ideas as subjective phenomena are, in their view, to be dealt with by Psychology. They belong exclusively to the private history of the individual. But ideas as having objective reference, a meaning for all minds capable of apprehending them, form the subject-matter of Epistemology. The spheres of these sciences are quite distinct from each other and from that of Ontology. The scientific law, *e.g.,* that the attraction of bodies for one another varies inversely with the square of their distances, is as distinct from the psychological occurrence in the consciousness of its dead discoverer as it is from the actual attraction itself. And, in so far as this law is part of a connected whole of meaning which we call the Copernican System of Astronomy, the term 'world of knowledge' sufficiently describes an actual fact. In that case Epistemology has a distinct field of inquiry, and the 'Hegelians' and 'Neo-Hegelians' cannot, without detriment to clear thinking, 'swamp it' in Metaphysics.

Our Epistemological critics would, no doubt, put their objection more forcibly. I have done what I could, and I now proceed to examine it.

The distinction between ideas as mere occurrences in consciousness and ideas as having objective reference seems to me quite valid. Mr Bradley has succeeded in putting this matter beyond reasonable dispute. The question that remains is, does this distinction justify the view that there exists, besides subjects and objects, a world of knowledge awaiting explanation at the hands of a science which is neither Psychology nor Metaphysics, but is, apparently, subsequent to the former, and certainly preliminary to the latter? Does there exist such a third sphere, or does it not rather consist of hypostasized abstractions? There are evidently thinkers and objects thought about; are there 'other' 'existential realities' — to use a phrase of our critics?

I do not think that there are. Ideas are not 'existential realities' in any sense, whether as psychological phenomena or as having objective reference. They are not divisible into two parts, one of which perishes, while the other has permanent existence. The objective reference is an essential characteristic of *every* idea as a phenomenon of consciousness and inseparable from it. The fact that we can and should distinguish these two *aspects* of ideas does not justify us in separating them, in making one fleeting and subjective and the other permanent and objective. Nor can we make ideas the subject of different sciences, except by a process of abstraction that becomes vicious if taken as ultimate. Prof. Seth tells us that 'the psychologist deals with psychical events merely as such'. 'It is only for the psychologist that mental states are interesting on their own account, as subjective realities or facts. To every one else they are interesting only for what they *mean,* for the knowledge they give us of a world beyond themselves' . . . 'We treat them consistently as significant, as ideas of something, as representative or symbolic of a world of facts. Now it is from this latter point of view that epistemology considers ideas'(*The Philosophical Review*, vol. i. pp. 131, 132). But it seems to me that psychology cannot deal with ideas 'merely as psychical events'. Apart from their objective reference, which Prof. Seth hands over to Epistemology, the psychologist could not recognize them as ideas. If he could, every idea would be the same as every other; perceptions, imaginations, memories, concepts, reasonings, as mere psychical events would be indistinguishable. In omitting the objective reference the psychologist would be endeavouring to deal with form without content, and the whole task of his science would be to mark the time of psychical occurrences, none of them having any character. His Epistemology would 'swamp' his Psychology. But, again, such an Epistemologist as Prof. Seth describes would be equally helpless. For it is evident that he could find no ideas having objective reference except those which are also phenomena of the individual consciousness. Or does Prof. Seth know of a world of thoughts without a thinker? If not, then his Epistemologist must take account of the fact that the ideas whose reference he would expound are psychical phenomena and nothing more; though, if they are ideas, they are psychical phenomena which have and must have objective meaning. In this respect Psychology would justly 'swamp' his Epistemology.

What, then, is to be said of such systems of thought as the ideal theory of Plato, or the astronomical theory of Copernicus or Newton? Simply, I would answer, that as *knowledge* or *ideas* they are psychical experiences of individuals, fleeting and subjective; and as having permanent meaning for mankind they are not ideas nor knowledge, but objective facts consisting of symbols, and capable of being interpreted into knowledge, or ideas, by the activity of individual minds. In this last respect they fall entirely into the world of external objects, and they are permanent objects of knowledge for exactly the same reasons as works of art, or plants and planets, are permanent objects of knowledge. They are related to intelligence and await its interpretation in precisely the same way. They are natural objects in the outer world, presented to intelligence in the same way as all other objects which have meaning. They occupy no sphere by themselves. They do not constitute a 'world of ideas' from which we must in some inexplicable way escape in order to find realities corresponding to them. They do not, therefore, await interpretation at the hands of a special discipline called Epistemology, but are objective facts whose ultimate nature is to be explained by Ontology. In themselves they are not knowledge. When intelligence interprets them, not before and not after, they may in a sense be called systems of ideas. But so may plants and stars.

Of course these systems of knowledge as outwardly symbolized, which is the *only* way in which they can be regarded as 'existential realities', form a special class of outer objects. In their case some form of matter — whether it be ink and paper as in books, or stones as in sculpture or architecture, or sounds and movements as in human speech — becomes informed with meaning which is foreign and accidental to it. The objective fact in these cases is a sign or symbol, that is, something whose essence is its meaning and whose *special* material form is more or less extraneous and contingent. But I do not think that this distinction is relevant here. Language, 'whether written or spoken, is not an outward fact of the same kind as the natural events whose meaning it is used to convey. Still it *is* an outward fact, and it is ultimately to be explained in the same way as other outward facts. And it is only as outward objects, capable of being interpreted, that systems of knowledge have any permanence and can be inherited from one generation by another. By the help of language, a system of objective signs, we inherit them from our predecessors just as we inherit their works of art, public buildings, canals and coal mines. What is handed down from age to age and accumulated is not knowledge but the *means* of knowledge; not ideas but objects which have meaning. That meaning must be elicited anew by every generation for itself. It is only when so elicited that there is knowledge, as we have consciousness of beauty when we appreciate a work of art, or a scientific law when we understand a physical fact or event.

It is equally manifest that there is no accumulation of knowledge in the individual. There are no ideas except those which occur serially. Each of these ideas is a transient psychical phenomenon which has more or less significance, according as it is a more or less complex unity of multiple elements. Being transient, ideas cannot be accumulated. All the objections urged by Mr Bradley against the Associationists are valid against all ideas alike, whether particular (were their particular ideas) or universal.

They perish with the process of knowing, and they can never be called into existence again. Of course that process may be repeated. The individual may go through similar intellectual activities over and over again with like results; but neither the activities nor their results are identically the same. They have no permanence. The permanent identity is on the one side the thinking subject, and on the other the objects thought of. The subject grows, but not his knowledge as such. Every intellectual act modifies *him*. Every process is organized into him in the form of developed faculty. But the thoughts themselves pass away, as other good or bad actions do. They are accumulated only in the same sense as a learner of the piano accumulates technical skill. Each thought vanishes like each movement of the fingers on the keys; but no thought vanishes before the result of the activity from which it sprung has been organized into the agent by the development of his powers. In a word, there exists no world of ideas any more than there exists a world of actions.

All this seems to me so plain and elementary that I press it at such length with some sense of shame. But, on the other hand, the metaphorical use of such phrases as 'world of knowledge' exercises such a tyrannical power in philosophy that very important results would follow the clear consciousness that they are metaphors — that the 'world of ideas', whether regarded as in 'imperturbable repose' with Lotze, or as 'wandering adjectives' with Mr Bradley, is a more or less solidly hypostasized abstraction, and nothing more. If this phantom world were swept off the boards altogether we should no longer need Epistemology in the sense of a theory of the nature and validity of the objective reference of ideas. It would then be clearly seen that what remains to be explained is the activity of knowing, the intellectual processes performed by individuals in virtue of an ontological relation between them and objects in the outer world. The task of philosophy would be to investigate the nature of this ontological relation, or of the 'single principle' which makes possible the intelligent processes in individuals. Logic would no longer seem to be an analysis of the relations of ideas to one another, but an exposition of intellectual processes. It would not be a theory of abstract conceptions, but an ontological inquiry, just as the physical sciences are. And if it should turn out in the last resource that every process is best explicable as a process of thinking, then Logic would itself be Ontology, or Metaphysics, as Hegel conceived it.

For this is what Hegel meant. To him the Universe was not a system of thoughts, but a thinking reality manifesting itself most fully in man. He has been regarded as setting in motion an 'unearthly ballet of bloodless categories', and then to have confounded these categories, these thought-determinations, these abstract ideas, with realities. He is accused of inventing a logical chain of mere thoughts, analogous to 'Plato's system of general notions or ideas', and then to have endowed these thoughts with a dynamic power. He is thus guilty as Plato was of a 'crude mythology', of substantiating mere ghosts, of taking a *mauvais pas* [false step] from the world of mere thoughts to a world of real things. 'The distinctive feature of the Platonic theory of Ideas', we are told by Professor Seth, reading Plato backwards, 'in which it is a type of a whole family of systems, Hegel's among the rest, I take to be its endeavour to construct existence or life out of pure form or abstract thought. Plato's whole account of sensible things is to name the general idea of which they are particular examples; Hegel's whole account of Nature is that it is a reflexion or realization of the abstract categories of Logic'. As against this view Professor Seth insists that knowledge is not reality, that the notion of Being is not existence, that the form or self-consciousness is neither man nor God, but an abstract thought. 'Hegel', he says, 'has taken the notion or conception of self-consciousness, and he conceives the whole process of existence as the evolution and ultimately the full realization of this notion. But it is evident', he adds, 'that if we start thus with an abstract conception our results will remain abstract throughout'. *Most* evident, I quite agree. To evolve things out of ideas is a manifestly hopeless endeavour. Out of thoughts can come nothing but thoughts. This matter is so evident as not to need discussion, or proof, or iteration. If Hegel and his followers, old and new, have attempted this task they are convicted, in my opinion, of manifest absurdity. *Ex nihilo nihil fit* [from nothing, nothing comes]. From a world of ideas which has no existence, which is a mere manifestation of a subjective process of intelligence, nothing can be deduced. Abstractions cannot yield even abstractions.

The truth of the matter is, however, that the critics of Idealism have been reading into that system their own views. They believe in this world of ideas; they desire a science of it; they wish to relate it to a world of realities. For them the categories are general ideas connecting other ideas, universal thoughts like beams supporting an edifice of thoughts. For Hegelians and Neo-Hegelians there are no general ideas which do not perish in the making. There are no categories in this sense, no thoughts which bind other thoughts to one another. There is no world of knowledge in the heavens above, or on the earth beneath, or in the water under the earth. Their universe is mind, not thoughts. Their categories are laws of the operations of intelligence, not connecting ideas. Their problem is to understand reality, to discover the nature of the fundamental principle of which all existences are revelations, not to constitute a theory of a world of abstract notions. That fundamental reality they pronounce to be the universal intelligence, whose operation they would fain detect in all things. They are as frank in their ontological intentions, as little troubled with Epistemology and the sphere of ideas, as if they were Materialists. The laws of thought are not for them the laws of *thoughts,* but the law of things. They do not wish to know the nature of knowledge, except in the sense of the process of knowing. Their attitude towards thought is that of science towards natural processes. Their explanation of thinking is as ontological as the physicist's explanation of gravitation. If their explanation is more full and true it is to that degree more intimately related to reality. If, as they hold, all reality is ultimately explicable as Spirit, or Intelligence, their Ontology *must* be a Logic, and the laws of things *must* be laws of thinking. And this is just what Hegel tried to prove in his Logic, in which he advances from being to thought. I am not concerned at present in defending this interpretation of the universe as a thinking activity. It may be quite as absurd to regard physical energy as intelligent action, as it is to regard the intelligent activity of man as the operation of mere physical force. To say, for instance, that gravitation is implicit, or obscure thinking, may be to speak nonsense, as it probably is for the Materialist to say that conscious action is nothing but the intricate movement of physical particles. It may be impossible either to level up or to level down, to regard Matter as Spirit or Spirit as Matter. In any case there is no doubt, in my opinion, that Idealism is committed to the view of the world as Spiritual, and that the interpretation of God, man and the world as *thoughts* is as foreign to it as their interpretation into rings of smoke.

If this is so then the arguments advanced by these epistemological critics against Idealism are simply beside the mark. If they are valid at all, which is very doubtful, they are valid against some fundamentally different system of philosophy. Indeed, the service of these critics to students of Hegel, in particular, is confined pretty much to the fact that they have unconsciously drawn attention to the point in which his theory differs essentially from previous systems. For I should say that the most significant advance made by Hegel consists, not so much in his reconciliation of knowledge and reality, as in his refusal to start — as previous philosophers did, and most of his critics still do — from their opposition. If we except Spinoza we may say that modern philosophy up to and including Kant has endeavoured to pass from the subject to the object, from thought to reality, or from reality to knowledge, from the object to the subject. Kant did more than anyone else to show that the object implied the subject, and he pointed out also, though less clearly, that the subject implied the object. But subject and object, thought and reality, were never completely reconciled by him. The things-in-themselves became more and more shadowy in his hands, but they never disappeared; in other words, the fact that reality and thought are *essentially* related became ever more clear to him as he wrote, but this relation was not at any time so essential to him as to be *constitutive* of both the related terms. He always took his start from their opposition. He discovered again and again that each term had meaning *only* in relation to its opposite. Sense was helpless without thought, thought without sense; conception without perception, perception without conception; the 'given' or the manifold, without reason and its categories; man and the world without God. But the great step which was implied in all this, but only *implied,* it was reserved for Hegel to take: the step, namely, of making the *opposition* of the terms subordinate and secondary to their unity, and of regarding them as elements of unity. Kant's task to the end was that of reconciling differences, that of Hegel was to differentiate a unity. Kant sought to bring thought and reality together, Hegel starts from the conception of a reality which is all-inclusive, manifesting itself both in the knowing subject and in the known object. Kant had demonstrated to him by his failure that to take either of the alternatives as a starting-point was to make the other inaccessible. Thought in Kant never quite got over to things, and things never revealed their inmost nature in thought, and, in consequence, an element of scepticism, euphemistically and sophistically called 'faith', was the last outcome. Hegel, therefore, thought to take his stand *behind* these alternatives, on the reality, the All, which manifests itself in both of them. And his relation to this reality is as frank as that of the Materialist, who also has the significant philosophical merit of at once taking his stand on the unity of things. His task was to discover what conception of this single principle, or fundamental unity, which alone *is*, is adequate to the differences that it carries within it. '*Being*', he found, leaves no room for differences; it is overpowered by them. Quantity, Quality, Measure — all forms of Essence; Substance, Cause, a cause which is also effect — all forms of external relation; even consciousness was inadequate. He found that the reality can exist only as Absolute Self-Consciousness, as a Spirit who is universal and who knows himself in all things. In all this he is dealing with Reality.

Starting with a conception of the Real, the All, which might satisfy a materialist, he moves on, ever dealing with that Reality, to the conclusion that it must be conceived as Spirit. To regard Hegel as dealing with thought-determinations, as generating abstract conceptions out of one another, as needing in the end to leap out of the sphere of mere thoughts into a sphere of reality, is to attribute to him that dualism by repudiating which *alone* he was able to gain his starting-point. Go where Hegel will, he cannot escape from the Reality. He finds it active in all thinking, in all being. No *idea* of the reality interposes between him and it. In his ideas he detects the working of that reality. Apart from it he cannot even think falsely. His incomplete conceptions are as truly *its* manifestations, the results of *its* activity in him, as the growth of the grass, or the evolution of worlds, are its manifestations. He finds the Absolute, God, in the development of the thought of mankind, in the rise and fall of nations, in the establishment and overthrow of social institutions in the movements of history, just as truly as did the Hebrew prophets, or Carlyle. His task is to find God everywhere, to justify 'the faith' — if I may use this word of what was to him a rational necessity, and not a conviction unjustified by reason — that the Absolute Spirit lives and moves in all things.

This conception, no doubt, brings with it sufficient difficulties. It involves the Absolute in the fate of the finite, and raises in a new form fundamental questions that lie at the root of human life. It may be so conceived as to confuse the human and the divine, to blunt the edge of the opposition between right and wrong, and to make sin and goodness meaningless by undermining the freedom on which their possibility rests. But it is questionable whether any theory confronts these difficulties so fairly, or throws more light upon them. And in any case it is certain that to urge against Hegel or his followers that they are occupied in evolving abstract ideas from each other, that they have shut themselves up in a cloud-land of mere conceptions, and have committed the preposterous mistake of taking knowledge of reality for reality itself, their own passing ideas for things, and their systems and books for the Universe, is an accusation that comes home to roost. It is the critics of Idealism who find ideas interpose between them and reality, and who cannot escape from this shadow of themselves. They, and not the Hegelians or the Neo-Hegelians, find themselves shut up in a world of their own thoughts and are occupied in the hopeless puzzle of getting out of it. They want a theory of thoughts, of their validity and value, as if by thinking they could prove their validity; or as if the *theory* of thoughts were any nearer reality than the thoughts themselves. It is to me the supreme merit of Hegel that he has indicated a way of deliverance from this endless and hopeless puzzle of getting out of thoughts by means of thoughts. And he has done so by planting *himself* to begin with in the system of the real. Instead of regarding reality as circling round *his* ideas, as his critics do, he has brought about the Copernican change. His ideas are the working of reality in him; apart from that reality he is helpless, in so far as he is its instrument, 'all things are his'. Consequently he has repudiated altogether 'the sphere of thoughts without a thinker', swept away the world of ideas that divides the thinking intelligence from its objects, left man and the world, thinkers and 'things thought about' fairly confronting one another without any unsubstantial medium to separate them, and done his part to rid modern philosophy of the sickly element of subjectivity. He has, therefore, no Epistemology, and he needs none. His theory is a theory of the real, as Metaphysics was in the hands of Aristotle. In establishing that theory he deprived both thinkers and things of the false independence attributed to them by Individualism, but he did not reduce them into phantoms called thought-determinations, or abstract ideas, or logical categories, nor cut them loose from existence. They remain 'existential realities' for him, for they belong to the system of reality. And the system to which they belong, the Real which manifests *itself* in them is to him, as it was to Aristotle, Spiritual, an intelligence which knows itself in all things. To him there is no activity which, ultimately, is not the activity of Spirit. And, in consequence, the laws of its operations are laws of thinking — not the laws of thoughts. On this account his Metaphysic is also a Logic, a science, not of the connexions of ideas, but of the *operation of mind.* In a word, Hegel speaks of thinking, his critics speak of thoughts, converting his process of Reality into abstract and unreal general notions and his Ontology into an Epistemology.

How such a perversion of his meaning and of the meaning of his idealistic followers has come about, I shall try to show in another article.

II

I have tried to show that the critics of Hegel and his followers have taken his theory of thinking to be a theory of thoughts, and converted his process of reality into an unsubstantial system of abstract ideas. I have also tried to show that the systems of ideas whose nature, validity and relation to reality the Epistemologists investigate do not really exist. What exists is a series of mental operations, activities of reality, as manifested in the subject who thinks and in the conditions, within him and without, which make his thinking possible. There are thinkers and things thought about; but there are no third entities. The mental processes performed by individuals do not leave behind them any products which can be regarded as having the apparent independence and real existence of things. The *only* result of mental activities is the modification of the mental faculty. Thinking develops the thinking powers, but it does not aggregate, either within the thinker or elsewhere, a heap, or mass, or series of ideas. Hence the phrases 'world of ideas', 'circle of ideas', 'system of knowledge', indicate no actual fact. They are substantiated abstractions, as unreal as a world or circle or system of deeds severed from their agents. Ideas pass away never to be recalled, just as truly as actions or sensations pass away. They are serial phenomena, which can neither be associated nor dissociated, for they have no permanence and no universality. None of them serve to connect others, and they form no system, and consequently no theory of them is possible. We may have a science of the process of thinking; but a science of the products of thought, a theory of knowledge and of the nature and validity of ideas, is possible only at the expense of substantiating what is fleeting, and of treating abstractions as if they were realities.

Now, there is a sense in which every science (and even Metaphysics) deals with the fleeting as if it were permanent, and with abstractions as if they were real. We *must* tear up the unity of the real and deal with aspects only, for the simple reason that we cannot think all things at once. It may, therefore, seem that the charge made against Epistemology may be directed in like manner against all human knowledge, which certainly never reflects the whole of being but is always incomplete. If 'ideas' severed from the subject who thinks them and from the objects which they mean are unreal, so also, it may be said, are the 'quantity' of the mathematician, the 'laws' and 'causes' of physics, and even the 'things' of common-sense. All these in their last resort are abstractions and myths. We may in fact say at once that all human thought is untrue and all its objects are unreal, for the former is incomplete and the latter are abstractions. But this is only a half-truth. If all knowledge is false in so far as it is only a partial revelation of reality, all knowledge is true in so far as it is *nothing but* a partial revelation of reality. If every fact and event is in its isolation only an appearance, every appearance in its place within the system of reality is itself real. The condemnation of the incomplete and partial as false and unreal itself depends on the presence of the complete and real. Hence no science is altogether false and no abstraction is altogether nothing. In other words, while every science is untrue in so far as it is inadequate to the reality which it investigates, it still does investigate reality. But the unique characteristic of Epistemology is that it postpones the investigation of reality to another matter; it must pronounce upon the nature and validity of knowledge before it can be sure that we are not foreclosed into a thorough-going scepticism. It must investigate ideas in order to show first of all whether or not their whole meaning is not false, and their objective reference a mere illusion. So that the ideas with which it deals, while not altogether unreal, are set up over against reality. In so far as they have meaning, or are more than psychical events, they cannot be even appearances, for they can find no place in a system of reality whose very existence is a matter of doubt. Epistemology, in a word, differs from every other form of knowledge in that it cuts itself entirely free of reality to begin with. It must not assume the reality of the objects to which the ideas refer, for this is the very problem it has to investigate. It has nothing to do with the reality of the ideas as psychical occurrences, for that is the business of Psychology. It thus abstracts from reality on both sides, and by dealing with the mere meaning of ideas seeks a place between Psychology and Metaphysics.

But this process of double abstraction from reality, this withdrawal into the world of mere meaning, destroys the very possibility of Epistemology. I shall try to show that it finds its problem by only *seeming* to retire from reality, and that in so far as it actually does retire from it, it can find neither its problem nor its solution. In other words, I shall try to show that the whole edifice of Epistemology rests on a contradiction, on an attempt, that is, to treat its first starting-point and basis as both real and unreal. I do not deny the possibility of a theory of knowledge in every sense. I deny this theory of knowledge, because of the abstraction which is vital to it and at the same time fatal to it. In order that we may have a true theory of knowledge we must undo the abstraction on which Epistemology rests. We must restore the relation of ideas to reality on both sides. We must regard ideas in connexion both with their psychical occurrence and with the actuality of their objects. We must take ideas, not as independent entities or mere meanings, but as manifestations of the activity of reality. We must, in a word, base our theory of knowledge on a theory of reality, and either regard it as a particular science dependent on Metaphysics, as a part of Psychology, or else, by pressing its hypotheses and categories home, identify it with Metaphysics.

The importance assumed by Epistemology in modern times demands that an attempt to cut its very root should be justified in detail. Epistemologists insist, not only against Idealism, but also against every other philosophy which professes to deal directly with reality, that before we can legitimately say one word as to its nature, or take one step towards constructing a Metaphysic, we must solve certain preliminary problems as to the nature and validity of knowledge. Prof. Seth puts the matter in this way: 'Is there any reality beyond the conscious states themselves and their connexions? If there is, in what sense can we be said to know it? Is knowledge, inference, or belief the most appropriate word to use in the circumstances?' (*Phil. Rev.*, i. p. 136). 'How, or in what sense, does the individual transcend his own individual existence and become aware of other men and things? It is this relatively simple and manifestly preliminary question that Epistemology has to take up. Subjective states are plainly our data; it is there we have our foot-hold, our *pied à terre*; but unless we can step beyond them, Metaphysics in any constructive sense can hardly make a beginning. Epistemology, if its results are negative, necessarily leads to a thorough-going scepticism; but if its results are positive, it only clears the way for metaphysical construction or hypothesis' (*Phil. Rev.*, i. p. 138).

Two doctrines are set forth with admirable clearness in these words, namely — first, that the problem of Epistemology is to explain the transition we make, or seem to make, in knowledge, from 'conscious states' to a reality beyond; second, that this problem of the nature of the transition must be solved before we can attempt to determine whether there is reality and what is its nature. In order to solve its problem, Epistemology is furnished with 'plain data'. These are 'subjective states', 'in which it has its foot-hold, its *pied à terre*'. But in this last statement I find a most serious difficulty. What meaning is attached to these 'subjective states', on which as the one fragment of solid ground the epistemologist plants his foot? Following the lead of Prof. Seth and other epistemologists, I accept the distinction on which they insist as against Idealists, the distinction, that is, between a fact or event, and the knowledge or the idea of the fact. We are particularly warned by these writers not to confuse reality in any form with our thoughts concerning it. Lotze is most emphatic in his view that feelings can never be the ideas of them. And this applies in a similar way to all the phenomena of consciousness. The distinction between a psychical occurrence and the consciousness of that occurrence is as broad as the distinction between any other event or fact and the *idea* of the event or fact. The *idea* of the toothache, or of love or hatred, or of the perception of an object, or of a volition, is no more the actual toothache, or love, or hatred, or perception, or volition, than the idea of Arthur's Seat is the actual Arthur's

Seat. It does not matter whether the fact be subjective or objective, it is never the idea of itself.

Of course this difference rests on the presumption made by Epistemologists that *ideas* of facts, psychical or otherwise, have sufficient substantiality to be opposed to the facts. Apart from this most questionable assumption no one can deny the distinction. I would myself insist upon it as a universal and necessary truth. To assert that a thought is the thing thought of, or that one psychical activity is another psychical activity, is tantamount to dissolving the continuity of being, and contradicts the first condition of thinking. Nothing can be anything but itself. The fact is the fact, the event the event, the thought the thought; and there is an end of the matter. No metaphysical theory can affect this fundamental truth. Even if it be true, as Idealists are supposed to say, that reality is thought, or thoughts; nevertheless, the thoughts *of* reality are not the thoughts which constitute reality; they are at the best *other* thoughts, and are either unreal or additions to the first reality. A complete idea of the Universe would not be the Universe; the idea would be the idea, and the Universe the Universe. And the latter would have to be enlarged so as to take the former into it, or the former would have to be shown to be an unreal abstraction.

In the meantime, I accept, then, in the fullest way the distinction between thought and reality on which our critics insist. Let us now see its bearing on their doctrine. If the actual fact or event is never the knowledge of it, then our 'subjective states' are not our knowledge of them. Both are facts, of course, and both are psychical facts; but they are different psychical facts; the one is the object known, the other is the knowledge of the object, both falling within Consciousness. Now, the question arises, which of these is the datum of the Epistemologist? In which does he find his 'foot-hold, his *pied à terre*'? Is it in the reality, or is it in the knowledge of it? Is it the subjective state as a psychical occurrence, or is it the reflective knowledge of that psychical state?

Let me put the difficulty in another way. The Epistemologist has a 'chasm to bridge over', and that chasm separates the sphere of knowledge from the sphere of reality. 'The chasm is not absolute', we are told, 'else knowledge would be for ever impossible'. Nevertheless 'he' (the knowing individual) 'does not pass over into the things, nor do the things pass over into him. At no point can the real world, as it were, force an entrance into the closed sphere of the ideal; nor does that sphere open at any point to receive into itself the smallest atom of the real world, *qua* real, though it has room within itself *ideally* for the whole Universe of God' (*Phil. Rev.*, i. pp. 515, 516). Granting, for the sake of argument, that both of these closed spheres exist, the question arises: Into which of these exclusive spheres do the 'subjective states' fall? In which of them does the Epistemologist find his 'foot-hold, his *pied à terre*'? Is it in the ideal sphere, or in the real sphere, or in both? There is, of course, a sense in which the 'subjective state' is both real and ideal. I mean that an idea is ideal as having meaning, and real as being a psychical event. This truth has by no means escaped Prof. Seth. 'Of course', he says, 'if we take reality in the widest sense, our cognitive states are also part of reality. The wildest fancy that flits through the mind exists in its own way, fills out its own moment of time, and takes its individual place in the fact-continuum which constitutes the universe'. But, as he tells us elsewhere, this existential side of the idea is of no interest to Epistemology. 'It is only for the psychologist, however, that mental states are interesting on their own account, as subjective realities or facts' (*Phil. Rev.*, i. p. 132). Epistemology deals only with their meanings, and 'conveniently neglects' their other side. As psychical events filling out their own moments of time they are 'parts of reality', examples of what is called above 'smallest atoms of the real world'. But being real 'they cannot force an entrance into the ideal sphere', and 'the ideal sphere cannot open at any point to receive them into itself'. They thus fall into two fragments, one of which is seized by Psychology and the other by Epistemology. Epistemology, being a system of ideas, cannot adopt them *qua* real. (Psychology in some mysterious way can, although it, too, is a system of ideas.) As fact, or as real events, they are shut out of the ideal sphere. Seeing that, *qua* real, they escape the clutch of Epistemology, Epistemology does in strictness not deal with *them* at all, but with ideas of them. But as the ideal is never real, as their spheres are entirely exclusive, how is Epistemology possible? If it starts from the subjective state as real, then the real and ideal are not separate. The Epistemologist actually knows *this* real thing. He has *this* reality in his hand immediately and directly; and the question which he asks, whether he can or cannot know reality at all, is absurd. He assumes as his starting-point that he does know it, and the only reasonable question he can ask is, whether, knowing one reality, he can or can not know some other reality. If, on the other hand, the Epistemologist cannot know facts but only ideas, if he starts not from the subjective state, or from the self, but from his idea of that state or self, then it may be asked, what kind of foot-hold or firm ground does he find in it? What special virtue lies in the idea of a subjective state more than in the idea of a stone, a stick, or griffin, that he should 'find in it his *pied à terre*'? The idea of the self is no more the self than the idea of the world is the world. Hence, if we refuse to play fast and loose with the reality of the subjective state, if we adopt and hold fast to the two exclusive spheres of the ideal and real, Epistemology seems to me to be in an inextricable dilemma. It cannot deal with the subjective state as real, for, *ex hypothesi* [as the case supposes], it has first to pronounce on the possibility of knowing any reality, on the validity of the objective reference of any idea. And, on the other hand, it cannot deal with the subjective state as a mere idea; because if it begins with an idea it must end with ideas. There would be no outlet from the sphere of ideas, for surely it is preposterous to seek such an outlet by having more ideas. It has no foot-hold, its very dream of reality would vanish, and with it its own problem.

But, it may be urged, there is a third possibility. These subjective states may have the unique characteristic of being both real and ideal; or mind may have the power of knowing in this instance the actual reality itself; or, in this instance, at this point, the ideal and the real spheres interpenetrate. And this is what Prof. Seth means when he insists that the chasm between the ideal and the real, which 'nothing can bridge over', is 'not absolute'. This is also implied in the use of the word 'datum'. 'Subjective states', it is said, 'are plainly our data'; and a datum manifestly means a reality that is also known, at least to some extent. A datum that is not real, and a datum that is not known, are obviously meaningless phrases.

Now I have no objection to the statement that 'subjective states are plainly our data'. I would add, however, that they are data only as psychical events 'filling their own moment of time, and taking their individual place in the fact-continuum which constitutes the universe'. They are data as 'parts of reality'. And I would add further that mountains and rivers, other men and other things, are data in precisely the same sense. If the real state of the subject and the idea of it, if the actual self and the knowledge of it, come together in the one case they come together in the other. Or, on the other hand, if the idea intervenes between us and mountains and rivers, the idea intervenes between us and the psychical states. If the actual Arthur's Seat eludes our grasp, so does the actual self. Idea and existence, thought and thing, are similarly related in all cases. If Reality sunders into two aspects, if it has both an ideal and existential side in one case, it has the same in all other cases. Reality, whatever it is, is consistent with itself; and if it has as its fundamental characteristic the function of appearing as idea in the case of subjective states, it has that characteristic always. If not, how would even the empty conception of any reality other than psychical states ever occur to us?

I do not expect, however, that Prof. Seth will admit this. Its admission is not consistent with his fixing on subjective states as in some special way giving us our foot-hold. So that the question at issue turns out to be this: Whether or not we know anything actual *besides* subjective states; or, in other words, whether Sensationalism be not, after all, the true philosophy. But I do not expect that Prof. Seth will admit this either; for it is inconsistent with his view that, besides an Epistemology which concerns itself primarily with subjective states, we may have a Metaphysical doctrine of reality in general which may be either Idealistic or Materialistic. Moreover, he knows the history of Philosophy too well to be ignorant of the fact that Sensationalism leads to 'thorough-going scepticism'. There is some confusion here which we must try to disentangle.

We have set aside two alternatives for Epistemology — the alternatives, namely, of starting with a mere idea, or with a mere fact; we have, in other words, thrown overboard the absolute exclusiveness of the real and ideal spheres, and accepted 'the subjective state' as in both spheres at once, that is, as a 'datum', or reality known. Now the problem arises, how can Epistemology, starting as it does with reality in one particular form, ask its primary question? Epistemology is defined by Prof. Seth as 'an investigation of knowledge as knowledge, or, in other words, of the relation of knowledge to reality, of the validity of knowledge. This, at least, is the fundamental question to which other Epistemological discussions are subsidiary' (*Phil. Rev.*, i. p. 130). 'Our cognitive states appear to refer themselves to a reality which we know by their means. Epistemology does not, like psychology, rest in the appearance. It seeks to determine whether the appearance is true, and, if true, in what sense precisely it is to be understood' (*Phil. Rev.*, i. p. 136). Will the reader compare this statement of the problem of Epistemology with the one quoted above? 'Is there any reality beyond the conscious states themselves? How, or in what sense, does the individual knower transcend his own individual existence and become aware of other men and things? &c.'. If he does compare these statements of the problem of Epistemology, I think it will become evident that Prof. Seth confuses two distinct questions, and that his Epistemology rests on that confusion. The first of these questions is, Can we pass from knowledge to reality? Or can we know *any* reality? The second of these questions is, Can we pass from subjective states as known realities to other realities, persons, or things? Can we know any reality *besides* subjective states? The first problem is concerned with the possibility of the transition from knowledge, *excluding all reality*, to reality; the second with the possibility of the transition from the knowledge which *includes* one species of actual facts to a knowledge of other facts. We may put the distinction less accurately but none the less fairly by saying that the transition in the one case is from ideas to reality, in the other case from reality to reality.

I think it is not necessary for me to insist that there is a fundamental difference between these problems, and that it should be made clear which of them is the real problem of Epistemology. Does Epistemology start within the ideal sphere and then try to get out of it to reality? Or does it start with a fact and, like every other science, investigate the relation of its assumed fact to other facts? If it does the first, then I need not repeat what I have already urged, that it can never reach reality, nor even ask whether there is reality or not. It is shut up in the ideal sphere. If it does the second, then it does not 'inquire into the nature of knowledge as knowledge, of the relation of knowledge to reality', but into the nature of reality, and of the relation of reality to reality.

The first question is unanswerable. We cannot get out of the circle of mere ideas, because we are never in it; and we cannot get into the sphere of reality, because we are never out of it. And the assumption of a 'datum', which is manifestly indispensable, shows that Epistemology itself proceeds from a reality and not from a mere idea. The second question is answerable; but it is not the question of Epistemology. It is the question of the relation of a part of reality to reality in general, a question which is asked by every science, and which definitely assumes that reality is knowable, and, so far, actually known.

But Prof. Seth cannot afford to distinguish these questions, nor can Epistemology. It *must assume* reality in some form in order to have a foot-hold. This is done in the second question, where the actuality of the subjective state is taken for granted. On the other hand, if Epistemology is to make a preliminary inquiry into the validity of the objective reference of knowledge it *must not assume* reality; and hence the first question is asked. Epistemology thus rests on a self-contradictory basis: it both must and must not assume reality. And we find in this very necessity an explanation of the extraordinary statements made by Prof. Seth, and quoted in my last article, that 'the chasm between knowledge and reality is not absolute', and yet 'that nothing can serve to bridge it over'. The radical unreasonableness of the science is concealed by these ambiguous ways of stating its problem.

That it is based on a contradiction which is hidden beneath a confusion may be shown in another way. This confusion lies in the phrase 'subjective states'. States may be 'subjective' in two senses. First, a state may be subjective in the sense of being a portion of the experience of an individual subject. Feelings and volitions as well as cognitive activities are subjective in this sense. Mine are mine, and yours are yours. Secondly, a state may be 'subjective' in a sense which is applicable to ideas only, and not to feelings or volitions. Subjective ideas are those whose objective reference is not valid. In a word, they are untrue ideas, or illusions. We may, and continually do, inquire into the validity of a subjective state in this second sense; that is, we investigate the truth of a part of our knowledge by reference to our view of reality as a whole; we test a part of our experience 'by reference to the conditions of the possibility of any experience, or, in other words, by reference to its fundamental principles. But subjective states in the first sense are neither true nor untrue; for they are *ex hypothesi* parts of the life of the individual; they are assumed to be facts.

Now Prof. Seth uses either of these senses at his convenience, and he saves his Epistemology only by doing so. At one moment, 'the subjective state' is a real experience, a part of the world of reality in which he finds his foot-hold. At the next moment 'the subjective state' is an idea whose objective reference may, or may not, be valid. It is a part of the ideal world. And it is only this ambiguity which gives 'the subjective state' its value for Epistemological theory. It makes it possible to start from reality while seeming to leave the question of the possibility of knowing reality untouched; for the subjective state is either ideal or real as we please. In fact, the unconscious movement of the Epistemologist may be justly described as follows. He first starts from the subjective state or idea, as a fact of experience; 'then he slips the existential side of the idea up his sleeve and treats it *merely* as having meaning; then he looks up and asks, where can we find the reality which corresponds to this meaning? It seems to me that we can justly demand greater explicitness on this fundamental matter of the problem which Epistemology seeks to solve. Which is its problem? Is it whether we can know any reality whatsoever, and, if so, how? Or is it 'whether we can know any reality besides subjective states, and, if so, how? Epistemology starts from the subjective state as real, or it does not. If it does not, then it starts *ex vacuo* [out of a vacuum], and although it is not dumb, it has nothing to say. It is shut up absolutely and irretrievably in a circle of ideas and has at no point any foot-hold or contact with reality. On the other hand, if it *does* start from a real fact as known, then it has assumed not only the possibility but the actuality of a positive relation between the real and the ideal. It is confessedly unable to get behind reality in order to set forth on its specific inquiry, and has assumed a datum. Its problem is, therefore, no longer that of the validity of knowledge, but that of the relation of one fact to another, and in this respect it is just like other special sciences. It sinks in fact into a part of Psychology, and, as such, it is dependent upon, instead of preliminary to, Ontology. Like Idealism, which it criticizes, it bases the cognitive relation of thinker and things upon their Ontological relation, instead of *vice versa*. It seeks to understand, and not to make, a connexion between the real and the ideal. It denies the chasm between the ideal and the real by treating the subjective state as both; and thus, instead of having two spheres mutually exclusive, it goes far towards showing that reality has two sides, the existential and the ideal, or, in other words, that the real reveals itself as ideal.

I conclude, then, that Epistemology, as an inquiry into the validity of knowledge in general, is an impossible science, and that it has seemed possible only because, under the guise of this inquiry, it really deals with quite another problem, namely, whether it is possible to know anything *besides* subjective states. This is not an Epistemological inquiry, but a Psychological one aspiring to be Metaphysical. Before examining this second inquiry, and in parting with Epistemology as the science of the validity of knowledge in general, I should like to say that there is an objection frequently urged against such a science which seems to be plain and unanswerable. It is that it is impossible by knowing to pronounce upon the validity of knowledge as a whole. We may test a part by reference to the whole or the principle of the whole, but we manifestly cannot test the whole by means of a part. I have not used this argument; Epistemologists have been appealed to so often from this side that I must conclude that they are deaf on it. The same argument might have been put in another way, namely, by simply asserting the incontrovertible fact that Reality is all-inclusive, and, as such, takes in even false ideas. But this also is admitted and ignored by Epistemologists. They manifestly carry reality with them as a criterion whereby to distinguish truth and error, and they use it in every judgment that they make. But this does not deter them in the least from asking where is reality, or whether it is or is not. These broad objections having failed, I had recourse to the more tedious process of analysing the claims of this pseudo-science, for which I offer this apology to the intelligent reader.

It remains now to examine the second problem, which pretends to be Epistemological, but which I have asserted to be a Psychological one aspiring to be Metaphysical — the problem, namely, whether we can know anything *besides* our own subjective states. This inquiry starts from reality as directly, if not as frankly, as Idealism itself; hence the choice offered us is not between an Epistemology and a Metaphysic, but between one Metaphysic and another. And I think, as already hinted, that the Metaphysic to which it leads is simply Sensationalism. This Sensationalism differs from that of Hume or Mill, only in that it has been sophisticated to the highest degree by its intercourse with Germany, and by its attempt, at least in Prof. Seth's hands, to attach itself both to German Idealism and to Scotch Realism of the rough and ready type of Reid. To prove this, I acknowledge, is a task I am loath to undertake. I am not sure whether it would be a service to philosophy to separate the elements of a theory which represents itself as a combination of Epistemological Realism with Ontological Idealism; which, in other words, as an Epistemology asserts that it deals with mere ideas, as a Realism asseverates that these ideas are true, as an Ontology proclaims that it deals with reality, and as an Idealism pronounces this reality to be either thought, or thoughts.

I shall content myself with examining its fundamental assumption — That we do know subjective states as *real facts,* that at first at least we know nothing else, and that what we require to discover is whether, and, if so, how we can know anything besides subjective states. The first characteristic of this theory I should like to point out is that it starts from a *particular* datum, regarded as indubitable — 'Subjective states are plainly our data'. In this respect it reminds us of Cartesianism, which also sought for something fixed and sure, however small, as a basis on which to erect its structure. It differs from it in putting a 'subjective state' in the place of the *'cogito ergo sum'* [I think, therefore, I am], and in regarding its subjective state as real as well as ideal.

Now the idea of basing a metaphysical theory on an indubitable datum is radically false, and involves a mechanical method of procedure and a mechanical view of both thought and reality. In other words, the assumption of such a datum implies that thought links its objects externally one to another, because in existence they are isolated and particular. And just because particulars alone exist and the connexions between them are thought-woven 'spider-webs', cognition never can correspond to its object. It thus, as the history of Associationism has proved, leads directly through the discrepancy of knowledge and reality to thorough-going scepticism. But modern logicians contend with considerable unanimity, and, it seems to me, with convincing cogency, that thought does not move from a fixed datum by external aggregation, but by differentiation from within and reintegration. It must of course have a datum; but its datum, so far from being fixed, only gradually reveals what it is in the progressive evolution of knowledge, and so far from being particular it is implicitly all-inclusive. Modern Metaphysics, in accordance with this logical theory, starts from a view of reality as a whole, and not from a fragment; and its task is to expound the inner articulation, the internal harmony of this whole, and not by any means, or in any way, to proceed from the knowledge of one thing to the knowledge of other things. So far as I can see, we are practically forced to choose between these two methods. Lotze and his followers, I need hardly say, mingle these methods as they mingle metaphysical doctrines. But if we recognize the opposition between them, it becomes obvious that we must either adopt Associationism with its external and contingent linking of fact to fact [beginning with a sure one, hopping on to others and assuring them through it, finding its universal both indispensable and untrue, obliged to have 'webs' and obliged to make them spider-films] — or if not we must regard the whole as given at first, and watch its process of inward development. And this second method, if it is consistently carried out, must refuse to characterize its datum except in terms of the revelation it makes of itself during the evolving process. Thus each of its successive characterizations is known to be only proximate, a mere starting-point for a better, it will find certainty, or rather will seek it, in the end and not in the beginning. It possesses no certain fact to begin with; but, on the contrary, it finds its particular fact guaranteed as fact only by reference to the whole system of reality within which the particular fact obtains a place, and in relation to which alone it is real.

The conception that 'certainty' is to be found only in a complete system, in a consistent view of the world as an organic whole, and not in erecting an edifice of knowledge on a fragmentary fixed datum by mechanical means, is due to Kant; and in it lies the living force which brought about the momentous revolution in modern philosophy. His attempt to discover the conditions of experience, the fundamental question of the Critique of Pure reason, as indicated or expressed in 'How synthetic *a priori* judgments are possible', signifies that he had, once for all, turned his back on the old method of philosophy which started from psychical phenomena, from ideas or impressions, and then sought realities corresponding to them; and that, beginning with the conception of knowledge as a whole, or, in other words, of knowledge wherever it can be found, he sought to lay bare its constitutive principle. It is quite true that in his hands the problem assumed what may be called an Epistemological rather than an Ontological form, and that in giving us his theory of knowledge he refused to pronounce upon the nature of reality, or things-in-themselves. But it is also true, in his hands, that the things-in-themselves were gradually deprived of all their significance, that the reality which he considered to be opposed to knowledge became a *caput mortuum* [dead thing], of no possible interest to anyone. He left nothing to distinguish his theory of knowledge from a theory of reality except the thin disguise of the word 'phenomenon'. Thus, whether we accept the higher or the lower interpretation of Kant, it remains true that the revolution in philosophy which he brought about consisted in a fundamental change of method; it consisted in setting forth from experience as a whole (or as such) to investigate its internal conditions, instead of first dogmatically asserting the existence of a fragmentary reality, then linking the rest of reality to it by means of the external categories of mechanism.

Now the attempt which Prof. Seth makes to start from 'subjective states as plain data' is simply a reversion to the old associative method employed by Hume and his school; and it argues that whatever else has been learnt from Kant, the supreme lesson he taught has not been taken to heart. Is it not plain, even yet, that if we begin with 'subjective states' we must either expand these subjective states so as to make them all-inclusive, or else leap from them into something absolutely different? Is it not indisputable that we must conclude either that there is *nothing but* subjective states, or, if there is, that it is absolutely unknowable, and not only unknowable but unbelievable, because inconceivable? We cannot proceed from the part to the whole except by discovering the principle of the whole in the part; we cannot proceed from subjective states to 'other persons and things' except by finding in our subjective states the principle of 'the other persons and things'. In the mid-stream of Metaphysics we cannot swap horses. Knowledge cannot 'leap', nor faith either, if it is 'according to knowledge'. On the other hand, if we do find the principle of the whole in our subjective states, then in dealing with them we are not dealing with 'plain data', but with the whole of reality implicit in these data which has to be made plain by further knowledge. We are establishing an Ontology and not an Epistemology. The datum has ceased to be a particular one. If it really were particular we could proceed from it to nothing else. We could not even know it, for thought is surely relative. I do not mean to deny that we know 'subjective states', or that they are data; but we know them and they are data for further knowledge, because in knowing them we know all reality — in part. Every datum, owing to the organic nature of reality, has in it the principle of the whole and exists only as its manifestation. In this respect a 'subjective state' is as good as any other datum; but it is no better. And the use of the term 'subjective' for a datum of knowledge is worse than useless, for it brings with it misleading associations. That which is a datum, I insist once more, cannot *ex vi termini* [from the end of life] be subjective in the sense employed by these writers. The subjective which is a datum for further knowledge is also objective; as a datum it contains in it the principle of the whole. We cannot, except by a process of abstraction and for such merely practical purposes as those of the special sciences, ignore its relation to the whole, tear it from its context, treat it as an isolated part. If we do so tear it, it will lose all its meaning; it will be nothing real, it will not have even the virtue of an interjection. Philosophy exists in order to correct the abstractions of ordinary thought and science. It is false to its peculiar mission if it neglects the reference in every datum to the whole of reality. For it matters not whether we start from the isolated subject or the isolated object; in isolating our datum we have mutilated and paralysed it. We cannot do without a datum, as our critics themselves urge; but every datum we can possibly assume is in its last resort a universal, and the distinction of subjective and objective, like every other, falls within it.

Idealism, in the Berkeleian sense, as a theory of the subjective in pursuit of the objective, is as false as Materialism which starts from a mere object and looks for a subject. And Epistemology, which is engaged with knowledge as distinguished from reality, and which, while pronouncing upon the nature of the former, postpones all questions as to the nature of the latter, is subjective Idealism in disguise. So far from being preliminary to Metaphysics, it is itself a Metaphysical theory and a false one. The 'subjective states' which it assumes are 'plain data', and, being data, afford a 'foot-hold' from which without break or leap we can proceed to further knowledge. Either Epistemology begins with these data as isolated particulars, and therefore *ends* with them; or else it begins with them as manifestations of a reality which, with all its apparent and even real differences, is fundamentally one and the same in them and in all other facts. In the latter case it is Metaphysics. It can *appear* to be something else, to be a science preliminary to Metaphysics, only because these subjective states which furnish the theory with its data are at once taken to be real and unreal. It seems to me plain that inasmuch as Reality (or, if the word is preferred, the Absolute) appears in every datum which we can assume, and inasmuch as we must assume a datum, seeing that thought cannot spin *in vacuo* [in a vacuum] on its own pivot, the search for a form of knowledge preliminary to Metaphysics is futile. No science can be preliminary to Metaphysics. In a strict sense there is no science of the form of knowledge besides Metaphysics; no theory of the not-real or the not-as-yet-real can be invented except by the suicide of reason, and even that would not invent it. All the special sciences are doing the work of Metaphysics, and doing it in an admirable way, even though, or even because, they attempt to justify neither their categories nor their hypotheses. They are in no sense its rivals; nor are they preliminary to it, except in the sense that partial knowledge is preliminary to completer knowledge. If Epistemology in its attempt to avoid being a Metaphysical theory likes to rank with them, and to deal with its data of 'subjective states' in their spirit, relating fact to fact in a consciously abstract way without aspiring to give a final account even of knowledge, I would have no objection to it. I would prefer to call it the Psychology of Cognition, and would be glad to know it more thoroughly, partly because in knowing it better I would *ipso facto* [by the same fact] know more of reality as a whole. But a science which postpones *all* reality and proceeds without any datum except bare ideas, which is the first form of Epistemology we have examined, or a science which proceeds with a datum regarded as real and yet as excluding the principle of the whole, which is the second form of it we have examined, seems to me to be radically impossible. We live and move because the whole universe helps us to do so. We know *any* reality because, so far as we do know it, we know all reality. Neither in thought nor in action can we find a 'foot-hold', a *pied à terre*, except in that which is related to the whole, because it is itself the manifestation of the whole. No preliminary science is either possible or necessary. Epistemologists, instead of standing shivering on the bank asking the futile question whether we can know or not, had better make the plunge. There is no way of learning to swim without going into the water. If they want really to think they must become Metaphysicians.

Five

William Mitchell

William Mitchell was born at the croft of Derrylane, Inveravon, in Banffshire on 22 March 1861, and not on 27th as his obituaries claim. He died in Adelaide, Australia, at the age of 101 on 24 June 1962, leaving a son, Sir Mark Mitchell, and a daughter, Mrs J.R. Thomson. Mitchell's father was a hill farmer who died when his son was only five years old. His mother Margaret Ledingham took the family to Elgin for the better educational opportunities. Mitchell attended the West End School at Drainie, and was selected with the future Prime Minister Ramsey Mac-Donald by the dominie to be a pupil teacher, in return for personal tuition in prerequisite subjects for university entrance. Mitchell entered Edinburgh University in 1880 and graduated with an MA first class honours in Philosophy (1886). He was taught philosophy by Campbell Fraser. Mitchell gained a DSc by thesis (1891) in the Department of Mental Science.

While an undergraduate he reluctantly had an article published in *Mind*. He was immediately appointed assistant to Henry Calderwood, professor of Moral Philosophy at Edinburgh, who had submitted Mitchell's undergraduate paper to *Mind*. At Edinburgh Mitchell was a lecturer in moral philosophy (1887–90), and an examiner in philosophy and English (1891–4). He lectured on Ethics and education at the University College of London (1891–4), and on the theory of Education at Cambridge University (1894). In 1892 he declined the opportunity of a chair at New Brunswick, Canada. He became dedicated to day training colleges and to raising the standards of primary school teachers in English Schools. He was later to become immensely influential in educational policy in South Australia.

In 1894 Mitchell was appointed to the Hughes chair of English Language and Literature and Mental and Moral Philosophy in the

University of Adelaide, South Australia. As if this was not enough, economics was added to his brief, which he taught until 1917. In addition, he taught education until 1909. He joked that he did not have a chair, but instead a sofa. He became Vice-Chancellor in March 1916 and resigned his chair in 1922. He remained vice chancellor until 1942 when he succeeded Sir George Murray as Chancellor. He retired in 1948 at the age of eighty-seven. He once remarked to J. J. C. Smart that his duties as VC took him ten minutes a day. He was the driving force behind developing the university from a single building, now named the Mitchell Building in his honour, to a large complex of buildings including the Barr-Smith Library. He endowed the University with its Chair in Biochemistry.

In 1924 and 1926 he gave two sets of ten lectures as the Gifford Lecturer in Aberdeen University He was knighted in 1927 for his services to the Commonwealth of Australia, and in 1934 he gave the philosophical address at the British Academy on 'The Quality of Life'. Among his honorary degrees are DSc in Philosophy, University of Edinburgh, and Doctor of Letters of the University of Western Australia. In 1898 Mitchell married Marjory Erlistoun, daughter of the Adelaide businessman and philanthropist R. Barr-Smith. She died in 1913.

William Mitchell was the only professor of philosophy among his contemporaries in Australia to be internationally renowned. He attracted the attention of such distinguished British Idealists as Norman Kemp-Smith, Sir Henry Jones, Bernard Bosanquet and the American Brand Blanshard. The book for which Mitchell gained his international reputation, *Growth and Structure of the Mind,* was published in 1907 by Macmillan. The reader's report (Macmillan Archives, British Library) by Henry Jones said that: 'It is not often that I have had the pleasure of approving a book so heartily. It is extraordinarily strong, and manifests throughout the most thorough philosophical grasp'. What distinguished Mitchell from fellow Idealist philosophers was that, like W. Dilthey, he placed psychology, rather than religion, literature or poetry, at the foundation of philosophy. He recognized long before Blanshard that one of the major defects of the Idealism of such thinkers as Bosanquet was the relative neglect of psychology, which they generally thought irrelevant to the theory of thinking. Psychology in his view was the proper introduction for philosophy, and while the two should not be confounded, they could not be clearly demarcated.

Biographical

Obituary, *The Times*, 26 June 1962.

Obituary, *The Adelaide Advertiser*, and *Adelaide Register*, 25 June 1962.

J.J.C. Smart, 'Sir William Mitchell, K.C. M.G. (1861–1962)', *The Australian Journal of Philosophy*, 40 (1962), pp. 261–3.

S.A. Grave, *A History of Philosophy in Australia* (Queensland: University of Queensland Press, 1978).

David Boucher, 'Practical Hegelianism: Henry Jones's Lecture Tour of Australia', *Journal of the History of Ideas* (1990), pp. 423–2.

Martin Davies, 'Sir William Mitchell and the "New Mysterianism"', *Australasian Journal of Philosophy*, 77 (1999), pp. 253–7.

David Boucher and Andrew Vincent, *British Idealism and Political Theory* (Edinburgh: Edinburgh University Press, 2000).

Martin Davies, *The Philosophy of Sir William Mitchell (1861–1962) A Mind's Own Place* (Lampeter: Edward Mellen, 2003).

Principal Works

William Mitchell, *Structure and Growth of the Mind* (London: Macmillan, 1907).

Nature and Feeling, The Macrossan Lectures, University of Queensland (Queensland: University of Queensland Press, 1929).

The Place of Minds in the World, 1924 Gifford Lectures (London: Macmillan, 1933).

'The Quality of Life' Henriette Hertz Lecture, British Academy, 1934.

William Mitchell Papers, University of Adelaide, Australia.

READING V

MORAL OBLIGATION[1]

he reason why, while Science makes a straight course, Philosophy makes a zigzag and doubling advance is that the one is aware from the first of the precise facts with which it has to deal, while the other labours under the disadvantage of having itself to determine what they are. Philosophy must somehow state its own problem, and it cannot do this without somehow first answering it. Could philosophy state with sufficient definiteness what it has to explain, its problem would be, if not

---

[1]   'Moral Obligation', *Mind*, vol. 11, issue 41 (Jan. 1886), pp. 35-48.

solved, at least on the certain road to solution. It has to give the *rationale* of experience. But then, what is experience? It certainly includes much illusion, and neither thought nor experience is at once adequate to expel it. Not our thought, which of itself is a criterion not of truth but of consistency. Not experience, for it embraces the illusions. If you merely pick and choose facts that will harmonize, you may give a certain *rationale* of these; but it is neither the philosophy of experience, nor, if derogatory to other facts, is it more a philosophy at all than an arbitrary generalization. That is why philosophy is so difficult to make and so easy to criticize. Theories are made which explain certain facts and the rest are fairly or foully thrust in along with them, while those that are too obstinate are treated as sour grapes and handed over to credulity. This is especially the case in respect of Ethics, the science of the practice of man as man, and still more in the case of Moral Obligation by which as man he isolates himself from the other animals and would unite himself with God.

Even for the purpose of mere criticism we must be sure that the facts we flourish are genuine realities and not illusions. But since we cannot adopt all the facts of experience, seeing many are illusory, we are in this dilemma. On the one hand we cannot pick and choose among the facts without adopting a theory to guide us; and on the other hand, we cannot find a theory except we begin from the facts. It is evident that no one part of our fact-experience can be condemned on the mere strength of another part. We can eliminate the contradictions of our thought by reference to the pure facts of experience. But how eliminate the contradictions among these facts themselves? We have to purify experience, yet experience is the only instrument; for it is the universal postulate from which alone reason can begin and to which alone it can return.

The consciousness of this circular progress of philosophical knowledge was especially evident to Hume, Kant and Fichte. Philosophy, they saw, must end where it began — illuminating, purifying, unifying, but never destroying or creating. And so, when none of the three could exhibit a rationally complete representation of the philosophical circle, they did not blind themselves to the deficiency. They did not strive to make experience correspond to their theories. Experience as such was their assumption, and their failure to complete the rational cycle in it was not obscured by charging experience with delusion in respect of that part of it which resisted them. So that philosophy was no *petitio principii* [case of begging the question] to them. They all consciously failed to find a metaphysic of knowledge, that is, of experience in general, which was also a metaphysic of ethics — of experience in practice. What they did was not to attenuate the latter but to leave thought and practice in isolation, each with an explanation of its own.

Now it is just in this respect that their successors have committed their most Vital error. The result of it is seen in the existence of so many self-existent systems, each gaining adherents among the unattached but seldom or never proselytizing at the expense of one another. We are accustomed to overlook the seriousness only from the commonness of the error. All plead the actual illusoriness and contradiction in experience. Are we, then, in the dilemma of either taking experience as we find it and maintaining our various beliefs however recalcitrant to theory, or of proceeding throughout on the logical fallacy of questioning and purifying our postulate — the standard of our truth? If these are the only alternatives, it is evident that Ethics must proceed in an eternal see-saw of equally possible contradictions. In a case where one refuses to question the validity of the feelings of Freedom, Obligation, Responsibility, while another explains them away, how can either be justified or condemned?

It would be a very easy matter to show that the philosophical interpretation of duty is not the interpretation of duty as I or all feel it, that the benevolence of altruistic Utilitarianism is to me no benevolence, and so on. Even supposing me to be right in such contentions, I am not justified in thus defending the testimony of my feelings to objective truth except from something in them which inevitably distinguishes them from feelings that are illusory. I may maintain with Reid and Hamilton that they cannot with logical consistency be rejected if anything else is accepted — that I am perfectly 'parsimonious' in accepting them; but if I do no more I have only chosen the other horn of the dilemma and cannot defend myself from the suspicion of delusion. Whether to criticize an ethical doctrine or to make one, it is equally necessary to discover what precisely is the postulate from which to begin. If no inviolable postulate can be found, our morality can only be a more or less systematized theory of practice as in Hume; or if it pro-

fesses to be anything else, it will fall into the logical chaos which
he was able to avoid.

It has already been said that no one fact of experience as such,
can have any claim of itself to superiority in comparison with any
other fact. The difference between contingent and necessary truth
is a difference not of the validity of fact as fact, but of the function
which we find facts displaying. The bare feeling of any characteristic of a particular fact is undoubtedly the key to its importance in
the unreflecting consciousness. But in philosophy no such subjective criterion can be applied without dogmatism. It is not subjective but objective certainty that we require, and the problem of
philosophy is just this: to convert our subjective certainty — our
faith in the uniformity of nature, in freedom, in subjection to
moral law — into objective certainty. How can I who feel bound to
obey a moral law say that every one is bound to obey it? I may analyse my state of consciousness to the utmost, but I can get nothing
beyond it in my analytical judgment. Whatever feelings of necessity, universality, immediacy I find it containing, I can only say
they are so for me. To say that I recognize the law itself as that
which contains necessity is still to say that *I* recognize only. So
long, indeed, as I merely adopt the subjective position of common
self-consciousness, so long is it possible for another to say that I
may be deluded. I, as an individual, cannot from a mere individual's standpoint — from the purest fact of my consciousness —
prove that I am capable (as I *am* capable) of legislating for the
world. As little, on the same conditions, can the world legislate for
me. What it legislates for me is no moral obligation but force,
unless it corresponds with what I legislate for myself. On the contrary, when I claim to legislate for society or society claims to legislate for me, both presuppose a system of law which is peculiar
neither to society as such — as a majority say — nor to me as an
individual.

In one sense then we can derive neither objective from subjective obligation nor subjective from objective. Yet in another sense
we do and must do both. The reason why criteria *of* actual truth
have so often failed is that they have seldom had a true objective
application given to them. This was the case with the Cartesian
criteria which aimed at obviating contradiction, but they never
could get beyond a subjective application. For the removal of
objective contradiction some transcendent principle had to be

assumed — either generally, as with Descartes, the perfection of God, or particularly, as with Spinoza, the agreement of the idea and its *ideatum* [the thing it stands for], and with Leibniz, a pre-established harmony.

Equally valueless for objective certainty are the criteria of necessity, universality and immediacy or 'apriority' as mere characteristics of a cognition. If, in the first place, one says that he *must* believe so and so because of his own nature or because of the self-evident nature of the cognition, he satisfies himself, but is quite unable to satisfy another till he show that this necessary perception of a cognition or perception of a necessary cognition is independent of him as a particular individual. He must, in short, somehow universalize either himself or the cognition. But, in the second place, that cannot be done by pointing to the *universality* of the conception; for the physical evolutionist will inquire as to its origin and then point to the uniformity of the circumstances of human life as its cause, whether it be true or delusive. And, in the third place, the *immediacy* or 'apriority' of a cognition equally fails to assure of objective validity. For, on the one hand, men differ in regard to the beliefs of which, nevertheless, each maintains that he has an intuitive or necessary knowledge; and, on the other hand, one can never know whether or not he is using absolutely a *priori* knowledge. As a matter of fact, most of our perfectly intuitive knowledge was demonstrative at one time of our life; and, as a matter of strong supposition if not of scientific demonstration, all our intuitive knowledge has had a similar history in the history of the race. Finally, all three criteria fail to give the transference from idea to fact, from conviction to truth, from subjectivity to objectivity. I may talk of a moral law which I for my part never excogitated or developed in me more than I do the light of the sun — a law which I find in everyone and which comes to me with a vividness and self-evidence that I cannot resist. But this alone will not prevent Hegel or Darwin from telling me that my inquiry should begin where I leave off. I cannot pass from conviction to truth by using the criteria of the former. The real criteria of both may be the same, but that is just what I have to prove, and I cannot prove it from an individualistic standpoint.

It is evident that we can assign reality or truth to the facts of which necessity, universality and immediacy assure us, only after we apply the question of evolution to them. Whence are they?

What is that subjective necessity which is objective and transforms convictions into realities? It is not the necessity of conception to any one, but its necessity for existence or experience; not
the fact that it is believed by all men, but that all experience
requires it; not its underivedness in any one's mind, not its priority in time, but that it is the logical *prius* [priority] of the particulars
from which it is thought to be derived. Our purpose is not to make
a transcendental justification of the ethical conceptions. What we
do is to assume this rather and to state its counterpart. That is to
say, we assume the existence of an ethical sphere of action and
develop the consequences of that assumption. If such a sphere of
action is denied, if, in other words, Sceptical or Egoistic Hedonism is maintained, there is nothing further to be said. For it is
quite possible to deny the validity of the whole scope of Morality.
One has only to brand the whole thing as delusion to be secure
against every demonstration, seeing that every proof must begin
with part of what is denied. I might exhibit the chaos into which
the world would fall were morality expelled and did only personal gratification remain, but no one could demonstrate that
such chaos was not the natural state and that order was not a
fraudulent imposition of schemers for their own behoof.

Proceeding then to constitute Ethics as concerned with a distinct round of experience, we apply our objective criterion and
ask — What is the principle which determines the science of Ethics as such? The sphere of morality is notoriously the home of subjective conviction. What, then, is it that justifies or purifies these
convictions to the individual in regard to their claim to actuality?
Whatever it is, it is inviolable *for Ethics.* That is the cardinal point
of this paper. We must find it in order to avoid the suspicion of
delusion and subjective dogmatism in our assertions of freedom
and in cases of conscience, as well as to justify our feelings of
remorse and devotion. When we have found it we cannot tamper
with it without begging the question, for it must be the universal
postulate in ethical determinations.

As we have already hinted, it is Moral Obligation. There are
many other elements without which morality would be impossible, but as these apply to other spheres of knowledge besides Ethics they are not the determiners of the ethical sphere as such.
Every science has both a general and a particular determination.
Thus the physical sciences are generally determined under logical

laws with reference to their generic element, while they are also particularly distinguished from one another. So in Ethics, though freedom is an indispensable characteristic, and even though it might be said that we should not have become aware of freedom but for morality, it is not freedom which constitutes Ethics as a separate branch of philosophy, seeing that we are as free in other spheres of experience to which morality as such does not extend. Nor is it the possession of self-evident practical laws or of an ideal; for we possess such in the sphere of prudence which is out of, or at least wider than, the sphere of Ethics. Finally, merit or demerit being the concomitant of freedom is likewise too wide, and responsibility is consequent upon obligation.

If, then, there is a distinct sphere in the round of human action — call it Ethics, as in this paper, or a branch of Ethics, it is no matter — it is determined from the rest of human action by moral obligation, which on that account becomes also the first determiner of its contents. When we say that Ethics exists for the enlightenment of our moral obligation, we do not mean that a doctrine of duty must always be the main feature of every system. We should rather expect it to be the least prominent part. But it should always be remembered that what affords the guiding line of the whole process, what enables us to get beyond our own subject to legislate in morals, and what makes society a legislator for us, is this obligation. However slightly therefore anyone treats of Duty, and this is naturally most apparent in Aristotle the founder of Ethics as a distinctive science, it is this conception which determines every other ethical idea. Our question, then, is — What theories of End, Freedom, Merit and Responsibility are consistent with the postulate which enables them to be ethical theories at all, and for the sake of whose ultimate enlightenment they ought to exist?

The character of any ethical system is known by the end, ideal or standard of action which it professes. Our question is — What must be the characteristics of the end by reason of its determination through obligation? It is just the converse of this question that is usually put. But every attempt to derive oughtness from rightness must, as we have shown, either end in an illogical system or destroy the possibility of a separate science of Ethics at all. The history of Ethics in England furnishes an apt illustration in the three stages represented, say, by Bentham, Bain and Spencer. Each begins by determining the right or end and subordinates to this what should have been the postulate. The result, of course, is that morality coalesces with prudence. The three stages are marked by the aspect which obligation comes to assume. Bentham expels it, Bain admits it in an external way by handing it over to the police, and Spencer absorbs it by identifying it with existence. No other conclusion than this was possible: what ought to be, is, and that not more as a philosophical reality than in even the most contingent action. If there is a science of ethical practice at all, obligation cannot be subordinated to the end but the end must be subordinated to obligation. And so we repeat our question — What are the necessary characteristics of the ethical end in view of the postulate of morality as such?

They are, that it be at once subjective and objective and equally valid and harmonious in both respects. It must be subjective, that is, it must present some interest to my desire before I could recognize it as a law to *me*. It must be objective, that is, it must present some interest external to my individual desires as such before I can recognize it as a *law* at all. An obligation is just the principle which expresses the equal validity of the same law as subjective and objective. The end must be subjective but not individualistic, and objective but not external.

With this criterion of ends determined by the necessary postulate of Ethics, let us inquire how far it is satisfied by the ordinary ideals of moral systems. It is apparent how the history of Hedonism has throughout its progressive career endeavoured to realize it. Beginning from the Sophistical position of unlimited subjectivity, which is to Ethics what Pyrrhonism is to Metaphysics, *i.e.,* what neither can answer in any other way than by neglect, Hedonism has sought to find some end which should be at once of equal subjective and objective validity. But, though it has passed from a formula of pure egoism to a formula of pure altruism, it has failed to find an end which shall preserve equally the rights of the subject and the rights of the object: and this, just because it has always been forced by its presupposition to occupy only one of the two standpoints, and has consequently been unable to do justice to the other, since of themselves they manifest no inherent connexion with each other. Not that this dilemma has not been seen. Every system of Utilitarianism has been an attempt to overcome it and nothing else. But it cannot be overcome till Mill's question — 'Why should I promote the general happiness?'

receives the answer — Because it is when and only when I promote the general happiness that I increase my own; in short, till there is no opposition between my own and my neighbour's good — till Egoism becomes Altruism and Altruism Egoism; till, that is, the collapse of Obligation or Ethics itself.

In such a hopeless condition Utilitarianism was bound to lie till it somehow should get out of itself and criticize the absolute value of its own end. Now this has been done in two opposite directions — by the Rational or Universalistic Utilitarianism, and by the Ethics of Physical Evolution.

We concern ourselves with these theories only in respect of their attitude to the necessary postulate of Ethics. The end we found must be such as to conserve the rights equally of the subject and of the object. Now it is to this condition that Utilitarianism has, in its two developments, sought however unconsciously to conform. They are both prompted by Mill's introduction of quality as the distinguishing feature in hedonical calculations; for that was really to oust happiness as such from being the determining end. Utilitarianism was forced, as Socrates had been, to apply the calculus, the 'measuring arte', with the purpose not merely of measuring pleasure but of constituting or determining its absolute value. And since the value of the pleasure which an object produces differs with the attitude of the individual towards it, it is the best attitude which becomes the end; in other words, it is the harmony of the subject and the object.

But now, what is required is not a mere assertion of the harmony but the *rationale* of it. This the Ethics of Physical Evolution has seen and seeks to give. But the Universalistic and Rational Utilitarianism really presents no end, but only an ideal fusion of the rights of the subject and the object, without discovering the ground or determiner, rather only the consequence, of the fusion. It begins with what was the common conclusion of the Stoics and Epicureans, and amalgamates without unifying the reasoning of both as justified by the presupposition of the conclusion. It gives no *rationale* of the connexion between Happiness as such — the right of the subject, and Virtue as such — the right of the object. Whether happiness causes virtue or virtue happiness remains still the antinomy of practical reason. Nor is Kant's barren conjecture further advanced. 'It is not impossible', he says, 'that morality of mind should have a connexion as cause with happiness (as an effect in the sensible world), if not immediate yet mediate, *i.e.*, through an intelligent Author of nature'.

The other development does present the required *rationale*, namely, in physical evolution. It is this which determines the true ethical end − human development towards the complete realization of function and adaptation to environment. At present it constitutes, says Mr Spencer, a Relative Ethics, but in the distance we see it will bring out an Absolute Ethics, in which, 'instead of each maintaining his Own claims, others will maintain his claims for him'. This is just what Utilitarianism has always sought, as it had to seek; but it has obviously been gained only by reading 'existence' for 'obligation', 'is' for 'ought'. Morality is taken from the individual and habited in an external determiner, or, to say the same thing, it is left with an individual who, in everything he does, exhibits the resulting product of a determination, to which in ultimate analysis he is found to be the passive subject, if anything more than the resultant himself. The ethical end is thus not for, but of, man. Not only is morality proper taken from the individual; what ghost of it remains is equally claimed in kind by the meanest object of his environment. Just as Clifford found it necessary so to extend the psychology of this evolution as to find the elements of consciousness in material operations, for the sake of the same consistency this physical ethics has to be similarly extended. Thus, while Spencer would apply moral distinctions only to the actions of sentient beings, his natural successors see no reason whatever for the limitation. 'Is a watch that won't go the less a bad watch', says a writer in *Mind*, 'because it neither made itself nor wound itself up? . . . Is a man the less a bad man because he only follows his bad will and did not originate it?'

The only other end we shall examine under the postulate of Obligation is Perfection. Now subjective perfection, the mere attainment of efficiency, is not the ethical end for the simple reason that it may not include the rights of the object. Accordingly all the famous systems of Perfection have had an objective as well as a subjective reference. This is prominent in the formulas − to realize, according to Aristotle, the perfect exercise of a perfect life; according to Kant, an absolutely good-will; and according to Hegel, universal self-consciousness. Each of these regards the perfection of the individual as only a constituent in the actual end which is at once internal and external, subjective and objective.

Society and the individual reach perfection, not by the former acting for itself — the doctrine proper to Physical Evolution, nor by
the latter acting for himself — the doctrine of Sophism or Egoism;
neither according to such impossible ideals as the former acting
for the latter — the ideal of the Absolute Ethics, or the latter acting
for the former — the ideal of modern Utilitarianism. Both are in
essential relation; and that for which obligation rests on each is
just the realization and thereby the perfection of that relation.
Only after discovering what that relation is, are these formulas
admissible, and then they are all admissible. The discovery can
emanate of course only from self-consciousness where we find an
identity of nature and interest with one another. Here we discover
that the relation is self-relation and that its perfection consists in
its infinity — in our self-satisfaction or freedom from external
determination. The perfection contemplated by Mr Spencer, on
the other hand, is the finite and necessitated ideal of a complete
external adjustment. The laws of morality are the expressions of
this ethical self-relation. What experience does is as little to produce them as to construct the ideal to which they point. It only
determines them to greater particularity and definiteness. They
are accordingly a *priori* without being abstract, and actual or concrete without being an external product.

The application of the postulate of Obligation has a double
function relatively to moral freedom. In the first place it assures of
the reality of that freedom, a thing which no demonstration could
do (except for metaphysical freedom) in view of possible doctrines of association and unconscious cerebration. In the second
place, it establishes the essential characteristics of moral freedom
without which no theory of it can be adequate. Confining ourselves to this latter function, we have to ask — What is the necessary characteristic of a moral agent in view of Obligation? The
answer can only be that man must, in the first place, have power
to perform every obligation, and, in the second place, that the
exercise or non-exercise of such power must depend on himself
alone. But for the former I should not recognize the law at all; but
for the latter it would be no law for me.

We need not examine any of the many theories of freedom that
are founded on a psychology which makes the realization of these
conditions impossible. If, as Spinoza says, 'the mind cannot determine the body to motion or rest or any other state', we need not

care to discover whether mind is a function of brain or has its dynamical power and the reason of its existence within itself. Our freedom must be able to express itself in the determination of phenomena.

So, too, if the metaphysic of knowledge necessarily excludes it. Kant came dangerously near this position and is often actually in it when representing the sensible world as self-determined, independently of the noumenal world. It is from this Kantian source that the undetermined will of Schelling and Schopenhauer is developed. Schelling, making the distinction between the noumenal and sensible worlds, defines free actions as those which proceed from the former. But before the noumenal *Ego* acts it must be disposed or determined to a specific nature. This nature we do not assume in time, and nothing we do in time can remove one particle of any essential evils it contains. Our sensible actions are therefore all inevitably determined. But we feel remorse in respect of them just because we know that we might noumenally have assumed another nature. Beyond the useless revealing of this noumenal freedom the feeling has no rational function. Similarly Schopenhauer is related to Kant, whom indeed Hartmann calls the father of theoretic as Schopenhauer is of practical pessimism. He lays the guilt of our actions on our character — a blind will — whose nature our actions reveal. We can never help acting as we do, seeing that willing always precedes knowing. Regarded from an external point of view our actions might have been different — that is, had our character been other than it is, or had we been some other person. When I regret, it is my constitution I regret. I can only be sorry I am not another. Such doctrines of freedom are divorced from obligation, which nevertheless is the Kantian postulate for proving the existence of freedom at all.

The interpreter of Kant has two courses open to him. He may suppose either that Kant represents the sensible world as completely determined in itself, or that he makes it dependent on the noumenal world in some vital way. If the former, then to make Kant consistent, the interpreter must deprive him of the noumenal world (to which he held tenaciously) as an unwarrantable, because an unnecessary, assumption; which is to deprive him of his whole doctrine of morals and leave him in intellectual agnosticism. In the other alternative, we must find in his work that he has some living connexion between the two worlds. If this be found, the latter can evidently be the only just interpretation.

Causality is one of the scientific categories or categories of ordinary experience, and so has its full application in the sensible or phenomenal world. We cannot apply it in the same sense to anything else without dogmatism — such dogmatism as is expressed in the current agnosticism which manipulates the common categories at will as in Mill's question, Who caused God? From the standpoint of science or experience we know only that causality is becoming, but in morals we find that becoming is only the phenomenal representation of causality. We find that causality is more than a mere time-relation. It is a determination of an object before it receives — before it can receive — the determination of time or of any other phenomenal relation. It is the logical *prius* of a phenomenon as such — the first predicate of every possible object of sensible experience. No phenomenon could be a phenomenon at all without it. On the one hand, then, we can represent the sensible world as complete and determined; and, on the other hand, we can point to the freedom of the cogitable world as expressed in it. In the former sense, we say motives cause volitions or resolves; in the latter, that I alone am their cause. Motives, I can say, become resolves just as I can say that a certain combination of gases becomes water. But analyse the antecedents in either case as I may, I can find no trace of the effect or of any causal nexus in them, for no phenomenon is adequate to express more than it is in itself. The causal nexus is not phenomenal. Before the time-relation of becoming, or, as we say, physical or phenomenal causation, is predicable of an object, the object must, like all phenomena, be causally determined by a transcendental unity implied in all systems of relation. The self-conscious agent in that unity *I* is the cause that determines my motives, my resolves and actions to be what they are. Motives become volitions and volitions become actions not in respect of any abstraction like a phenomenal succession, but by reason of the unity which gives them their first determination — and which we have called the causal determination — to be phenomena at all.

Such a function moral obligation postulates for will as the first of its two characteristics, namely, that it have power to fulfil its obligations. We proceed to the second, that the exercise and non-exercise of such power must depend on the agent — the subject of obligation. Under the former we have seen how he is free in his phenomenal relations, *i.e.*, How he *can*. We must now discover how he is free in his essential or self-relation, *i.e.*, How *he* can.

As it is the confusion of will and desire which creates the difficulty of conceiving the personal manifestation of freedom, so it is the confusion of will and knowledge which makes it difficult to keep man in his individuality. The history of ethics shows that it is hardly possible to escape from identifying will and desire without identifying will and knowledge. Thus the earliest moral speculators, the Sophists, committed the former error, being immediately followed by Socrates who committed the other; and so on through all the ancient systems. The modern course was opened by Descartes with the former error; Spinoza added the other, and so on again till the present time when the doctrine of Evolution claims to resolve the difficulty — the physical, by uniting reason to desire, *i.e.*, under the form of physical necessity; the dialectical, by uniting desire to reason, *i.e.*, under the form of freedom. We confine ourselves to the latter.

To say with Green that 'in the sense in which thought and desire enters into an act of will, each is the whole act', or that 'will is equally and undistinguishably desire and thought', is just to say that a man never acts but for an end he desires, and that he is free when that end is rational. Now, while this is a correct representation of the acts of men, it is not the freedom with which we are more immediately concerned. This metaphysical or general freedom when demanded from a man, as is done by obligation, postulates a particular freedom in him. The one is the freedom of God which we are commanded to realize, the other is the freedom which we demand for the purpose of performing that command. Obligation thus postulates both this objective and this subjective freedom. It could not impose the latter without presuming the former, nor if it imposed the former without presuming the latter would it be any longer obligation at all. The significance of freedom in Ethics as a science is the state of the individual before the harmony of thought and desire, before ideal freedom has been realized. That it can be realized we presume under the postulate of obligation. How it is realised we also know. It is through self-reflection, through thereby recognizing the limitations of impulse, that man becomes superior to impulse and is released from physical necessity. Man shows his freedom when by such absolute reflection he harmonizes reason and desire in the satisfaction of moral obligations — when practical reason is his sole guide and he acts under the idea of this complete self-satisfaction.

This distinction between the distinctively metaphysical or objective and the distinctively ethical or subjective freedom is not to be confounded either with Hegel's distinction between absolute and formal freedom or with that between determination and indifference. Absolute freedom is that which has been described. It has itself for its object, is wholly self-related and becomes determinate through no external impulse but by its own infinite self-reflection. The formal freedom has a limited or contingent content and is variously denominated by Hegel as caprice, arbitrariness, wilfulness. It is free at all just because it consciously transcends limitations; but its transcendence is finite and relative, for its reflection is not self-directed but proceeds from impulse to impulse, from cause to consequence, thereby being partly determined from without. Now the will must in action be always one or other of these two, that is, it must manifest itself either in absolute or in formal freedom. But obligation, as it applies to the individual before such manifestation of his will, applies to a state in which it is possible for the individual either to identify himself with the universal reason and be free or to refuse to do it. A murderer sentenced to death, says Hegel, is free only when he wills to get hung. We with the postulate of obligation, if in this case it applies, if the harmony of desire and knowledge is attainable, claim for him a freedom which shall enable him to attain it.

Nor is this distinction of subjective and objective will to be compared with that absurd outstart of much current discussion as to freedom — 'Will is either determined or undetermined, that is, indifferent; now, if it is not determined', and so on. The alternative is perfectly good in Psychology, but except for the misconception it breeds it has precisely the same importance to Philosophy as the fact that it was fair yesterday but it rains today. Indifference, indeed, is generally itself a form of determination and is always on a level with it in the case of a self-conscious being. Man has always subjective freedom — the power to realize or not his proper or objective freedom. If he does not so realize himself in his actions, he is *indifferent* to his proper self or is *determined* by the blind force of his external relations. If he does realize his objective freedom, he is indifferent to the blind force of his external relations and is determined — determining them — according to his proper self.

I ought now to examine in the same way the ideas of Merit and Responsibility, but it is better to close here as these subjects have lately become too prominent in ethical literature to be adequately treated within the limits of this paper. For the present purpose, too, a critical discussion is unnecessary. Merit and Responsibility are the necessary consequents or complements of the ideas already discussed. It is just as legitimate to reject them (in the only sense in which anybody gives them any meaning and value), on the ground of Physical Ethics, as it would be for a man who had gone round the world to deny the existence of some place which could not have lain in his way. Nor are these ideas in any way inconsistent with the fact that to make the moral law square with the appetites is, as Kant says, 'to corrupt at the source the fountain of Duty and to banish and cloud all its dignity'; seeing that in ethics they spring from and are determined by that very fountain of Moral Obligation.

Six

David George Ritchie

David George Ritchie was born in Jedburgh, Scotland on 26 October 1853, into a cultured family which included among its number academics and clergymen. He was the only son of three children born to George Ritchie and Elizabeth Bradfute Dudgeon. His father was the parish minister, elected as a moderator to the general assembly of the Church of Scotland in 1870. There were family connections with the Carlyles and in 1889 Ritchie edited the *Early Letters of Jane Welsh Carlyle*. Ritchie had two sisters and led a sheltered existence that his biographer insinuates had damaging psychological effects, making him nervous of disposition and craving sympathetic companionship. He was educated at Jedburgh Academy, and entered Edinburgh University in 1869 where he was introduced to philosophy by Alexander Campbell Fraser and Henry Calderwood. While at Edinburgh he attended a botany class which stimulated a life-long interest that was to find expression in his ethical and political writings. His main subject was classics in which he graduated with first class honours in 1875. He then went to Balliol College, Oxford, where he gained a first in Classical moderations (1875) and in the 1878 final Greats examinations. Ritchie had originally intended to enter the clergy, but his irritation with orthodox religion and passion for philosophical idealism and socialism led him to reject the vocation. Instead, in the same year he became a fellow of Balliol, and in 1881 was made a tutor at Balliol from 1882–6. While at Oxford he was influenced by both T.H. Green and Arnold Toynbee. Ritchie was unsuccessful in his application for the chair of Logic, Rhetoric and Metaphysics at St Andrews in 1891 against Henry Jones and W.R. Sorley. Sorley lost out by one vote to Jones and went on to chairs at Cardiff, Aberdeen and Cambridge (where he influenced the young Michael Oakeshott). When Jones left St Andrews in 1894 Ritchie was appointed to the chair. He was awarded an hon. LL.D. by Edinburgh University in 1898, and in 1898–9 he was president of the Aristotelian Society.

One of Ritchie's colleagues described him as a socialist and 'zealous' democrat whose way of thinking seemed to have little in common with ordinary people. He was an early member of the Fabian Society, but left in the mid 1890s. He was at the forefront in criticizing the application of naturalistic theories of evolution to society. His *The Principles of State Interference* was one of the most widely read political tracts in the English speaking world.

Ritchie was married twice. The first time to Flora Lindsay Macdonell in 1881 who gave birth to a daughter. In 1889, the year after Flora died, he married Ellen S. Haycraft with whom he had a son. Ritchie died after a short illness on 3 February 1903 at St Andrews, where he is buried.

Biographical

E.S. Haldane, 'Ritchie, David George (1853–1903)', *Dictionary of National Biography 1901–1911*.

Robert Latter, 'Memoir' in *Philosophical Studies* by David D. Ritchie (London: Macmillan, 1905).

William Sweet, 'Ritchie, David George' in *Dictionary of Nineteenth Century British Philosophers*, ed. W.J. Mander and Alan P.F. Sell (Bristol: Thoemmes, 2002), pp. 953–7.

Principal Works

Darwinism and Politics (London: Swan Sonnenschein, 1889)

The Principles of State Interference (London: Swan Sonnenschein, 1891)

Darwin and Hegel with other philosophical studies (London: Swan Sonnenschein, 1893)

Natural Rights (London: Swan Sonnenschein, 1894).

Studies in Political and Social Ethics (London: Swan Sonnenschein, 1902).

Collected Works of David Ritchie, ed. Peter Nicholson (Bristol: Thoemmes, 1998), 6 vols.

READING VI

THE POLITICAL PHILOSOPHY OF T.H. GREEN[1]

I: *Political Philosophy in England*

In no country has there been through many centuries a more continuous discussion of the questions of practical politics than in England. In no country has the interest in politics been diffused more widely through the whole community. But there has been no corresponding activity in the philosophical study of the nature of society and the State. Hobbes and Herbert Spencer are almost the only two English philosophers who have treated politics as an integral part of a complete philosophical system: and it might be shown that the monarchical prejudices of Hobbes and the individualist prejudices of Spencer have hindered them from even so adequate a treatment of the nature of the State as their philosophical theories admitted.[2] We can hardly reckon the brilliant political Essays of Hume in this connection, for Hume was professedly a destroyer of systems, and his attention to politics and to history went along with his despair of metaphysics. The political writings of Locke and of John Stuart Mill have not only a permanent interest for the student of political ideas, but have exercised in different ways a direct influence on

---

[1] 'The Political Philosophy of Thomas Hill Green' in *Principles of State Interference* (London: Swan Sonnenschein, 1891), 127–151.

[2] With regard to Mr Spencer see Essay I [of *The Principles of State Interference*].

the course of political events; but this influence was direct, very much because both Locke and Mill wrote on politics more as politicians than as philosophers. Locke makes no explicit link between his theory of knowledge and his theory of government, though both were given to the world at about the same time; in fact, the ideas of a 'law of nature' and 'natural rights', on which his political doctrines rest, belong to that manner of thinking which the analytic method of the Essay contributed in the long run to discredit. Hume attacked the idea of 'social contract' by using just such weapons as Locke had used in attacking 'innate ideas'. In the case of Mill the careful reader can trace the connection between the psychical atomism (for he treats sensations as if they were psychical atoms) which forms the fundamental assumption in his theory of knowledge and the individualism out of which his practical interest in human well-being helped him partially to escape; but, though Mill himself was fully aware of the ultimate interdependence of different departments of human thought and human prejudice, and though he regarded himself as fighting for the same cause of progress in his *Logic* and *Examination of Hamilton* on the one hand, and in his *Liberty* and *Representative Government* on the other, yet the two sets of works are obviously addressed to different classes of readers, and it requires the diligence of the student to see more than a biographical connection; and, in any case, Mill was concerned with practical questions about the limits of government-action and the arrangement of representative bodies, not with the primary and more strictly philosophical questions about the nature of the State. In fact, the intense preoccupation of the most vigorous English minds in the immediately practical problems of legislation and administration has diverted attention from an investigation of the ultimate principles on which government is based. And, while it has been an enormous advantage that those amongst us who have written about government have themselves had some practical acquaintance with what legislation and administration mean, we have lost something, not only in clearness of theory but in consistency and firmness of practice, because the elementary terms of political discussion have passed current without having their value scientifically tested. In Germany, on the other hand, some of the very best energy of philosophical thinking has been devoted to the doctrine of rights and the nature and functions of the State; but, owing to the fact that political liberty is not yet very well known in Germany, we may occasionally complain (echoing the complaint of Aristotle) that the Sophists, or Professors, who profess to teach *politikai* [art of politics], or *Staatslehre*, have no practical experience of their subject, while the practical politicians of our own country have not raised their knowledge of the State from the domain of experience to that of thought.

This scarcity of English political philosophy gives a peculiar importance to the portion of the late Professor Green's *Philosophical Works*, which contains his 'Lectures on the Principles of Political Obligation'.[3] The same metaphysical subtlety, which had been already applied to the Theory of Knowledge and the Theory of Ethics, is here directed to a criticism of political theories and to the attempt thereby to arrive at a more adequate doctrine of political rights and obligations. To those who knew Professor Green personally, this part of his *Works* has an additional and very special significance; for here we have the meeting-point between the speculative and the practical interests, which to onlookers might seem to be two divergent channels in which his life ran, but which in his own mind were united and tended in the same direction. The painstaking pursuit of philosophical truth and the endeavour in all things to be the good citizen and the honest politician were equally characteristic of the man, and sprang from a common source of earnestness and sincerity. His conscience was equally exacting in speculation and in practice. His philosophical thinking was to him no mere exercise of intellectual ingenuity, but provided the basis of his conduct and influenced the details of his actions to an extent very rare even amongst those whom we consider the most conscientious of men. He neither despised the small matters of local politics, nor forgot the wider interests of mankind. He went straight from the declaration of the poll, when he was elected a town councillor, to lecture on *The Critique of Pure Reason*. He was robbed of his sleep by thinking about the Eastern Question, and dreading lest the country should be driven, by motives 'of which perhaps a diffused desire for excitement has

[3]   *Works of Thomas Hill Green, late Fellow of Balliol College, and Whyte's Professor of Moral Philosophy in the University of Oxford.* Edited by R.L. Nettleship, Fellow of Balliol College, Oxford. Vol. II. London: Longmans. 1886. (see pp. 308–the end.)

been the most innocent',[4] into what he regarded as an indefensible and unrighteous war. His strong opinions on the liquor traffic were in his own mind directly connected with his conception of the ethical end and the nature of rights.

II: The Relation Between Philosophy and Politics

The late Mark Pattison[5] thought it must have been due to 'a certain puzzle-headedness' on the part of the Professor that he, 'a staunch Liberal', should have imported into Oxford 'an *a priori* philosophy, which under various disguises aims at exempting Man from the order of nature, and making him into a unique being whose organism is not to be subject to the uniform laws which govern all other Being that is known to us'. It was, in any case, from no want of thinking and puzzling over problems, that Professor Green was at once 'a staunch Liberal' and an '*a priori* philosopher'. Mark Pattison's phrase, '*exempting* Man from the order of Nature', must be challenged on behalf alike of Kant and Green, who by no means deny that Man is a part of Nature, and that human actions are natural events, but who do deny that Man can be understood if he be considered as *merely* a part of Nature and his actions *merely* as natural events. But that question must be left for the present.

There is a remarkable passage in the *Autobiography* of J.S. Mill (pp. 273–5), where he says:

> The difference between these two schools of philosophy, that of Intuition and that of Experience and Association, is not a mere matter of abstract speculation; it is full of practical consequences, and lies at the foundation of all the greatest differences of practical opinion in an age of progress. The practical reformer has continually to demand that changes be made in things which are supported by powerful and widely spread feelings, or to question the apparent necessity and indefeasibleness of established facts; and it is often an indispensable part of his argument to show how those powerful feelings had their origin, and how those facts came to seem necessary and indefeasible. There is therefore a natural hostility between him and a philosophy which discourages the explanation of feelings and moral facts by circumstances and association, and prefers to treat them as ultimate elements of human nature; a philosophy which is addicted to holding up

---

[4]   Cp. *Philosophical Works*, ii. p. 476.
[5]   See his *Memoirs*, pp. 167, 242.

favourite doctrines as intuitive truths, and deems intuition to be the voice of Nature and of God, speaking with an authority higher than that of our reason. In particular, I have long felt that the prevailing tendency to regard all the marked distinctions of human character as innate, and in the main indelible, and to ignore the irresistible proofs that by far the greater part of those differences, whether between individuals, races or sexes, are such as not only might but naturally would be produced by differences in circumstances, is one of the chief hindrances to the rational treatment of great social questions, and one of the greatest stumbling blocks to human improvement. This tendency has its source in the intuitional metaphysics which characterized the reaction of the nineteenth century against the eighteenth, and it is a tendency so agreeable to human indolence, as well as to conservative interests generally, that unless attacked at the very root, it is sure to be carried to even a greater length than is really justified by the more moderate forms of the intuitional philosophy. That philosophy, not always in its moderate forms, had ruled the thought of Europe for the greater part of a century. My Father's *Analysis of the Mind*, my own *Logic*, and Professor Bain's great treatise, had attempted to re-introduce a better mode of philosophizing, latterly with quite as much success as could be expected; but I had for some time felt that the mere contrast of the two philosophies was not enough, that there ought to be a hand-to-hand fight between them, that controversial as well as expository writings were needed, and that the time was come when such controversy would be useful.

These considerations Mill assigns as his special reason for attacking Sir William Hamilton.

Sir William Hamilton was a Whig, it is true (and a Whig in those days was still a Liberal); but undoubtedly the doctrine of 'intuitive truths' has served as a convenient formula under which time honoured delusions and abuses have been sheltered from the attacks of critical analysis and reforming zeal. The 'intuitional metaphysics' of this country and the so-called 'spiritualist' philosophy, which flourished in France under the restored monarchy, have both been associated with the maintenance of existing ideas and institutions in society, politics and religion. The supporters of these Intuitionalist systems very often pointed to the triumphs of the Kantian Criticism and sometimes of the post-Kantian Idealism in Germany, glad to use the sanction of great names where they were available, without committing themselves to speculative theories which had the reputation of being vaguely 'dangerous'. Those, too, who first introduced the

names and theories of the German philosophers were generally
enlisted on the side of the reaction against the French Revolution
— Coleridge most conspicuously, De Quincy and others following in the same line. In Thomas Love Peacock's *Nightmare Abbey*
the 'Kantian' philosopher, Mr Flosky, is represented as an
extreme obscurantist reactionary; his very name, by an old-
fashioned etymology, signifying 'the lover of darkness'. Certainly
Hegel was a Prussian Conservative, and Schelling seemed to lead
the way through mysticism back into the fold of the Catholic
Church; but people would appear to have forgotten how the aged
Kant, with tears in his eyes, said his *Nunc dimittis* [departure] on
hearing of the proclamation of the French Republic, and how
Fichte was the intellectual father of German Socialism. Mill and
Pattison might also have remembered that Hobbes was an Abso-
lutist, and that Hume became more and more a Tory without
becoming less a sceptic; and it has not yet been explicitly proved
that there is a logical connection between 'philosophic doubt' and
support of the Tory party. From a man's philosophical speculations we cannot always predict his attitude in practical politics.
But the mistake in the statements both of Mill and Pattison lies in
the assumption that the *a priori* philosophy of Kant and his followers is identical with the 'intuitional metaphysics' which had been
the familiar object of attack to the English Empiricists. The resemblance between the answers to Hume of Kant and of Reid is slight
and superficial, compared with the difference between them.
And the attitude of Hegel to the problems of knowledge and of
life is distinct both from the old metaphysics and from the new
empiricism. The German Idealist is equally distasteful to the
defender of 'innate ideas' or 'intuitive truths' and to their assail-
ant — because he is apt to be misunderstood by both. And, if we
pass to the more practical application of philosophy, there would
be more reason for classing Hegel and his followers along with
Comte than with the obscurantist theologians whom Pattison dis-
liked and the obstructionist Conservatives whom Mill opposed.
Comte, it is true, presents a double face: he is both of the Revolution and against it. And the same remark really applies to Hegel.
Hence it is no wonder that opposite parties should have started
from the same great school, and that Catholic and Positivist, Conservative and Socialist should have found weapons in the same
armoury. Which is the truer interpreter it is of course important to

decide; and it does not always follow that the initiator of new ideas will himself be the best judge of their practical tendency.

Another side to the mistake in Pattison's remark about Green is the failure to appreciate fully the change that has come over English Liberalism. During the last century and the earlier part of the present century, the friends of social and political reform were engaged in a struggle mainly against mischievous interference with individual liberty on the part of a government which chiefly represented the influence and interests of a hereditary ruling class: thus Liberalism came to be identified with the criticism and removal of repressive laws and institutions, and an intellectual basis for such a policy was naturally found in a philosophy of critical analysis. It was in the same spirit that Locke, the father of English Empiricism, criticized the doctrine of innate ideas and the doctrine of the divine right of kings. And this alliance between Empiricism in philosophy and Liberalism in politics continued with few exceptions to the time of John Stuart Mill, whose philosophical creed remained, on the whole, in its intellectual aspects what his father had taught him, however modified by emotional sympathies, but whose political ideas underwent a greater change than he himself was aware of. The efforts of Liberals having passed from the merely negative work of removing mischievous State-action to the more positive task of employing the power of a government, which is now, more or less, the real representative of the 'general will', in behalf of the well-being of the community, it is natural and necessary that the intellectual basis of the new political creed should be found in a philosophy of construction, and not in one of merely negative criticism and analysis. Thus there is a real affinity between the newer stages of Radicalism and a political philosophy such as that of Hegel or of Comte, apart from the special influence of Prussian bureaucracy in the one case and the admiration for mediaeval Catholicism in the other, which are, after all, elements belonging more to the idiosyncrasy of the philosophers than to the essence of the ideas of which they are the most notable representatives.

III: *Kant and Aristotle — The Ethical End*

These remarks must not, however, be taken as implying that Professor Green was only 'the importer' (to adopt Mark Pattison's phrase) of a German philosophy. It is rather common to hear him classed as one of 'the English school of Hegelians'. He would certainly not have acknowledged the title himself, and it is really inaccurate — unless it be very carefully qualified. If we are to connect him with any particular names of philosophers, it would be least misleading to say that he corrected Kant by Aristotle and Aristotle by Kant. Now, this is just what might have been said of Hegel himself; for, if Hegel had no other claims to distinction, he would have this, that first of modern philosophers he really understood and appreciated the Greeks, referring to Hegel, Green is reported to have said, 'It must all be done over again' — *i.e.* he admitted the general validity of Hegel's objections to the subjective, and, in appearance, merely psychological method of Kant, and to the survivals (from the old metaphysics) in Kant's system of ways of thinking and speaking, of which Kant himself had implicitly made an end; but he considered the Hegelian attempt to read off the whole secret of the Universe, to fill up the whole contents of the eternal Self-consciousness, premature and over-hasty, and he set himself to do some small part of the vast work in a more modest spirit and with special reference to the English theories which he found occupying the field.[6]

There is a brief reference to Greek philosophy in the lectures on Political Obligation (§39), where it is said that, just because Plato and Aristotle regarded man as finding his end in the end of the State, they laid the foundation for a true theory of rights. In the *Prolegomena to Ethics* it was argued that Greek ethics were defective, not in defining the end as self-satisfaction or self-realization (*energeia psyches* [mental activity]), but because, in the stage of moral and social progress then attained, this self-realization was only possible to a few, and so here it is said: 'Practically it is only the Greek man that Aristotle regards as *phusei polites* [having a political nature], but the Greek conception of citizenship once established was applicable to all men capable of a common interest'. As Aristotle concludes his 'Ethics' by passing on to Politics, because the good life can only be fully realized by the citizen of

[6]   It is worth calling attention to the very great degree in which the questions discussed and the phraseology adopted in the 'Lectures on Political Obligation' are determined by Locke's *Treatise of Civil Government*. Green's polemic against Locke's theory of knowledge has not prevented his sympathy with the most *politically* important English book on the nature of government.

the good State, so Green's view of ethics is completed by his view of Politics; because he conceives that the function of the State is to make it possible for men to realize themselves, which they can only do by attaining a good that is a common good. In the ethical writings the phrase, 'self-satisfaction' or 'self-realization' is perhaps the more conspicuous, in the political 'common good' (which, however, is used quite as much in the ethical); but it is just because to Green these terms are identical expressions of the end for man that his ethics can escape the reproach of being only the Egoistic Hedon- ism he professedly rejected come back under a disguised form. 'If the end be self-realization', it might be objected, 'does it not depend entirely on the individual what he chooses to do? The pleasure-seeker might say he was realiszing himself quite as much as the patriot or the philanthropist, and how can you prove him wrong?' He can only be proved wrong if it be shown that the self in a human being is something other than a mere series of feelings, and so in its true nature other than a mere subject for pleasurable sensations. And Green argues that the self is other than a mere series of feelings just because it is what renders possible the consciousness of a series of feelings: the self-consciousness, which is manifested in them, must yet be other than they; for, as J.S. Mill himself had seen, it was a 'paradox' that what is only a series of feelings should be aware of itself as a series.[7] In this fact of self-consciousness, discovered by examination of mental phenomena, Green finds the metaphysical basis of Ethics; on the other side the interpretation of self-realization as the realization of a common good is what makes the connection between Ethics and Politics. 'The good which a man seeks for himself is not a succession of pleasures, but objects which, when realized, are permanent contributions to a social good which thus satisfies the permanent self'.[8] Thus, the practical tests which Green applies to determine the rightness of any proposed course of conduct, either for the individual or for the State, seem to coincide with those which would be proposed by the Utilitarian. Of this he is quite aware,[9] but he considers that he has a logical justification for

---

[7] Cp. Mill's *Examination of Hamilton*, p. 248 (5th edition).

[8] *Prolegomena to Ethics*, § 234 (Analysis).

[9] Cf. 'Lectures on Political Obligation' (in *Philosophical Works*, vol.ii.), §23, of which Mr Nettleship's analysis is: ' The utilitarian theory so far agrees

applying the test of social well-being to which the Utilitarian, with his Hedonist starting-point, has no claim, and that, having defined the end as the realization of a permanent self-satisfaction, he escapes the difficulties attending the balancing of pleasures and pains. The practical benefits conferred by Utilitarianism on political and social conduct he is most ready to acknowledge, but he maintains that the significant part of Bentham's famous formula was not 'the greatest happiness', but the reference to *the greatest number*, and especially the added clause, 'Every one to count for one and no one for more than one'.[10] This he holds to have been the main source both of the beneficence and of the unpopularity of Utilitarianism. 'The healthful influence of Utilitarianism has arisen from its giving a wider and more impartial range to the desire to do good, not from its stimulating that desire'.[11] When we look to politics rather than to ethics, we shall see the reason why Green would have found himself, in the case of so many questions, on the same platform with John Stuart Mill, and that without the least sacrifice of philosophical consistency. He would have agreed with a follower of Locke or of Rousseau in demanding, for instance, an extension of the franchise; but he would have agreed with Bentham and Mill in objecting to any talk about 'natural rights': he would have preferred to put the matter on the ground of social expediency. But while Mill would *ultimately* have brought the question back to some consideration of pleasures and pains, Green would have insisted that the social expediency was determined ultimately, not by the probable effects on the greatest number of pleasures of an individual consistently with those of other individuals, but on the scope given to the individual for exercising all his capacities of self-development, all true self-development implying, however, the well-being of a community; for man, as we often repeat without fully understanding what we say, is essentially 'a social animal'. The convenience of Bentham's formula is the readiness with which it supplies a means of checking and criticizing individual and class prejudice and selfishness. And formulae for ordinary rough use need not be philosophically unassailable. There is no

---

with that here advocated that it grounds existing law, not on a "natural" law prior to it, but on an end which it serves'.

[10] *Prolegomena to Ethics*, § 213.

[11] *Prolegomena to Ethics*, § 331 (Analysis).

reason why the Idealist, after making clear his objections to Hedonism, should not join hands with the Utilitarian. In fact, an ethical system like Green's is really, on its practical side, J.S. Mill's Utilitarianism with a securer basis and a criterion provided, which Mill cannot logically provide, for distinguishing the different *qualities* of pleasures. Mill, we know, would himself prefer the higher pleasures. But what justifies him in considering those to be the best pleasures for other people? To say that the common good is the end may seem more vague than to say that pleasure is the end; but to say that pleasure is the end is in reality quite as vague and is more open to objection, because the vagueness is less obvious, and therefore more misleading.

IV: 'Freedom' — Negative and Positive

Besides 'self-realization' and a 'common good' as phrases for the ethical, which is also ultimately the political end, Green is willing to allow Hegel's term 'freedom'. In a special discussion of the 'different senses of 'freedom' as applied to will and to the moral progress of man',[12] which may be taken as intermediate between the *Prolegomena to Ethics* and the political lectures, he distinguishes between a generic sense of 'freedom', in which it applies to *all* will — whatever be the character of the object willed ('freedom' meaning, simply, self-determination or acting on preference) — and a *particular* sense, according to which acts are only 'free' in so far as the self-realizing principle in man tends to be realized — *i.e.* in so far as the objects of reason and of will tend to coincide.[13] Free acts are rational acts. In this sense Hegel's dictum, that the object of the State is freedom, is accepted, but only as the statement of an ideal to which actual States, so far as they are well regulated, tend to approximate.

'Hegel's account of freedom as realized in the State does not seem to correspond to the facts of society as it is, or even as under the alterable conditions of human nature, it ever could be; though undoubtedly there is a work of moral liberation, which society,

---

[12]   See *Philosophical Works*, vol. ii. pp. 308–33.
[13]   Cp. Spinoza's use of *libertas* as equivalent to the rule of reason, *potentia intellectus*.

through its various agencies, is constantly carrying on for the individual'.[14]

Now it is obvious that freedom in this sense as the ideal end of the State is very different from the 'freedom' to which Locke considered that man had a 'natural right' in which a well-managed State ought to secure him.[15] This freedom is the mere negative freedom of being left alone, and corresponds to the generic sense of freedom in morals. It is a mere means to the attainment of the freedom which is itself an end. The distinction shows what Green's attitude to the questions about State-action and *laissez faire* was likely to be. State-action, he holds, is expedient just in so far as it tends to promote 'freedom' in the sense of self-determined action directed to the objects of reason, inexpedient so far as it tends to interfere with this. The direct legal enforcement of morality cannot be considered expedient or inexpedient: it is impossible. The morality of an act depends on the state of the will of the agent, and therefore the act done under compulsion ceases to have the character of a moral act. It wants the negative condition of morality.[16] But on the other hand, there is no *a priori* presumption in favour of a general policy of *laissez faire*, because in a vast number of cases the individual does not find himself in a position in which he can act 'freely' (*i.e.*, direct his action to objects which reason assigns as desirable) without the intervention of the State to put him in such a position — *e.g.*, by ensuring that he shall have at least some education. Terms like 'freedom', 'compulsion', 'interference', are very apt to be misleading. As Green points out, ' "compulsory education" need not be "compulsory", except to those who have no spontaneity to be deadened': and it is 'not as a purely moral duty on the part of a parent, but as the prevention of a hindrance to the capacity for rights on the part of children, that

[14] *Philosophical Works*, ii. p. 314.
[15] Locke, however, sees that the freedom which means 'being left alone by other individuals' does not mean 'being left alone by the State'. He at least is free from the delusion that the equal freedom of all can be obtained by an absence of legislation. See the passages quoted in *note* on p. 85 [of *The Principles of State Interference*].
[16] The same holds, of course, with regard to religion, if religion is anything more than ritual observance. There is a story that some Tory Churchman (who must have been born two centuries too late) said to the late Professor Thorold Rogers: 'Religion must be compulsory, or else there will be no religion at all'. 'I cannot see the difference', was the answer.

education should be enforced by the State'.[17] The 'interference' may be interference in behalf of individual liberty — even in the negative sense of liberty. So also, when interference with 'freedom of contract' is spoken of, we must consider not only those who are interfered with, but those whose freedom is increased by that interference.[18]

It would be out of place here to give a detailed account of the way in which Green works out his own theory of political obligation and doctrine of rights by a criticism of Hobbes, Spinoza, Locke, Rousseau, and Austin — a criticism which is probably more valuable ad suggestive than any dogmatic treatise on political science. The foregoing exposition may, at least, serve to make it clear that, whether Professor Green was mistaken or not in his development of Kantian and Aristotelian philosophy, or in his sympathy with Radical politics, he was at least thoroughly and perfectly consistent. The State has, in his view, not the mere policeman's business of stepping in to arrest the wrongdoer, not the sole function of ruthlessly enforcing fulfilment of contracts, whatever these contracts may be and between whomsoever made; but the duty of providing such an environment for individual men and women as to give *all*, as far as possible, an equal chance of realizing what is best in their intellectual and moral natures. Material well-being *alone* might hinder, instead of furthering, this end; but we need not be afraid of weakening moral responsibility by making a moral and *human* life possible to those for whom at present it is practically hopeless. The politician is thus not inconsistent, who, after opposing all such State-action as 'tended to strengthen some at the cost of others' weakness', supports such measures of compulsion as shall secure to all, as far as possible, true freedom — *i.e.*, 'a positive power or capacity of doing or enjoying something worth doing or enjoying, and that, too, something that we do or enjoy in common with others'.[19] No better expression of Professor Green's social ideal can be found

---

[17] *Lectures on Political Obligation*, § 209.

[18] There is a popular lecture of Prof. Green's on *Liberal Legislation and Freedom of Contract*, published by Slatter & Rose, Oxford, 1881, republished in *Works*, vol. iii. pp. 365–86. The philosophical doctrines of the College lectures will be found to underlie the popular lecture, which serves as an excellent commentary on them.

[19] *Liberal Legislation and Freedom of Contract*, p. 9. (*Works*, vol. iii. p. 371.)

than in words of his that have already been quoted as typical by Professor Caird:

> I confess to hoping for a time when the phrase ['the education of a gentleman'] will have lost its meaning, because the sort of education which alone makes the gentleman in any true sense will be within the reach of all. As it was the aspiration of Moses that all the Lord's people should be prophets, so with all seriousness and reverence we may hope and pray for a condition of English society, in which all honest citizens will recognize themselves and be recognized by each other as gentlemen.[20]

This is certainly a democratic, some would call it a Socialist, sentiment. It is only one outcome of the recognition that the ethical end of self-realization is an end for all human beings, and that we must get rid of those barriers of class and caste which we are in the habit of saying that Christianity has broken down.

READING VII
'THE RIGHTS OF ANIMALS'[21]

In his article under this title in the January number, Mr Salt lays down his opinions without discussing what the word 'right' means; he simply repeats the dogma, which he has asserted before, that 'if man has rights, animals have the same — in kind'. He admits that there is a difference between human and non-human animals in degree. What these categories of 'degree' and 'kind' may mean, and whether they are mutually exclusive, Mr Salt omits to inquire. The difference between water at 20°F and water at 40°F is a difference in 'degree'; but you can stand on the one and will sink in the other. So, though we may admit that the intelligence of a man differs only in degree from the intelligence of a guinea-pig, it does not follow that, if the former has rights, the latter has them also *in the same sense of the term*.

(1) 'Rights', properly, is a legal term. Mr Salt argues that because the State protects some animals from cruelty or destruction, it has conferred legal rights upon them. This seems to me an inaccurate use of words. In my book on 'Natural Rights' (p. 108) I wrote — 'Because a work of art or some ancient monument is pro-

[20] *The Work to be done by the new Oxford High School?*: A Lecture addressed to the Wesleyan Literary Society, Dec. 19, 1881. (*Works*, vol. iii. p. 475.)
[21] 'The Rights of Animals', *International Journal of Ethics*, vol. 10 (1899/1900), pp. 387–9.

tected by law from injury, do we speak of the "rights" of pictures or stones?' Mr Salt considers my logic at fault here; he says I have 'overlooked the fact that pictures and stones are *not* protected by law — against the owners'. Mr Salt has not taken the trouble to understand my illustration. I spoke of the case where works of art *are* protected, *i.e.*, where they belong to the State or to some public body, and are therefore protected against injury from individuals. Unfortunately, works of art and ancient monuments are often in unintelligent or careless private ownership, responsible only to public opinion, and in such cases they are not legally protected against the neglect or stupidity of their owners. By punishing cruelty to animals which are private property, the State has so far interfered with absolute private ownership: the owner may kill his cat or his dog, but he may be punished for ill-treating it. He may not practice vivisection without a license, etc. Certain wild birds may not be killed at certain seasons, because the State has taken them under its charge. These are perhaps the closest parallel to State-owned pictures or monuments, though the latter are more completely protected because individually more valued. Mr Salt admits that the ill-used cab-horse cannot sue in a law court; nevertheless, he considers the horse a 'person'. Mr Edward Carpenter, whom Mr Salt calls 'a great teacher', tells us 'it is the same *human* creature that flies in the air and swims in the sea, or walks biped on the land'. If all living things are 'human' and 'persons' what do the words mean? Is a sponge a 'person', or is it several persons? And if we find a poor dog suffering from parasites, are we to respect these 'persons'? There are some difficult question of casuistry here.

(2)   In the sense of 'moral rights', *i.e.*, the sense in which a right is guaranteed by public opinion, it may seem more reasonable to talk of animals having 'the right to be kindly treated' or 'of our duty to the animals'. I hold it to be much more accurate to speak of our having duties of kindness towards animals — these duties being owed to human society and enforced, more or less, by it. And Mr Salt implicitly acknowledges the propriety of this distinction (though he scoffs at it) by calling himself a 'Humanitarian', not an 'Animalarian'.

(3)   In a metaphorical sense we may be said to acknowledge special rights, *i.e.*, special claims upon us, in domestic animals, and most of all in pets, to whom we give names and so a

quasi-human, quasi-personal character. They are quasi-persons, because we have admitted them to a sort of membership of the family circle. All rights — legal, moral or metaphorical — rest upon membership of a society.

But, it should be observed, that in the sense in which we may allow ourselves to talk of 'duties to animals' and 'rights' of animals to be well treated and painlessly killed when it is necessary, *in* the *same sense* (I admit differences of degree) we may speak of our duties to an ancient building, a beautiful landscape, an historic oak, a family heirloom — duties which are really and strictly owed to humanity, but which we may think of as owed to inanimate things, so far as interesting or pleasing to humanity. We may also speak of duties to logic and to accuracy of language, though Mr Salt does not seem to care much about such duties. I feel more sense of 'duty' to a beautiful plant than to the wretched parasites that are injuring it, more sense of duty to an old book than to the mice who are enjoying it; though the parasites and the mice are 'persons' to Mr Salt. In both cases my duty is really a duty to humanity. Mr Salt, however, professes to look at matters from the animal's point of view. He objects to animals being kept in captivity, however kindly treated. 'To live one's own natural life, to realize one's self, is the true moral purpose of man and animal equally'. If a tiger comes out of his cage, to live his own natural life and realize himself, Mr Salt would be well-advised to keep out of his way. 'Treat the animal as you would willingly be treated if you were such an animal', is a maxim quoted with approval by Mr Salt. Is he ready to treat the tiger, as the tiger would wish to be treated — not a vegetarian diet, but to a diet of vegetarians? But about the *jus animalium* [law of the jungle] I have said quite enough in my book on 'Natural Rights' — more than was necessary in the opinion of some of my critics.

Seven

Richard Burden Haldane

Richard Burden Haldane was born in Edinburgh on 30 July 1856. His father Robert was an Edinburgh lawyer with a country residence at Cloan, Perthshire, where Richard spent late Spring and Summer each year during childhood, and much of his later life. His mother was Mary Elizabeth Burden-Sanderson of West Jesmond, Northumberland. Richard's brother John Scott Haldane and sister Elizabeth Sanderson Haldane were also important nineteenth-century Scottish philosophers. In religion the family was of the Calvinist anti-episcopacy persuasion. Richard was educated at preparatory school in Edinburgh, and then the Edinburgh Academy. He entered Edinburgh University at the age of sixteen, but was not at ease with any of his studies. He felt uncom-

fortable with the coldly practical philosophy of Hamilton, much
in fashion in Edinburgh, and was persuaded at the age of eighteen
to study with Hermann Lotze in Göttingen, whom he came to
admire greatly. He returned to Edinburgh University in 1874 and
studied philosophy under Campbell Fraser, graduating with an
MA, first class honours. He then applied himself to studying law.
He went to London where his specialized knowledge of Scottish
Law made him invaluable to his fellow countrymen, and was
called to the Bar at Lincoln's Inn in 1879. He became passionately
interested in politics, believing that education and social reform
should be at the forefront of Liberal policies, and in 1885 he was
elected to Parliament as the member for East Lothian and served
in that capacity until 1911. He continued to practise law, becoming a Queen's Councillor in 1890. Between 1905 and 1912 he was
Secretary of State for War. He was elevated to a peerage in 1911
and was Lord Chancellor from 1912 to 1915, when he was forced
to resign because of adverse public perception of his German
sympathies. He gradually became estranged from the Liberal
Party, and in 1924 was briefly once again Lord Chancellor in
Ramsey MacDonald's government. His political activities were
mainly devoted to the establishment of regional universities and
to the reform of the army.

At Edinburgh University Haldane made lifelong friends with
Andrew Seth and W.R. Sorley, ensuring that he permanently
maintained his philosophical interests. In 1883 he edited the
Idealist 'testament', *Essays in Philosophical Criticism* with Andrew
Seth, and throughout the '80s continued to develop his own
philosophical position, taking the opportunity in 1890 with his
brother John to renew his links with German philosophy. His acu-
men as a philosopher was acknowledged in being issued the invitation to deliver the Gifford Lectures at the University of St
Andrews, 1902–4. Haldane here, for the first time, formally presented his fully-developed philosophical position. He gave
numerous addresses that were informed by his philosophical outlook, many of which he published in collections of his writings.
He was elected a Fellow of the Royal Society in 1906 and Fellow of
the British Academy in 1914.

Biographical

Richard Burden Haldane, *An Autobiography* (London: Hodder and Stoughton, 1929).

Major-General Sir Frederick Maurice, *Haldane 1856–1915: The Life of Viscount Haldane of Cloan* (London: Faber and Faber, 1937) and *Haldane 1915–1928: The Life of Viscount Haldane of Cloan* (London: Faber and Faber, 1939).

Dudley Sommer, *Haldane of Cloan: His Life and Times 1856–1928* (London: Allen and Unwin, 1960).

Stephen E. Koss, *Lord Haldane: Scapegoat for Liberalism* (New York: Columbia University Press, 1969).

Edward M. Spiers, *Haldane: An Army Reformer* (Edinburgh University Press, 1980).

Principal Works

The Pathway to Reality (London: John Murray, 1903–4).
The Reign of Relativity (London: John Murrary, 1921).
The Philosophy of Humanism (London: John Murray, 1922).
Human Experience (London: John Murray, 1926).
Selected Essays and Addresses (London: John Murray, 1928).

READING VIII

HIGHER NATIONALITY[1]

It is with genuine pleasure that I find myself among my fellow lawyers of the New World. But my satisfaction is tempered by a sense of embarrassment. There is a multitude of topics on which it would be most natural that I should seek to touch. If, however, I am to use to any purpose the opportunity which you have accorded me, I must exclude all but one or two of them. For in an hour like this, as in most other times of endeavour, he who would accomplish anything must limit himself. What I have to say will therefore be confined to the suggestion of little more than a single thought, and to its development and illustration with materials that lie to hand. I wish to lay before you a result at which I have arrived after reflection, and to submit it for your consideration with such capacity as I possess.

---

[1] 'The Higher Nationality: A Study in Law and Ethics': An address delivered before the American Bar Association at Montreal on 1 September 1913. *The Conduct of Life* (London: John Murray, 1914), pp. 99–136.

For the occasion is as rare as it is important. Around me I see assembled some of the most distinguished figures in the public life of this Continent; men who throughout their careers have combined law with statesmanship, and who have exercised a potent influence in the fashioning of opinion and of policy. The law is indeed a calling notable for the individualities it has produced. Their production has counted for much in the past of the three nations that are represented at this meeting, and it means much for them today.

What one who finds himself face to face with this assemblage naturally thinks of is the future of these three nations, a future that may depend largely on the influence of men with opportunity such as are ours. The United States and Canada and Great Britain together form a group which is unique, unique because of its common inheritance in traditions, in surrounding, and in ideals. And nowhere is the character of this common inheritance more apparent than in the region of jurisprudence. The lawyers of the three countries think for the most part alike. At no period has political divergence prevented this fact from being strikingly apparent. Where the letter of their law is different the spirit is yet the same, and it has been so always. As I speak of the historical tradition of our great calling, and of what appears likely to be its record in days to come, it seems to me that we who are here gathered may well proclaim, in the words of the Spartans, 'We are what you were, we shall be what you are'.

It is this identity of spirit, largely due to a past which the lawyers of the group have inherited jointly, that not only forms a bond of union, but furnishes them with an influence that can hardly be reproduced in other nations. I will therefore venture to look ahead. I will ask you to consider with me whether we, who have in days gone by moulded their laws, are not called on to try in days that lie in front to mould opinion in yet another form, and so encourage the nations of their group to develop and recognize a reliable character in the obligations they assume towards each other. For it may be that there are relations possible within such a group of nations as is ours that are not possible for nations more isolated from each other and lacking in our identity of history and spirit. Canada and Great Britain on the one hand and the United States on the other, with their common language, their common interests and their common ends, form something resembling a single society. If there be such a society, it may develop within itself a foundation for international faith of a kind that is new in the history of the world. Without interfering with the freedom of action of these great countries or the independence of their constitutions, it may be possible to establish a true unison between Sovereign States. This unison will doubtless, if it ever comes into complete being, have its witnesses in treaties and written agreements. But such documents can never of themselves constitute it. Its substance, if it is to be realized, must be sought for deeper down in an intimate social life. I have never been without hope that the future development of the world may bring all the nations that compose it nearer together, so that they will progressively cease to desire to hold each other at arm's length. But such an approximation can only come about very gradually, if I read the signs of the times aright. It seems to me to be far less likely of definite realization than in the case of a group united by ties such as those of which I have spoken.

Well, the growth of such a future is at least conceivable. The substance of some of the things I am going to say about its conception, and about the way by which that conception may become real, is as old as Plato. Yet the principles and facts to which I shall have to refer appear to me to be often overlooked by those to whom they might well appear obvious. Perhaps the reason is the deadening effect of that conventional atmosphere out of which few men in public life succeed in completely escaping. We can best assist in the freshening of that atmosphere by omitting no opportunity of trying to think rightly, and thereby to contribute to the fashioning of a more hopeful and resolute kind of public opinion. . . .

The chance of laying before such an audience as this what was in my mind made the invitation which came from the Bar Association and from the heads of our great profession, both in Canada and in the United States, a highly attractive one. But before I could accept it I had to obtain the permission of my Sovereign; for, as you know, the Lord Chancellor is also *Custos Sigilli*, the Keeper of that Great Seal under which alone supreme executive acts of the British Crown can be done. It is an instrument he must neither quit without special authority, nor carry out of the realm. The head of a predecessor of mine, Cardinal Wolsey, was in peril because he was so daring as to take the Great Seal across the water to Calais, when he ought instead to have asked his Sovereign to put it into Commission.

Well, the *Clavis Regni* [Royal Key] was on the present occasion put safely into Commission before I left, and I am privileged to be here with a comfortable constitutional conscience. But the King has done more than graciously approve of my leaving British shores. I am the bearer to you of a message from him which I will now read:

> I have given my Lord Chancellor permission to cross the seas, so that he may address the meeting at Montreal. I have asked him to convey from me to that great meeting of the lawyers of the United States and of Canada my best wishes for its success. I entertain the hope that the deliberations of the distinguished men of both countries who are to assemble at Montreal may add yet further to the esteem and goodwill which the people of the United States and of Canada and the United Kingdom have for each other.

The King's message forms a text for what I have to say, and, having conveyed that message to you, I propose in the first place to turn to the reasons which make me think that the class to which you and I belong has a peculiar and extensive responsibility as regards the future relations of the three countries. But these reasons turn on the position which Courts of Law hold in Anglo-Saxon constitutions, and in entering on them I must recall to you this character of the tradition that tends to fashion a common mind in you and me as members of a profession that has exercised a profound influence on Anglo-Saxon society. It is not difficult in an assemblage of lawyers such as we are to realize the process by which our customary habits of thought have come into being and bind us together. The spirit of the jurisprudence which is ours, of the system which we apply to the regulation of human affairs in Canada, in the United States, and in Great Britain alike, is different from that which obtains in other countries. It is its very peculiarity that lends to it its potency, and it is worthwhile to make explicit what the spirit of our law really means for us.

I read the other day the reflections of a foreign thinker on what seemed to him the barbarism of the entire system of English jurisprudence, in its essence judge-made and not based on the scientific foundation of a code. I do not wonder at such reflections. There is a gulf fixed between the method of a code and such procedure as that of Chief-Justice Holt in *Coggs* v. *Bernard*, of Chief-

Justice Pratt in *Armory* v. *Delamirie*, and of Lord Mansfield when he defined the count for money had and received. A stranger to the spirit of the law as it was evolved through centuries in England will always find its history a curious one. Looking first at the early English Common Law, its most striking feature is the enormous extent to which its founders concerned themselves with remedies before settling the substantive rules for breach of which the remedies were required. Nowhere else, unless perhaps in the law of ancient Rome, do we see such a spectacle of legal writs making legal rights. Of the system of the Common Law there is a saying of Mr Justice Wendell Holmes which is profoundly true: 'The life of the law has not been logic; it has been experience. The felt necessities of the time, the prevalent moral and political theories, intentions of public policy, avowed or unconscious, even the prejudices which judges share with their fellow-men, have had a good deal more to do than the syllogism in determining the rules by which men should be governed. The law embodies the story of a nation's development through many centuries, and it cannot be dealt with as if it contained only the axioms and corollaries of a book of mathematics'. As the distinguished writer whom I have quoted tells us, we cannot, without the closest application of the historical method, comprehend the genesis and evolution of the English Common Law. Its paradox is that in its beginnings the forms of action came before the substance. It is in the history of English remedies that we have to study the growth of rights. I recall a notable sentence in one of Sir Henry Maine's books. 'So great', he declared, 'is the ascendancy of the Law of Actions in the infancy of Courts of Justice, that substantive law has, at first, the look of being gradually secreted in the interstices of procedure'. I will add to his observation this: that all our reforms notwithstanding, the dead hands of the old forms of action still rest firmly upon us. In logic the substantive conceptions ought of course to have preceded these forms. But the historical sequence has been different, for reasons with which every competent student of early English history is familiar. The phenomenon is no uncommon one. The time spirit and the spirit of logical form do not always, in a world where the contingent is ever obtruding itself, travel hand in hand. The germs of substantive law were indeed present as potential forces from the beginning, but they did not grow into life until later on. And therefore forms of action have thrust them-

selves forward with undue prominence. That is why the understanding of our law is, even for the practitioner of today,
inseparable from knowledge of its history.

As with the Common Law, so it is with Equity. To know the
principles of Equity is to know the history of the Courts in which it
has been administered, and especially the history of the office
which at present I chance myself to hold. Between the law and
equity there is no other true line of demarcation. The King was the
fountain of justice. But to get justice at his hands it was necessary
first of all to obtain the King's writ. As Bracton declared "*non
potest quis sine brevi agere.*" But the King could not personally look
after the department where such writs were to be obtained. At the
head of this, his Chancery, he therefore placed a Chancellor, usually a bishop, but sometimes an archbishop and even a cardinal,
for in these days the Church had a grip which to a Lord Chancellor
of the twentieth century is unfamiliar. At first the holder of the
office was not a judge. But he was keeper of the King's conscience,
and his business was to see that the King's subjects had remedies
when he considered that they had suffered wrongs. Consequently he began to invent new writs, and finally to develop remedies which were not confined by the rigid precedents of the
Common Law. Thus he soon became a judge. When he found that
he could not grant a Common Law writ he took to summoning
people before him and to searching their consciences. He
inquired, for instance, as to trusts which they were said to have
undertaken, and as the result of his inquiries rights and obligations unknown to the Common Law were born in his Court of
Conscience. You see at a glance how susceptible such a practice
was of development into a complete system of Equity. You would
expect, moreover, to find that the ecclesiastical atmos- phere in
which my official predecessors lived would influence the forms in
which they moulded their special system of jurisprudence. This
did indeed happen; but even in those days the atmos- phere was
not merely ecclesiastical. For the Lord High Chancellor in the
household of an early English monarch was the King's domestic
chaplain, and as, unlike his fellow servants in the household, the
Lord High Steward and the Lord Great Chamberlain, he always
possessed the by no means common advantage of being able to
read and write, he acted as the King's political secretary. He used,
it seems, in early days to live in the palace, and he had a regular

daily allowance. From one of the records it appears that his wages were five shillings, a simnel cake, two seasoned simnels, one sextary of clear wine, one sextary of household wine, one large wax candle, and forty small pieces of candle. In the time of Henry II the modern treasury spirit appears to have begun to walk abroad, for in the records the allowance of five shillings appears as if subjected to a reduction. If he dined away from the palace, *si extra domum comederit*, and was thereby forced to provide extras, then indeed he got his five shillings. But if he dined at home, *intra domum*, he was not allowed more than three shillings and six-pence. The advantage of his position was, however, that, living in the palace, he was always at the King's ear. He kept the Great Seal through which all great acts of state were manifested. Indeed it was the custody of the Great Seal that made him Chancellor. Even today this is the constitutional usage. When I myself was made Lord Chancellor the appointment was effected, not by Letters Patent, nor by writing under the Sign Manual, nor even by words spoken, but by the Sovereign making a simple delivery of the Great Seal into my hands while I knelt before him at Buckingham Palace in the presence of the Privy Council.

The reign of Charles I saw the last of the ecclesiastical chancellors. The slight sketch of the earlier period which I have drawn shows that in these times there might well have developed a great divergence of Equity from the Common Law, under the influence of the Canon and Roman laws to which ecclesiastical chancellors would naturally turn. In the old Courts of Equity it was natural that a different atmosphere from that of the Common Law Courts should be breathed. But with the gradual drawing together of the Courts of Law and Equity under lay chancellors the difference of atmosphere disappears, and we see the two systems becoming fused into one.

The moral of the whole story is the hopelessness of attempting to study Anglo-Saxon jurisprudence apart from the history of its growth and of the characters of the judges who created it. It is by no accident that among Anglo-Saxon lawyers the law does not assume the form of codes, but is largely judge-made. We have statutory codes for portions of the field which we have to cover. But those statutory codes come, not at the beginning, but at the end. For the most part the law has already been made by those who practice it before the codes embody it. Such codes with us arrive only with the close of the day, after its heat and burden have been borne, and when the journey is already near its end.

I have spoken of a spirit and of traditions which have been apparent in English law. But they have made their influence felt elsewhere. My judicial colleagues in the province of Quebec administer a system which is partly embodied in a great modern code, and partly depends on old French law of the period of Louis XIV. They apply, moreover, a good deal of the public and commercial law of England. The relation of the code to these systems has given rise to some controversies. What I have gathered, however, when sitting in the Judicial Committee of the Privy Council, is that a spirit not very different from that of the English lawyers has prevailed in Quebec. The influence of the judges in moulding the law, and of legal opinion in fashioning the shape which it should take, seem to me to have been hardly less apparent in Quebec than elsewhere in Canada. Indeed the several systems of our groups of nations, however those systems have originated, everywhere show a similar spirit, and disclose the power of our lawyers in creating and developing the law as well as in changing it, a power which has been more exercised outside the legislature than within it. It is surely because the lawyers of the New World have an influence so potent and so easily wielded that they have been able to use it copiously in a wider field of public affairs than that if mere jurisprudence. It is very striking to the observer to see how many of the names of those who have controlled the currents of public opinion in the United States and Canada alike have been the names of famous lawyers. I think this has been so partly because the tradition and spirit of the law were always what I have described, and different from that on the Continent of Europe. But it has also been so because, in consequence of that tradition and spirit, the vocation of the lawyer has not, as on the Continent of Europe, been that of a segregated profession of interpreters, but a vocation which has placed him at the very heart of affairs. In the United Kingdom this has happened in the same fashion, yet hardly to so great an extent, because there has been competition of other and powerful classes whose tradition has been to devote their lives to a Parliamentary career. But in the case of all three nations it is profoundly true that, as was said by the present President of the United States in 1910, in an address delivered to this very Association, 'the country must find lawyers of the right sort and the old spirit to advise it, or it must stumble through a very chaos of blind experiment'. 'It never', he went on to add, 'needed lawyers who are also statesmen more than it needs them now — needs them in its courts, in its legislatures, in its seats of executive authority — lawyers who can think in the terms of society itself'.

This at least is evident, that if you and I belong to a great calling, it is a calling in which we have a great responsibility. We can do much to influence opinion, and the history of our law and the character of our tradition render it easy for us to attain to that unity in habit of thought and sentiment which is the first condition of combined action. That is why I do not hesitate to speak to you as I am doing.

And having said so much, I now submit to you my second point. The law has grown by development through the influence of the opinion of society guided by its skilled advisers. But the law forms only a small part of the system of rules by which the conduct of the citizens of a state is regulated. Law, properly so called, whether civil or criminal, means essentially those rules of conduct which are expressly and publicly laid down by the sovereign will of the state, and are enforced by the sanction of compulsion. Law, however, imports something more than this. As I have already remarked, its full significance cannot be understood apart from the history and spirit of the nation whose law it is. Moreover it has a real relation to the obligations even of conscience, as well as to something else which I shall presently refer to as the General Will of Society. In short, if its full significance is to be appreciated, larger conceptions than those of the mere lawyer are essential, conceptions which come to us from the moralist and the sociologist, and without which we cannot see fully how the genesis of law has come about. That is where writers like Bentham and Austin are deficient. One cannot read a great book like the *Esprit des Lois* [*The Spirit of the Laws*] without seeing that Montesquieu had a deeper insight than Bentham or Austin, and that he had already grasped a truth which, in Great Britain at all events, was to be forgotten for a time.

Besides the rules and sanctions which belong to law and legality, there are other rules, with a different kind of sanction, which also influence conduct. I have spoken of conscience, and conscience, in the strict sense of the word, has its own court. But the tribunal of conscience is a private one, and its jurisdiction is limited to the individual whose conscience it is. The moral rules enjoined by the private conscience may be the very highest of all. But they are enforced only by an inward and private tribunal. Their sanction is subjective and not binding in the same way on all men. The very loftiness of the motive which makes a man love his neighbour more than himself, or sell all his goods in order that he may obey a great and inward call, renders that motive in the highest cases incapable of being made a rule of universal application in any positive form. And so it was that the foundation on which one of the greatest of modern moralists, Immanuel Kant, sought to base his ethical system, had to be revised by his successors. For it was found to reduce itself to little more than a negative and therefore barren obligation to act at all times from maxims fit for law universal, maxims which, because merely negative, turned out to be inadequate as guides through the field of daily conduct. In point of fact that field is covered, in the case of the citizen, only to a small extent by the law and legality on the one hand, and by the dictates of the individual conscience on the other. There is a more extensive system of guidance which regulates conduct and which differs from both in its character and sanction. It applies, like law, to all the members of a society alike, without distinction of persons. It resembles the morality of conscience in that it is enforced by no legal compulsion. In the English language we have no name for it, and this is unfortunate, for the lack of a distinctive name has occasioned confusion both of thought and of expression. German writers have, however, marked out the system to which I refer and have given it the name of 'Sittlichkeit'. In his book, *Der Zweck im Recht* [*The Purpose of Right*], Rudoplh von Jhering, a famous professor at Göttingen, with whose figure I was familiar when I was a student there nearly forty years ago, pointed out, in the part which he devoted to the subject of 'Sittlichkeit', that it was the merit of the German language to have been the only one to find a really distinctive and scientific expression for it. 'Sittlichkeit' is the system of habitual or customary conduct, ethical rather than legal, which embraces all those obligations of the citizen which it is 'bad form' or 'not the thing' to disregard. Indeed regard for these obligations is frequently enjoined merely by the social penalty of being 'cut' or looked on askance. And yet the system is so generally accepted and is held in so high

regard, that no one can venture to disregard it without in some
way suffering at the hands of his neighbours for so doing. If a man
maltreats his wife and children, or habitually jostles his fellow-cit-
izen in the street, or does things flagrantly selfish or in bad taste,
he is pretty sure to find himself in a minority and the worse off in
the end. Not only does it not pay to do these things, but the decent
man does not wish to do them. A feeling analogous to what arises
from the dictates of his more private and individual conscience
restrains him. He finds himself so restrained in the ordinary
affairs of daily life. But he is guided in his conduct by no mere
inward feeling, as in the case of conscience. Conscience and, for
that matter, law overlap parts of the sphere of social obligation
about which I am speaking. A rule of conduct may, indeed,
appear in more than one sphere, and may consequently have a
twofold sanction. But the guide to which the citizen mostly looks
is just the standard recognized by the community, a community
made up mainly of those fellow-citizens whose good opinion he
respects and desires to have. He has everywhere round him an
object-lesson in the conduct of decent people towards each other
and towards the community to which they belong. Without such
conduct and the restraints which it imposes there could be no tol-
erable social life, and real freedom from interference would not be
enjoyed. It is the instinctive sense of what to do and what not to do
in daily life and behaviour that is the source of liberty and ease.
And it is this instinctive sense of obligation that is the chief foundation of society. Its reality takes objective shape and displays
itself in family life and in our other civic and social institutions. It
is not limited to any one form, and it is capable of manifesting
itself in new forms and of developing and changing old forms.
Indeed the civic community is more than a political fabric. It
includes all the social institutions in and by which the individual
life is influenced — such as are the family, the school, the church,
the legislature, and the executive. None of these can subsist in isolation from the rest; together they and other institutions of the
kind form a single organic whole, the whole which is known as
the Nation. The spirit and habit of life which this organic entirety
inspires and compels are what, for my present purpose, I mean by
'Sittlichkeit'. 'Sitte' is the German for custom, and 'Sittlichkeit'
implies custom and a habit of mind and action. It also implies a lit-

tle more. Fichte[2] defines it in words which are worth quoting, and which I will put into English: 'What, to begin with', he says 'does "Sitte" signify, and in what sense do we use the word? It means for us, and means in every accurate reference we make to it, those principles of conduct which regulate people in their relations to each other, and which have become a matter of habit and second nature at the stage of culture reached, and of which, therefore, we are not explicitly conscious. Principles, we call them, because we do not refer to the sort of conduct that is casual or is determined on casual grounds, but to the hidden and uniform ground of action which we assume to be present in the man whose action is not deflected and from which we can pretty certainly predict what he will do. Principles, we say, which have become a second nature and of which we are not explicitly conscious. We thus exclude all impulses and motives based on free individual choice, the inward aspect of "Sittlichkeit", that is to say morality, and also the outward side, or law, alike. For what a man has first to reflect over and then freely to resolve is not for him a habit in conduct; and in so far as habit in conduct is associated with a particular age, it is regarded as the unconscious instrument of the Time Spirit'.

The system of ethical habit in a community is of a dominating character, for the decision and influence of the whole community is embodied in the social habit. Because such conduct is systematic and covers the whole of the field of society, the individual will is closely related by it to the will and spirit of the community. And out of this relation arises the power of adequately controlling the conduct of the individual. If this power fails or becomes weak the community degenerates and may fall to pieces. Different nations excel in their 'Sittlichkeit' in different fashions. The spirit of the community and its ideals may vary greatly. There may be a low level of 'Sittlichkeit'; and we have the spectacle of nations which have even degenerated in this respect. It may possibly conflict with law and morality, as in the case of the duel. But when its level is high in a nation we admire the system, for we see it not only guiding a people and binding them together for national effort, but affording the most real freedom of thought and action for those who in daily life habitually act in harmony with the General Will.

---

[2]   *Grundzüge des Gegenwärtigen Zeitalters, Werke,* Band vii., p. 214.

Thus we have in the case of a community, be it the city or be it the state, an illustration of a sanction which is sufficient to compel observance of a rule without any question of the application of force. This kind of sanction may be of a highly compelling quality, and it often extends so far as to make the individual prefer the good of the community to his own. The development of many of our social institutions, of our hospitals, of our universities, and of other establishments of the kind, shows the extent to which it reaches and is powerful. But it has yet higher forms in which it approaches very nearly to the level of the obligation of conscience, although it is distinct from that form of obligation. I will try to make clear what I mean by illustrations. A man may be impelled to action of a higher order by his sense of unity with the society to which he belongs, action of which, from the civic standpoint, all approve. What he does in such a case is natural to him, and is done without thought of reward or punishment; but it has reference to standards of conduct set up by society and accepted just because society has set them up. There is a poem by the late Sir Alfred Lyall which exemplifies the high level that may be reached in such conduct. The poem is called *Theology in Extremis*, and it describes the feelings of an Englishman who had been taken prisoner by Mahometan rebels in the Indian Mutiny. He is face to face with a cruel death. They offer him his life if he will repeat something from the Koran. If he complies, no one is likely ever to hear of it, and he will be free to return to England and to the woman he loves. Moreover, and here is the real point, he is not a believer in Christianity, so that it is no question of denying his Saviour. What ought he to do? Deliverance is easy, and the relief and advantage would be unspeakably great. But he does not really hesitate, and every shadow of doubt disappears when he hears his fellow-prisoner, a half-caste, pattering eagerly the words demanded. He himself has no hope of heaven and he loves life —

> Yet for the honour of English race
> May I not live or endure disgrace:
> Ay, but the word if I could have said it,
> I by no terrors of hell perplext.
> Hard to be silent and have no credit
> From man in this world, or reward in the next;
> None to bear witness and reckon the cost;
> Of the name that is saved by the life that is lost.
> I must begone to the crowd untold

Of men by the cause which they served unknown,
Who moulder in myriad graves of old;
Never a story and never a stone
Tells of the martyrs who die like me
Just for the pride of the old countree.

I will take another example, this time from the literature of
ancient Greece. In one of the shortest but not least impressive of
his *Dialogues*, the 'Crito', Plato tells us of the character of Socrates,
not as a philosopher but as a good citizen. He has been unjustly
condemned by the Athenians as an enemy to the good of the state.
Crito comes to him in prison to persuade him to escape. He urges
on him many arguments, his duty to his children included. But
Socrates refuses. He chooses to follow, not what anyone in the
crowd might do, but the example which the ideal citizen should
set. It would be a breach of his duty to fly from the judgment duly
passed in the Athens to which he belongs, even though he thinks
the decree should have been different. For it is the decree of the
established justice of his City State. He will not 'play truant'. He
hears the words, 'Listen, Socrates, to us who have brought you
up'; and in reply he refuses to go away, in these final sentences:
'This is the voice which I seem to hear murmuring in my ears, like
the sound of the flute in the ears of the mystic; that voice, I say, is
murmuring in my ears, and prevents me from hearing any other.
And I know that anything more which you may say will be vain'.

Why do men of this stamp act so, it may be when leading the
battle line, it may be at critical moments of quite other kinds? It is,
I think, because they are more than mere individuals. Individual
they are, but completely real, even as individual, only in their
relation to organic and social wholes in which they are members,
such as the family, the city, the state. There is in every truly organized community a Common Will which is willed by those who
compose that community, and who in so willing are more than
isolated men and women. It is not, indeed, as unrelated atoms
that they have lived. They have grown, from the receptive days of
childhood up to maturity, in an atmosphere of example and general custom, and their lives have widened out from one little
world to other and higher worlds, so that, through occupying successive stations in life, they more and more come to make their
own the life of the social whole in which they move and have their
being. They cannot mark off or define their own individualities

without reference to the individualities of others. And so they unconsciously find themselves as in truth pulse-beats of the whole system, and themselves the whole system. It is real in them and they in it. They are real only because they are social. The notion that the individual is the highest form of reality, and that the relationship of individuals is one of mere contract, the notion of Hobbes and of Bentham and of Austin, turns out to be quite inadequate. Even of an everyday contract, that of marriage, it has been well said that it is a contract to pass out of the sphere of contract, and that it is possible only because the contracting parties are already beyond and above that sphere. As a modern writer, F.H. Bradley of Oxford, to whose investigations in these regions we owe much, has finely said:[3]

> The moral organism is not a mere animal organism. In the latter (it is no novel remark) the member is not aware of itself as such, while in the former it knows itself, and therefore knows the whole itself. The narrow external function of the man is not the whole man. He has a life which we cannot see with our eyes, and there is no duty so mean that it is not the realization of this, and knowable as such. What counts is not the visible outer work so much as the spirit in which it is done. The breadth of my life is not measured by the multitude of my pursuits, nor the space I take up amongst other men; but by the fullness of the whole life which I know as mine. It is true that less now depends on each of us, as this or that man; it is not true that our individuality is therefore lessened, that therefore we have less in us.

There is, according to this view, a General Will with which the will of the good citizen is in accord. He feels that he would despise himself were his private will not in harmony with it. The notion of the reality of such a will is no new one. It is as old as the Greeks, for whom the moral order and the city-state were closely related; and we find it in modern books in which we do not look for it. Jean Jacques Rousseau is probably best known to the world by the famous words in which he begins the first chapter of the *Social Contract*: 'Man is born free, and everywhere he is in chains. Those who think themselves to be the masters of others cease not to be greater slaves than the people they govern'. He goes on in the next paragraph to tell us that if he were only to consider force and the effects of it, he would say that if a nation was constrained to obey and did obey, it did well, but that whenever it could throw off its

[3] *Ethical Studies*, p. 170 [and pp. 188–9 of 2nd. edition, 1927].

yoke and did throw it off, it acted better. His words, written in 1762, became a text for the pioneers of the French Revolution. But they would have done well to read further into the book. As Rousseau goes on we find a different conception. He passes from considering the fiction of a Social Contract to a discussion of the power over the individual of the General Will, by virtue of which a people becomes a people. This General Will, the *Volonté Générale*, he distinguishes from the *Volonté de Tous*, which is a mere numerical sum of individual wills. These particular wills do not rise above themselves. The General Will, on the other hand, represents what is greater than the individual volition of those who compose the society of which it is the will. On occasions this higher will is more apparent than at other times. But it may, if there is social slackness, be difficult to distinguish from a mere aggregate of voices, from the will of a mob. What is interesting is that Rousseau, so often associated with doctrine of quite another kind, should finally recognize the bond of a General Will as what really holds the community together. For him, as for those who have had a yet clearer grasp of the principle, in willing the General Will we not only realize our true selves but we may rise above our ordinary habit of mind. We may reach heights which we could not reach, or which at all events most of us could not reach, in isolation. There are few observers who have not been impressed with the wonderful unity and concentration of purpose which an entire nation may display — above all, in a period of crisis. We see it in time of war, when a nation is fighting for its life or for a great cause. We have seen it in Japan, and we have seen it still more recently even among the people of the Balkan Peninsula. We have marvelled at the illustrations with which history abounds of the General Will rising to heights of which but few of the individual citizens in whom it is embodied have ever before been conscious even in their dreams.

In the life of Themistocles Plutarch tells us how even in time of peace the leader of the Athenian people could fashion them into an undivided community and inspire them to rise above themselves. It was before the Persians had actually threatened to invade Attica that Themistocles foresaw what would come, Greece could not raise armies comparable in numbers to those of the Persian kings. But he told his people that the oracle had spoken thus: 'When all things else are taken within the boundary of

Cecrops and the covert of divine Cithaeron, Zeus grants to Athena that the wall of wood alone shall remain uncaptured, which shall help thee and thy children'. The Athenian citizens were accustomed in each year to divide among themselves the revenue of their silver mines at Laurium. Themistocles had the daring, so Plutarch tells us, to come forward and boldly propose that the usual distribution should cease, and that they should let him spend the money for them in building a hundred ships. The citizens rose to his lead, the ships were built, and with them the Greeks were able at a later date to win against Xerxes the great sea-fight at Salamis, and to defeat an invasion by the hosts of Persia which, had it succeeded, might have changed the course of modern as well as ancient history.

By such a leadership it is that a common ideal can be made to penetrate the soul of a people, and to take complete possession of it. The ideal may be very high, or it may be of so ordinary a kind that we are not conscious of it without the effort of reflection. But when it is there it influences and guides daily conduct. Such idealism passes beyond the sphere of law, which provides only what is necessary for mutual protection and liberty of just action. It falls short, on the other hand, in quality of the dictates of what Kant called the Categorical Imperative that rules the private and individual conscience, but that alone, an Imperative which therefore gives insufficient guidance for ordinary and daily social life. Yet the ideal of which I speak is not the less binding; and it is recognized as so binding that the conduct of all good men conforms to it.

Thus we find within the single state the evidence of a sanction which is less than legal but more than merely moral, and which is sufficient, in the vast majority of the events of daily life, to secure observance of general standards of conduct without any question of resort to force. If this is so within a nation, can it be so as between nations? This brings me at once to my third point. Can nations form a group or community among themselves within which a habit of looking to common ideals may grow up sufficiently strong to develop a General Will, and to make the binding power of these ideals a reliable sanction for their obligations to each other?

There is, I think, nothing in the real nature of nationality that precludes such a possibility. A famous student of history has

bequeathed to us a definition of nationality which is worth attention: I refer to Ernest Renan, of whom George Meredith once said
to me, while the great French critic was still living, that there was
more in his head than in any other head in Europe. Renan tells us
that 'Man enslaved neither by his race, nor by his language, nor by
the direction of mountain ranges. A great aggregation of men,
sane of mind and warm of heart, creates a moral consciousness
which is called a nation'. Another acute critic of life, Matthew
Arnold, citing one still greater than himself, draws what is in
effect a deduction from the same proposition. 'Let us', he says,[4]
'conceive of the whole group of civilized nations as being, for
intellectual and spiritual purposes, one great confederation,
bound to a joint action and working towards a common result; a
confederation whose members have a due knowledge both of the
past, out of which they all proceed, and of each other. This was the
ideal of Goethe, and it is an ideal which will impose itself upon the
thoughts of our modern societies more and more'.

But while I admire the faith of Renan and Arnold and Goethe in
what they all three believed to be the future of humanity, there is a
long road yet to be travelled before what they hoped for can be
fully accomplished. Grotius concludes his great book on War and
Peace with a nobler prayer: 'May God write', he said, 'these lessons — He Who alone can — on the hearts of all those who have
the affairs of Christendom in their hands. And may He give to
those persons a mind fitted to understand and to respect rights,
human and divine, and lead them to recollect always that the min-
istration committed to them is no less than this, that they are the
Governors of Man, a creature most dear to God'.

The prayer of Grotius has not yet been fulfilled, nor do recent
events point to the fulfilment as being near. The world is probably
a long way off from the abolition of armaments and the peril of
war. For habits of mind which can be sufficiently strong with a
single people can hardly be as strong between nations. There does
not exist the same extent of common interest, of common purpose, and of common tradition. And yet the tendency, even as
between nations that stand in no special relation to each other, to
develop such a habit of mind is in our time becoming recogniz-
able. There are signs that the best people in the best nations are

---

[4]   *Preface to the Poems of Wordsworth.*

ceasing to wish to live in a world of mere claims, and to proclaim on every occasion 'Our country, right or wrong'. There is growing up a disposition to believe that it is good, not only for all men but for all nations, to consider their neighbours' point of view as well as their own. There is apparent at least a tendency to seek for a higher standard of ideals in international relations. The barbarism which once looked to conquest and the waging of successful war as the main object of statesmanship, seems as though it were passing away. There have been established rules of International Law which already govern the conduct of war itself, and are generally observed as binding by all civilized people, with the result that the cruelties of war have been lessened. If practice falls short of theory, at least there is today little effective challenge of the broad principle that a nation has as regards its neighbours duties as well as rights. It is this spirit that may develop as time goes on into a full international 'Sittlichkeit'. But such development is certainly still easier and more hopeful in the case of nations with some special relation, than it is within a mere aggregate of nations. At times a common interest among nations with special relations of the kind I am thinking of gives birth to a social habit of thought and action which in the end crystallizes into a treaty, a treaty which in its turn stimulates the process that gave it birth. We see this in the case of Germany and Austria, and in that of France and Russia. Sometimes a friendly relationship grows up without crystallizing into a general treaty. Such has been the case between my own country and France. We have no convention excepting one confined to the settlement of old controversies over specific subjects, a convention that has nothing to do with war. None the less, since in that convention there was embodied the testimony of willingness to give as well as to take, and to be mutually understanding and helpful, there has arisen between France and England a new kind of feeling which forms a real tie. It is still young, and it may stand still or diminish. But equally well it may advance and grow, and it is earnestly to be hoped that it will do so.

Recent events in Europe and the way in which the Great Powers have worked together to preserve the peace of Europe, as if forming one community, point to the ethical possibilities of the group system as deserving of close study by both statesmen and students. The 'Sittlichkeit' which can develop itself between the peoples of even a loosely connected group seems to promise a sanction for International Obligation which has not hitherto, so far as I know, attracted attention in connection with International Law. But if the group system deserves attention in the cases referred to, how much more does it call for attention in another and far more striking case!

In the year which is approaching, a century will have passed since the United States and the people of Canada and Great Britain terminated a great war by the Peace of Ghent. On both sides the combatants felt that war to be unnatural and one that should never have been commenced. And now we have lived for nearly a hundred years, not only in peace, but also, I think, in process of coming to a deepening and yet more complete understanding of each other, and to the possession of common ends and ideals, ends and ideals which are natural to the Anglo-Saxon group, and to that group alone. It seems to me that within our community there is growing an ethical feeling which has something approaching to the binding quality of which I have been speaking. Men may violate the obligations which that feeling suggests, but by a vast number of our respective citizens it would not be accounted decent to do so. For the nations in such a group as ours to violate these obligations would be as if respectable neighbours should fall to blows because of a difference of opinion. We may disagree on specific points and we probably shall, but the differences should be settled in the spirit and in the manner in which citizens usually settle their differences. The new attitude which is growing up has changed many things, and made much that once happened no longer likely to recur. I am concerned when I come across things that were written about America by British novelists only fifty years ago, and I doubt not that there are some things in the American literature of days gone past which many here would wish to have been without. But now that sort of writing is happily over, and we are realizing more and more the significance of our joint tradition and of the common interests which are ours. It is a splendid example to the world that Canada and the United States should have nearly four thousand miles of frontier practically unfortified. As an ex-War Minister, who knows what a saving in unproductive expenditure this means, I fervently hope that it may never be otherwise.

But it is not merely in external results that the pursuit of a growing common ideal shows itself when such an ideal is really in men's minds. It transforms the spirit in which we regard each other, and it gives us faith in each other

> Why, what but faith, do we abhor
> And idolize each other for —
> Faith in our evil or our good,
> Which is or is not understood
> Aright by those we love or those
> We hate, thence called our friends or foes.

I think that for the future of the relations between the United States on the one hand and Canada and Great Britain on the other, those who are assembled in this great meeting have their own special responsibility. We who are the lawyers of the New World and of the old mother country possess, as I have said to you, a tradition which is distinctive and peculiarly our own. We have been taught to look on our system of justice, not as something that waits to be embodied in abstract codes before it can be said to exist, but as what we ourselves are progressively and co-operatively evolving. And our power of influence is not confined to the securing of municipal justice. We play a large part in public affairs, and we influence our fellow-men in questions which go far beyond the province of the law, and which extend in the relations of society to that 'Sittlichkeit' of which I have spoken. In this region we exert much control. If, then, there is to grow up among the nations of our group, and between that group and the rest of civilization, a yet further development of 'Sittlichkeit', has not our profession special opportunities of influencing opinion, which are coupled with a deep responsibility? To me, when I look to the history of our calling in the three countries, it seems that the answer to this question requires no argument and admits of no controversy. It is our very habit of regarding the law and the wider rules of conduct which lie beyond the law as something to be moulded best if we co-operate steadily, that gives us an influence perhaps greater than is strictly ours, an influence which may in affairs of the state be potently exercised for good or for evil.

This, then, is why as a lawyer speaking to lawyers, I have a strong sense of responsibility in being present here today, and why I believe that many of you share my feeling. A movement is in progress which we, by the character of our calling as judges and as advocates, have special opportunities to further. The sphere of our action has its limits, but at least it is given to us as a body to be the counsellors of our fellow-citizens in public and in private life alike. I have before my mind the words which I have already quoted of the present President of the United States, when he spoke of 'lawyers who can think in the terms of society itself'. And I believe that if, in the language of yet another president, in the famous words of Lincoln, we as a body in our minds and hearts 'highly resolve' to work for the general recognition by society of the binding character of international duties and rights as they arise within the Anglo-Saxon group, we shall not resolve in vain. A mere common desire may seem an intangible instrument, and yet, intangible as it is, it may be enough to form the beginning of what in the end will make the whole difference. Ideas have hands and feet, and the ideas of a congress such as this may affect public opinion deeply. It is easy to fail to realize how much an occasion like the assemblage in Montreal of the American Bar Association, on the eve of a great international centenary, can be made to mean, and it is easy to let such an occasion pass with a too timid modesty. Should we let it pass now, I think a real opportunity for doing good will just thereby have been missed by you and me. We need say nothing; we need pass no cut and dried resolution. It is the spirit not the letter that is the one thing needful.

I do not apologize for having trespassed on the time and attention of this remarkable meeting for so long, or for urging what may seem to belong more to ethics than to law. We are bound to search after fresh principles if we desire to find firm foundations for a progressive practical life. It is the absence of a clear conception of principle that occasions some at least of the obscurities and perplexities that beset us in the giving of counsel and in following it. On the other hand, it is futile to delay action until reflection has cleared up all our difficulties. If we would learn to swim, we must first enter the water. We must not refuse to begin our journey until the whole of the road we may have to travel lies mapped out before us. A great thinker declared that it is not Philosophy which first gives us the truth that lies to hand around us, and that mankind has not to wait for Philosophy in order to be conscious of this truth. Plain John Locke put the same thing in more homely words when he said that 'God has not been so sparing to men to make them two-legged creatures, and left it to Aristotle to make them rational'. Yet the reflective spirit does help, not by furnishing us with dogmas or final conclusions, or even with lines of action that are always definite, but by the insight which it gives, an insight that develops in us what Plato called the 'synoptic mind', the mind that enables us to see things steadily as well as to see them whole.

And now I have expressed what I had in my mind. Your welcome to me has been indeed a generous one, and I shall carry the memory of it back over the Atlantic. But the occasion has seemed to me significant of something beyond even its splendid hospitality. I have interpreted it, and I think not wrongly, as the symbol of a desire that extends beyond the limits of this assemblage. I mean the desire that we should steadily direct our thoughts to how we can draw into closest harmony the nations of a race in which all of us have a common pride. If that be now a far-spread inclination, then indeed may the people of three great countries say to Jerusalem, 'Thou shalt be built', and to the Temple, 'Thy foundation shall be laid'.